FLIGHT TO AMERICA

STUDIES IN SOCIAL DISCONTINUITY

Under the Consulting Editorship of:

CHARLES TILLY
University of Michigan

EDWARD SHORTER
University of Toronto

William A. Christian, Jr. Person and God in a Spanish Valley

Joel Samaha. Law and Order in Historical Perspective: The Case of Elizabethan Essex

John W. Cole and Eric R. Wolf. The Hidden Frontier: Ecology and Ethnicity in an Alpine Valley

Immanuel Wallerstein. The Modern World-System: Capitalist Agriculture and the Origins of the European World-Economy in the Sixteenth Century

John R. Gillis. Youth and History: Tradition and Change in European Age Relations 1770 – Present

D. E. H. Russell. Rebellion, Revolution, and Armed Force: A Comparative Study of Fifteen Countries with Special Emphasis on Cuba and South Africa

Kristian Hvidt. Flight to America: The Social Background of 300,000 Danish Emigrants

James Lang. Conquest and Commerce: Spain and England in the Americas

Stanley H. Brandes. Migration, Kinship, and Community: Tradition and Transition in a Spanish Village

FLIGHT TO AMERICA

THE SOCIAL BACKGROUND OF 300,000 DANISH EMIGRANTS

Kristian Hvidt

Head Librarian
Danish Parliamentary Library
Copenhagen, Denmark

ACADEMIC PRESS *New York San Francisco London*

A Subsidiary of Harcourt Brace Jovanovich, Publishers

ACADEMIC PRESS, INC.
111 Fifth Avenue, New York, New York 10003

United Kingdom Edition published by
ACADEMIC PRESS, INC. (LONDON) LTD.
24/28 Oval Road, London NW1

Library of Congress Cataloging in Publication Data

Hvidt, Kristian.
    Flight to America.

    (Studies in social discontinuity)
    Bibliography: p.
    1.   Denmark—Emigration and immigration.   2.   United
States—Emigration and immigration.   3.   Danes in the
United States.   I.   Title.   II.   Series.
JV6714.H9   301.32'8'489073   73-18996
ISBN 0–12–785348–0

PRINTED IN THE UNITED STATES OF AMERICA

CONTENTS

PREFACE

This book began with the discovery of 58 thick volumes containing handwritten registers of the Danes who went overseas in the years after 1868. Behind the dry pages stating names and personal data for over 300,000 individuals who made this great decision, I saw a fantastic panorama of social history—a human drama for each person who gave up his home, his family, and his native surroundings for a foreign and little-known world beyond the seas. Scores of questions and problems arose from the pages of the registers. What sort of people made the decision? Why did they leave? What motive forces, what push in Danish society made them go? Mass emigration spread like a contagious fever all over Europe, and also attacked Denmark. A silent stream of people in the prime of life left the country; the phenomenon was of more significance to both Denmark and the overseas countries than many government crises or even wars.

To describe emigration in a scholarly way is impossible without statistical material. The official statistics on emigration from Denmark were very poor. Therefore my first task was to build up a new statistical basis. This was done by computer processing of data on the police registers for 172,000 emigrants who left Denmark before 1900.

By using this vast material I have tried to describe the development and structure of Danish emigration compared to that of other countries, especially the other Scandinavian countries. The following chapters, then, should reveal a wider perspective than just from Denmark alone. It is my hope that this book will be read not only as a general account of Danish emigration but also as a contribution to the international discussion on the motive force for all the millions of Europeans who left for America. In analyzing the social background of the emigrants one also perceives a way of viewing the social and economic transformation caused by industrialization. Through this study it becomes evident that the internal migration to the urban areas and the overseas emigration constituted two sides of the same phenomenon: the rural exodus in common for all Europe.

The original Danish version of this book—a doctoral dissertation for the University of Copenhagen—also included some chapters on the pull factor in emigration, and especially the influence of the propaganda spread by the great Atlantic shipping companies. I have included here one section of this material showing to what extent money and prepaid tickets sent home from America were additional incentives to emigration.

At the end of the volume I have provided bibliographic data on the most important literature mentioned in the text. For more detailed references one can refer to the Danish edition (*Flugten til Amerika eller drivkræfterne i dansk masseemigration 1868–1914,* Århus, 1972).

I am greatly in debt to all who have worked on this manuscript, first to the two translators, Anne Zeeberg and Virginia Laursen, and later the editorial staff of Academic Press who so carefully processed my manuscript into a book.

FLIGHT TO AMERICA

The 19 counties of Denmark before 1970.

1

INTRODUCTION

It seems a safe rule of thumb that the appearance of each great new culture in history was preceded by a period of large-scale migrations that brought together peoples of different origins. From such melting pots came new cultural castings. Before the Greek city–states rose to eminence, the Aeolian, Doric, and Ionic peoples migrated south from the Danube. From their meeting with the indigenous Greeks arose one of the most refined civilizations in world history. The same happened in Italy. Northern tribes mixed with existing Italian, possibly Etruscan, peoples, creating the basis for the Roman republic. The first three centuries after the fall of Rome are obscure to us, though during that time great migrations again prepared the way for a major change. A new, European culture slowly emerged, clearly the offspring of the old, yet having its own unique features.

Just as the hordes coming down over the Alps toward Caesar's Rome foreshadowed the empire's dissolution 400 years later, the great discoveries of the sixteenth century signaled the break-up of European world dominance in the twentieth century. Posterity will judge whether or not we may speak of the flowering of an American culture. However, an extended period of migration took place prior to America's ascendence to its present position of world power. The century between 1814 and 1914 saw the largest migration in the history of mankind, with more than 50 million Europeans setting out for America or other overseas destinations.

Naturally the restructuring of the nineteenth-century world cannot be ascribed to mass migrations alone; capitalism and the industrial revolution played a large role in forming modern society. But it is surprising to see how much modern historians have emphasized these factors as causes for the development of the United States and Europe, to the virtual exclusion of any consideration of emigration. For example, Dudley Dillard scarcely mentions emigration in his *Economic Development of the North Atlantic Community,* in which he sets out to explain the association between Europe and the United States over the last two centuries. He devotes a scant quarter page out of 592 to the subject, and one-third of this pittance is spent on explaining that immigration into the United States delayed the formation of an organized American trade union movement! To the extent that Dillard is representative of the literature, we are faced with a serious distortion, resulting in a disregard of migratory movements that typifies the narrowness of much economic history.

The same indifference on the part of economic historians also appears in Danish historiography. The only comprehensive economic history of Denmark, that by Erling Olsen (1962), does not mention emigration. Admittedly the importance of Danish overseas emigration should not be overestimated, but it would not be unreasonable to expect some reference to the 300,000 Danes out of a total population of 2 million who left their homeland in a period of less than 50 years.

It is with these 300,000 Danes that this book deals. They are only a small fraction of the great mass of people who crossed the oceans—a host of anonymous, silent individuals who influenced history without creating picturesque heroes, without deeds of valor. There was no glamour in the suffering they endured in the holds of ships or the misery of their new homes. Satisfaction for them was a chance to see their children or grandchildren enjoy some of the happiness they themselves had pursued. Each of them acted out his own miniature drama, and the total had far greater consequences for the modern world than did most of the kings, emperors, or wars described in history books.

This fascinating perspective forms the starting point for the present inquiry into mass migrations before 1914 as seen from a Danish point of view. It is to be hoped that the Danish material will also throw light over emigration as a European phenomenon. My inspiration for this study came from the excellent survey of the work on this subject that F. Thistlethwaite presented to the international history conference in Stockholm in 1960. In his talk, Thistlethwaite stressed the fact that the great international migrations before 1914 had been made the subject of intensive study by historians in the receiving countries, especially in the United States, while very little attention had been paid to the problems of the originating countries. A review of the situation distinctly called for monographs that dealt with the emigration problems of separate European countries, and that based descriptions of the phenomena on local social and economic features.

When studying countries such as England, Ireland, Norway, and Sweden, the scholar is faced with such overwhelming amounts of material that it is beyond the power of any person to cover the subject in one monograph. But Denmark is a small country, and it should be possible to present a complete survey. Danish emigration before 1914 never reached the overwhelming dimensions that it did in Norway or Sweden. In addition, the Danish archives contain unusually comprehensive material hitherto as a whole untouched, yet complete and representative enough to support a sociohistorical analysis. But without the groundwork which has been done in Norway or Sweden, the present work had to start from scratch, and it has been necessary to limit the subject. Consequently certain aspects of Danish emigration before 1914 will not be treated in this book. Both the demographic and sociohistorical aspects of emigration and the individual biographical approach are justifiable historical methods, but the story of why Jens Hansen went to America and what happened to him there has been disregarded in this study, except in cases where the fate of an individual person seems to be characteristic of a large number of emigrants.

The ideal way to describe emigration from a particular area would be to use the historical sources to follow the emigrants on their journey, as the Swedish author Vilhelm Moberg did in fictional form in his famous trilogy about a dozen emigrants from Sweden and their lives in Minnesota. It would mean depicting their social positions in Denmark, their motives for leaving, their voyages, and their later lives in the country to which they emigrated. This method must be virtually excluded in a broad survey of emigration from a whole nation, and would really be practicable only in dealing with single persons or groups who left letters and diaries. Therefore the process of transforming emigrants into immigrants will be touched on only where I believe it possible to add something new to a complex field hitherto unexplored by Danish historians. Danish assimilation is badly in need of a competent separate treatment.

I owe a word of explanation to the reader about the statistical basis of this book. After May of 1868, the police had to control contracts between emigration agents and the prospective emigrants. The data of each contract were written in great alphabetized volumes running in two parallel series, one for the emigrants going directly from Copenhagen to overseas countries, and another for emigrants passing indirectly via English or German harbors. For each emigrant the following information has been used and computerized:

1. Year and month of departure
2. Sex
3. Traveling alone or in group
4. Occupation
5. Age
6. Place of last residence
7. Destination

On the computer tape is processed information about 172,022 Danish emigrants leaving between 1868 and 1900, representing approximately 90% of the total Danish emigration during the period.[1] Where no other references are given for the tables and figures included in this volume, they are taken from this data base.

Historically the concept of emigration, i.e., voluntary individual removal from one region to another, belongs to the centuries following the great land discoveries. For the European countries that had financed and carried out the explorations, exploitation of the newly discovered lands became a concern of the state. Overseas territories were not opened to free immigration, for, in accordance with the prevailing mercantile tenets, absolutist governments were anxious to retain their population size. Emigration to the colonies was therefore limited to a comparatively small number of people who usually were employed and instructed by chartered trading companies. The relations between the colonies and the mother countries were largely determined by the migration policy of the individual countries. Thus it has been maintained that one of the major causes for the collapse of the Spanish colonial empire was the strict prohibition of emigration for permanent settlement, a policy that allowed people to be sent out to the colonies for only a limited period.

The first waves of emigration actually began toward the beginning of of the seventeenth century. Periods of religious intolerance overcame economic and political principles, and this caused migration both within the boundaries of Europe (for instance, out of France after the revocation of the Edict of Nantes in 1685) and major population transfers overseas. The story of religious dissenters leaving England under King James to

---

[1] A detailed account as to method and source value of the material can be found in the Danish edition of this book: *Flugten til Amerika eller drivkræfterne i masseudvandringen fra Danmark 1868–1914*, Århus, 1972.

settle in New England is well known and can be considered the starting point of a new type of colonial venture. Small-scale colonies of self-selected and individually motivated emigrants, which within a short time created relatively prosperous societies, provided the basis for later large-scale emigration from Europe. The tension between the individualism and unlimited resources of the New World and the political, economic, and social pressures of the Old World supplied a background for westward migration. But the restrictions that the European countries put on migration, combined with extremely underdeveloped transportation, held back the avalanche for yet another century and a half. Actual mass emigration did not take place until after the Napoleonic wars.

The increase in emigration from Europe came immediately after the end of the Napoleonic wars; from the very beginning it was a spontaneous, individual migration without distinct religious or political features. Statistical information concerning the first period is extremely unreliable, resting on nothing but the official American statistics of the immigration. According to this source, the average annual arrivals of the 1820s amounted to 15,100 persons for the United States. For the 1830s the figure rose to 59,900 per year. By the 1840s, the great exodus had started, especially since the Irish Potato Famine had forced a large percentage of the Irish population to emigrate. The annual average number of immigrants from Europe was now 171,000, and if we take the second half of this decade alone we get a figure as high as 256,000. Table 1.1 gives a

TABLE 1.1

Annual Average Emigration from Europe, 1851–1915 (in thousands) [a]

	From Europe	Portion from Scandinavia
1851–1855	342.3	6.9
1856–1860	197.1	4.5
1861–1865	219.3	9.7
1866–1870	345.9	39.3
1871–1875	370.7	22.1
1876–1880	258.0	23.2
1881–1885	661.3	58.4
1886–1890	737.7	60.8
1891–1895	674.8	48.1
1896–1900	543.2	22.1
1901–1905	1038.9	53.9
1906–1910	1436.7	43.7
1911–1915	1365.3	28.6

[a] From United Nations Population Studies, Number 17. *The Determinants and Consequences of Population Trends.* New York: United Nations, 1953, p. 110.

very clear impression of the way emigration from Europe (to the United States, Australia, and other overseas countries) soared to immense new heights during the next decades. The Scandinavian emigration figures are shown to give an idea of their size relative to the total numbers.

After 1850, increases in emigration occurred in waves that would suddenly rise, recede, and then be succeeded by others. The first such wave came in the second half of the 1840s and peaked about 1853. The next began after the end of the American Civil War and culminated in the beginning of the 1870s. From about 1880, a veritable flood suddenly occurred, and the annual number of emigrants leaving European ports more than doubled. These record numbers peaked in 1887, with European emigrants reaching about 900,000, and yet the figure is still small compared to the tidal wave that began just after the turn of the century, when European emigration reached a peak amounting to almost 1.5 million emigrants. Whether this accelerating trend would have continued if not interrupted by World War I is impossible to judge. But a glance at the dynamic development after 1850 seems to indicate a certain self-accelerating element in the movement that, at least from a European perspective, could have been stemmed only by such a wholly exceptional and shattering event as a world war. Peace brought about different conditions in Europe, and in America general immigration restrictions in the form of the quota system of the 1921–1924 legislation were introduced. As late as 1920–1925, European emigration was of considerable size, nearly 50% of its pre-war level, but after that it fell to a very low figure. However, this large-scale emigration, a movement which in the course of 74 years from 1846 to 1914 deprived Europe of approximately 52 million of its population, proved to be a unique phenomenon—the human aspect of the great discovery of the open space of the New World.

The fluctuating development of emigration since 1815 was to a very large extent the consequence of the "new" economic system, liberalism. Before 1800 capital export and emigration had gone hand in hand, but afterward they operated as separate elements. However, the epidemic nature of a kind of emigration fever had its own influence on fluctuations in emigration. Ideas of slipping free of the fetters of the more or less fixed social structure of Europe in 1800 spread just as rapidly as did new political concepts. People sought to break with the system; the difference was that the emigrants selfishly turned their backs on their homelands, abandoning hopes of reform within Europe, whereas those infected with a political mission organized in the hope that group agitation could improve their situation. The spread of the idea of migration among individual members of a static society is an unexplored field with broad sociological implications.

Early nineteenth-century village society consisted of very small population groups with an intellectual horizon that barely extended a few miles beyond the village limits, and perhaps not even to the next town. If a person or a family broke loose from a group as confined as this, and sold everything in order to move to town and start a new life, others in the village were not necessarily led to do the same thing. But the fixed pattern of the village had been broken through the departure of this one person, and for those left behind the world had been widened. Psychologically, even one departure sowed the idea of possibilities other than the acceptance of a lot determined by birth. This mental seed could begin as the awareness of a means of escape from unbearable poverty, and might later develop into a feeling that even normal conditions were intolerable and were sufficient cause for a man to burn his bridges. Such mental germination might take months, or it might take decades. The seed might lie dormant during periods of acceptable conditions in the village, but once hardship recurred it would sprout forth again. An entirely new picture of a world with immense perspectives would be introduced when a neighbor emigrated to Australia or America, and would be enlarged further every time a letter came from the emigrants. It would certainly make the young who stayed behind wonder, "What is there to tie us to our native place?"

The late eighteenth-century reform legislation in Denmark had already helped to breach formerly static population patterns. First of all, the abolition of peasant bondage had given the rural population the freedom to move; but equal importance must be ascribed to the abandonment of common-field cultivation. The movement of a family away from the village community severed some of the invisible ties that had bound these small groups of people together, but the individual farms were also becoming independent of the group mentality. An additional and not insignificant consequence of the new pattern of cultivation was the reduction of the vicar's position as the spiritual guardian of the parish, a development that local government reforms advanced further during the first half of the nineteenth century. This change in turn forms an important part of the background for the religious revivals that took place after 1820.

Attempts at a sociological explanation of the emergence of a tendency to migrate assume a society without crises or catastrophies, a society characterized by reasonably satisfactory conditions. But such crises did after all occur, and then the thought of moving or emigrating might arise not only from the influence of neighbors—it would be a last resort, a chance for survival. Both the Irish Potato Famine and, to some extent, the enclosure movement in England, with the resulting accumulation of an unemployed population in towns, exemplify this type of crisis. The underlying conditions that account for such natural and social crises also constitute the prime feature behind emigration: the demographic revolution after 1800. The sources of this enormous increase in population, which demographers have made the subject of lively polemics, seem to have been as follows: As far back as the seventeenth century, the birthrate was at an unusually high level, where it remained until the last quarter of the nineteenth century. The factor that caused the increase in population was a drop in the death rate from about 1800, a descending curve which was particularly steep in the middle of the nineteenth century and which still continues downward. The particularly marked increase in population during the period 1800–1875 resulted, therefore, from the conjunction of a high-level birthrate and a decline in the death rate—especially among infants. From about 1880, the situation altered, since a large-scale decrease in the birthrate occurred during the following decades. What is striking evidence of the nineteenth-century population explosion as a special European phenomenon is that although Europe suffered a migration loss of more than 50 million persons during this period, its share of the world population nevertheless increased from 20.7 to 25.2%.

Pressure from a surplus European population might have been absorbed through the contemporary industrial revolution. But actually, industrialization lagged behind population growth during most of the nineteenth century. The surplus rural population looked to the urban culture for employment, but the transformation of craft trades to mass production did not keep pace with the rush of people to the towns. This resulted in an excess urban population exerting an even greater pressure than that found in the rural districts.

As might be expected, emigration began first from the coastal areas of western Europe, where seamanship and acquaintance with overseas lands were the greatest. But in the course of the nineteenth century, emigration fever penetrated deep into central Europe. Even before World War I, it permeated one country after another from the west coast toward the east and south. For a long time the most important ports of departure were English, and after 1846 Irish ports also played a substantial role. The British Isles were always the largest and most important source of people for the settlement of the New World. Of the 52 million emigrants registered throughout the period 1846–1932, 35% came from Britain and the surrounding islands

The huge wave of emigrants from Ireland which broke upon the American shore in 1846–1847 has often been the subject of historical discussion. But it is a much less recognized fact that this emigration was not confined to those few years: It continued with only a slightly lessened volume almost to the end of the century. In most years, 1 or 2% of the population emigrated, so that the number of inhabitants fell from 8 million to about 4 million between 1840 and 1900. Also, the Irish case was fundamentally different from the English in many ways. Irish emigration was mainly a result of agricultural problems, while English emigration was caused by urban overpopulation. English emigration was to some degree characterized by organized exploitation of a surplus population, while Ireland presented a sad contrast of a wild, disorganized flight from famine—the product of a hopeless economic structure ignored by government authorities.

The German states formed another new source of emigrants from Europe, that began about 1832, grew from 1843 on, and became even more important after 1850–1855. During the first years a deliberate attempt was made to direct the stream of emigrants in the hope of establishing genuine German colonies in the manner of the English settlements. But the Germans never succeeded in using emigration as a political instrument. During the peak period in the 1870s and 1880s, the main sources of emigration were the northeastern sections of Germany: first and foremost Mechlenburg–Schwerin, Pomerania, Posen and Schleswig–Holstein. But compared to the emigration from the British Isles, that from Germany and Schleswig–Holstein remained relatively small; whereas 35 out of 100 emigrants from Europe spoke English, only 9 were German speaking.

Scandinavian emigration increased shortly after the German rush set in, but did not really reach sizable proportions until the end of the American Civil War, when it became comparable to the northwestern section of Europe. Even so, from an overall European perspective, the total emigration from Scandinavia made a relatively small contribution: For the period up to the First World War, the Scandinavian share of the entire European emigration amounted to 4.4%. Only in one 5-year period (1866–1870) did the number of emigrants from the three Scandinavian countries rise to more than 10% of the total for Europe. For the entire period 1840–1914, the number of Scandinavian overseas emigrants was some 2,168,000 persons. Although there is some uncertainty attached to the statistical data, especially from the early part of the period, the distribution among the three countries seems to have been:

Denmark	309,000	persons
Sweden	1,105,000	persons
Norway	754,000	persons

Out of the total only about 125,000 emigrants belong to the period 1810–1865, while the rest left during the years 1865–1914. There is no difficulty in detecting the boom in Scandinavian emigration.

Though it was noted earlier that northwestern Europe was pervaded by emigration fever, a distinct reservation must be made with regard to

Figure 1.1. Emigrants waiting for a ship in the harbor of Hamburg. Steerage passengers often had to wait for days, sometimes weeks, before departure on the voyage to New York. They were accommodated by the shipping companies in poor shelters like the one pictured above. (This photograph dates from the late 1890s and is part of the collection of the Genealogical Society, Salt Lake City, Utah.)

France. Here emigration never really made an impression, and during the entire period in question France was the one European country which could boast a positive balance of migration, i.e., an immigration that exceeded emigration. All in all, French overseas emigration during the period 1851–1908 was approximately 490,000, a very low figure for a country with such a large population. This phenomenon has naturally caused demographers to see a close relationship between emigration and population increase, since France, in contrast to the rest of Europe, had a very low birthrate from the very beginning of the nineteenth century. The annual increase in France was about 4 per 1000, while the corresponding figure for Denmark and Norway, for example, was 9 per 1000. France can hardly have been suffering from overpopulation, as was the case in England, and to some extent in Scandinavia. The moderate increase in France could be absorbed within the rural and urban structure, a process that created great dislocations in many other parts of Europe.

    Along with other factors, the striking contrast between population development in France and in the rest of Europe has led social scientists, especially sociologists, to consider the possibility that large-scale emigration served as a sociopolitical safety valve for the European nations. Those who comprised the surplus population faced towns filled with hosts of unemployed on one hand and, on the other, land patterns that left little room for the newcomer. As already mentioned, emigration was not the only alternative for the dissatisfied: Political activism provided another potential reaction to European conditions. Many an emigrant may have been involved in political movements, and then have left home after his original hopes were crushed by disappointments. By leaving their home countries, these 52 million emigrants may have taken the sting out of many revolutionary attempts in Europe. With some justice, one might maintain that emigration hampered the growth of revolutionary socialism in Europe after 1948. A large number of workers did not unite to follow the summons of the Socialist Manifesto, but spread throughout countries beyond the seas. It would be very hard to provide statistical proof for this hypothesis under the circumstances, but it certainly looks probable. These 52 million people were dissatisfied: They were a host of people distinguished by adjustment difficulties, and they came, as we shall see, mostly from the towns—from the very areas that supplied the best fuel for socialism.

The ratio between increase in population and emigration in England and in France might lead to the conclusion that there was a connection between the two elements. Other individual instances seem to confirm the idea—for example, the fact that among the Scandinavian countries Norway had the highest increase in population and also the highest percentage of emigrants. But if the theory is applied to a wider range of European countries, the question becomes far more complicated. It is impossible to establish a direct relationship between increase in population and emigration, especially for the countries of eastern Europe. Here we find a rate of increase after 1800 which greatly surpassed that of western Europe. In particular, the European part of Russia shows very high figures. Despite a high death rate, which never showed any sign of subsiding throughout the nineteenth century, the excess of births was so astonishingly high that the Russian population of 38 million in 1814 increased to 140 million about 100 years later.

But despite the enormous increase in population, eastern European countries did not join the great emigration until quite late. These huge masses of people first began to move in the late 1880s, but by then they swelled to a wave that completely overshadowed the one from western Europe. Between 1906 and 1914, the annual emigration from Russia, Austria–Hungary, and the Balkans was well over half a million. At about the same time the emigration rush reached southern Europe, particularly Italy, which itself yielded an average annual emigration of 402,000 persons between 1906 and 1910. The annual figure for Spain and Portugal was approximately 200,000. Emigrants from southern Europe, however, differed significantly from those of other countries by being what we might call birds of passage. Most of them came home again after a year. After 1900, the fare had become so cheap that it paid for poor Italian rural laborers to go to Argentina, say, in the fall to work during the harvest, and then return to their families the next spring. The very large figures for Italy consequently include a considerable number of repeating migrants, a point to be kept in mind when Italy, for the entire period between 1846 and 1932, appears as the second largest source of emigrants among the European countries, surpassed only by England.

In an overall view then, mass emigration from Europe came in two large waves, the first from western Europe, which began about 1845, and the second from eastern Europe, which began about 1890, outdistanced the figures for western Europe in 1896, and culminated between 1906 and 1914. In earlier works on this subject, a sharp distinction was made between the "early" wave of emigration from western Europe and the "later" wave from the Slavic and Latin regions. This distinction was maintained categorically in the large-scale inquiry into United States immigration and its consequences, undertaken by the Dillingham Committee, which was appointed by Congress and which reported in 1907 in no less than 21 volumes. The Committee argued that the later immigration differed in almost every respect from the early one, and that social conditions in the United States had been deeply influenced by this Latin–Slavic element.

It is true that the eastern European exodus had met difficulties of assimilation on a much larger scale than had the western European. While German, English, and Scandinavian emigrants settled in all parts of the country and rather evenly divided themselves between farming and industry, the Slavic and Italian immigrants accumulated in the important industrial centers in the East, and practically none of them entered farming. In this respect the Committee was right. But when they tried to establish statistically that there was a fundamental difference of "quality" between immigrants from the early and the later wave, the work of the Committee (and also that of many later scholars) seems to rest on faulty premises. This problem has been discussed by the Manchester scholar, Maldwyn Jones (1965). For instance, when the Committee arrived at the conclusion that many more men than women came from the eastern European countries and that a higher proportion of the later immigrants were unskilled workers and illiterate persons, it was partly a result of the Committee's statistical manipulations. They grouped the nations according to "early" and "late" migration and drew their conclusions from each group as a whole. The opposite procedure, dealing with each nation as a separate unit, gives completely different results. With the second method it becomes apparent, for example, that the percentage of men is higher among German, English, and Scandinavian immigrants than among the Jews, Austro-Hungarians, and Portuguese. Furthermore, Jones shows that a comparison between the composition of the western European emigration of the 1880s and that of the southern European emigration during the years just after 1900 is misleading, since these two waves of emigration demonstrate emigration in two different stages of development. That is to say, emigration from a certain area starts with one composition by sex, age, trade, etc., and in the course of some years these factors develop and change. In the 1880s, the western European emigration was an "old" phenomenon, whereas the eastern European flow was relatively new in 1907 when the Dillingham report was published. Therefore it would have been more correct if the comparison had been made between the western European emigration of the 1850s and the eastern and southern European emigration just after the turn of the century. That would have constituted an evaluation of the two phenomena at the same stage, and would have proved the existence of more or less the same pattern in the two emigrations. The Danish source material also sheds light on the changes in character that emigration from a certain area undergoes after the earliest emigrants have settled abroad.

The fact that large-scale emigration developed at different times in different European countries gives substance for thought. When an account of the mass emigration from Hungary, which showed a huge expansion during the last years of the 1890s, states that this great wave was caused by "unregulated land ownership, unsatisfactory administration of justice, low wages, and lack of education," this sounds like very probable reasoning. But this social pressure was not a new factor that had developed in Hungary toward the end of the 1890s. It was an old phenomenon which, probably as early as the 1860s, could have been sufficient cause to set a mass emigration moving; that is, it could have been simultaneous with the Scandinavian emigration. Social and economic causes alone are apparently insufficient. Other, imponderable factors must be taken into account—in part external influences that cause the idea of emigration to spread to the susceptible strata of the population, in part the fact that the population has reached a certain stage of intellectual development.

The student of pre-1914 emigration deals with numerical quantities of no mean order—great numbers of individuals, each of whom made a weighty decision that changed everything for him. But the enormous figures in themselves do not give a satisfactory impression of the degree to

TABLE 1.2

Annual Overseas Emigration per 100,000 of Population [a]

	1861–1870	1871–1880	1881–1890	1891–1900	1901–1908
Denmark	108	205	391	224	282
Sweden	228	234	701	415	428
Norway	581	470	963	454	855
England (+Scotland)	284	401	566	358	526
Ireland	1465	1024	1492	1010	1108
Germany	167	154	289	101	48
Austria–Hungary	11	31	108	155	450
Italy		99	323	491	1039
Russia	1	7	33	51	157

[a] From Sundbarg, *Emigrationsutredningen*, Vol. IV. Stockholm, 1910, p. 110.

which the emigration fever seized the populations of the individual countries. The figures are dead unless viewed in relation to the population
which the emigrants left. Consequently it is necessary to use a concept
that we shall call intensity of emigration: a figure that states the relative
number of persons of a given section of population who emigrated during
a certain period. Table 1.2 shows Gustav Sundbärg's calculations of the
intensity of emigration for several of the most important emigrant-
supplying countries in Europe. The figure of 108 for Denmark for the
decade 1861–1870, for instance, means that an annual average of 108
Danes for each 100,000 of the population emigrated between 1861 and
1870.

These figures give an idea of the emigration centers of Europe—regions
from which the highest percentages of the population left home. Ireland,
of course, has the highest figures of all: Over the entire period of 47 years,
an annual average of more than 1 out of 100 went overseas. Perhaps
more surprising is the fact that Norway comes next after Ireland in intensity of emigration. England and Sweden alternate as third and fourth on
the list. Denmark comes much further down the list, but with higher figures than Germany. Actually, nations are not rational units for analysis
of emigration data. Intensity figures for an area as large as Germany will
always hide the fact that emigration was concentrated in certain regions
while others were virtually unaffected. National boundaries seem to have
been of consequence for emigration only in those few cases where national
conflicts arose; as far as Germany was concerned, this was distinctly the
case with Alsace–Lorraine and North Schleswig.

2

MASS EMIGRATION
AND PUBLIC OPINION

The relatively inconsequential role that national frontiers played in mass emigration was due above all to the nearly uniform reaction by different governments: None of them tried to obstruct the large-scale departure. The migration of the 50 million took place during the golden period of liberalism, when the mere thought of encroachment on the freedom of the individual was anathema.

Before 1800 the situation was quite the opposite. The economists of the mercantile system viewed the state as a whole, the individual inhabitants being the raw material from which the nation was built. The economists of that period regarded the king's subjects first and foremost as a means of income. A strong increase in population, sometimes advanced by calling in foreigners (Huguenots, Jews, Dutch, etc.), was seen as a path to prosperity. Emigration was consequently regarded as a kind of crime, since the emigrating farmer or townsman would be robbing his country of his labor. Only where emigration was aimed at overseas colonization would it be permissible. Thus England encouraged emigration to the southern states, but in return the emigrants were compelled to trade only with England, their production providing English industry with raw materials.

Denmark, Norway, and Sweden all maintained the same mercantilist principles concerning emigration as did England and France. That view was expressed most clearly in a Swedish ordinance of 1768, which said:

> Although natural duty obliges all to love their home country and to remain there and to earn an honest living, some evil-minded persons, lacking these natural feelings of duty, have illegally left their country to go to foreign places with the treacherous hope of being able to support themselves more easily.

Fifteen years earlier a similar ordinance had been issued in Denmark. In 1753 Frederick V issued a warning to the population not to be led astray by the emissary who was traveling around the king's "duchies and provinces." This "general order regarding emigration to foreign colonies in America" threatened punishment of any person who employed "flattering temptations and malicious seductions," but did not state any definite prohibition of emigration. Neither does the Danish ordinance of May 16, 1760, concerning punishment of those who "seduce factory workers or transport them secretly out of the country." This ordinance is known to have been employed at least once. That was in 1786 when two persons in Copenhagen, Elias Hoel and Johan Zimmerman, had engaged in recruitment of colonists for a Russian colony at Cherson in Russia. For this activity Hoel was sentenced to forced labor for 1 year, while the other man was acquitted. The authorities did not go as far as to prohibit emigration, as was done in England, where several acts during the 1720s prevented craftsmen from leaving the country. Admittedly, these prohibitions very quickly proved to be of little avail, since the culprit obviously was no longer present when the sentence was to be executed. But the law had many other means of keeping the king's subjects in the country, the most effective of which was peasant bondage. The maintenance of a military draft offered another excuse for a strict population policy.

However, during the last decades of the eighteenth century, the rigorous mercantilistic population policy was relaxed. The principles of natural rights, as formulated by Locke and extended by the French philosophers, penetrated into the realm of legislation. The French Declaration of the Rights of Man in 1789 asserted "the right of free travel and free movement," and the Constitution of 1791 referred to "the freedom to go, to stay, and to depart." In the following decades the liberalistic view of the right to migrate spread throughout the whole of Europe. A kind of transitional system was introduced in Prussia in 1794, when it was laid down in the General Law that any person wanting to emigrate would be obliged to pay one-tenth of his possessions by way of "departure money"; the same system as was to be practiced in a much aggravated form against Jewish emigrants in Nazi Germany.

In Denmark there seems to have been a change in the direction of a more liberal emigration policy as early as 1792. This became apparent when a London organization sent recruiters to Hamburg and Altona, equipped with ships in order to enlist people for an American emigration project called the Genesee Association. One ship with emigrants from Germany and Schleswig–Holstein had already left for Philadelphia when the authorities of Hamburg and Prussia decided to stop this activity and proposed that the Danish Prefect of Altona do the same. The Danish Prefect refused on grounds of principle: The Danes were a free people, unbound by restrictions and so satisfied with conditions that their sovereign had no need to adopt measures against emigration.

After the Napoleonic Wars the right to free emigration was laid down in the constitutions of several European countries: in three German states even before 1820, in Bavaria in 1818, in Württemberg in 1819, and in Hessen–Darmstadt in 1820. In Prussia, where military service was a matter of major importance, this freedom was not given statutory form until the 1850 constitutional amendment (Section 11), which remained in force until 1918. But up until the turn of the century the Prussian authorities were hostile toward emigration by young men fit for military service. When the question of protection of German emigrants against exploitation en route was brought up in the Prussian Landestag in 1863, Bismarck answered that the entire thing ought to be brought to an end because emigration itself was treason against the fatherland, and consequently the country could hardly be under any obligation to protect emigrants.

In Denmark freedom to emigrate never entered the statute book, but by the 1830s it seems, to judge from a number of documents from ministeries and departments, that it was tacitly accepted. Adam Smith's theory of a natural economic harmony based on the concept of an "economic man" who always gravitates toward higher wage levels to his own and society's benefit formed the ideological background for abolition of all emigration restrictions. The view was thus established, and is still accepted, that the decisive factor in emigration was economic, i.e., the difference between the wage levels of the Old World and the New.

It is necessary to stress here that very often emigrants made up their minds on the basis of hypothetical calculations of an expected increase of income, and only in very few cases was the decision made in line with the experienced businessman's calculation of profits. Many unpredictable elements might mislead Adam Smith's "economic man." Especially during the beginning of the emigration period, the emigrants found it very difficult to estimate the real wages in the immigration country, i.e., the relation between wages paid and cost of living. Very likely many of them were unaware of the problem. Many newcomers were sorely disappointed by the wages offered them. An inquiry in the United States in the years 1905–1907 showed that the wages of newcomers were approximately 54% below the average wage for Americans and in the case of Italian workers as low as 20% of what was paid to the average "American" worker. All the same, that 20% might have constituted an increased income for a destitute Italian rural laborer. But after 1900, we find that the enormous immigration into the United States caused real wages there to fall until they were roughly at the European level. If we put the real wages of Europe in 1899 at 100, the corresponding figure for America in 1905 was 109, in 1911 only 93, but by 1913, 103.

However, we should not forget that higher income levels were not the goal of all overseas emigrants. Admittedly, about three-fifths of the 52 million leaving Europe went to the rich United States, but a not insignificant number went to areas which at that time were regarded as underdeveloped countries compared to the United States. Both Brazil and Australia, for instance, fall into this category.

While Adam Smith, as far as we know, did not subject international migrations and their consequences to separate examination, these problems were taken up by the somewhat younger economist Malthus. For his theories of population growth and the lack of opportunities for corresponding increases of production, overseas migration was necessarily an important point. But the possibility of a systematic cultivation of the American prairie and the Argentinian pampa did not cause Malthus to change his pessimistic prophecy. He thought that emigration might for a time ease the pressure from the surplus population of the emigration countries, but the improvement would be only temporary, since the "holes" would soon be filled as a result of earlier marriages and, consequently, an increased birthrate. Malthus was well aware that emigration was advantageous in that it brought larger areas under cultivation; but anticipating the acceleration in food production that was to come from the new wheat and corn-producing areas was hardly within the range of his imagination.

There is a certain continuity from the Malthusian theory of population increase to the Walker theory of 1891, which was of considerable importance in demographic discussion around the turn of the century. Francis A. Walker, director of the Bureau of Census of the United States, maintained that natural fertility was dependent on the pressure of population. The larger the influx from abroad, the more the fertility of the settled population would decrease. In other words, Walker maintained that the population of the United States would have shown the same increase as was actually the case even if no immigration into the country had occurred. So immigrants did not add to the American population, but replaced unborn Yankees. It is true that the birthrate of the "native stock" of Americans was on the wane during the nineteenth century, but modern scholars see this more as a result of urbanization and industrialization than of the influx of immigrants. However, the theory gained widespread acceptance before 1914, and was one of the most powerful arguments in those political circles which wanted to stop immigration into the United States—a policy that the first Quota Law made a reality in 1921.

It was not merely a political concept of personal freedom that formed the basis for the liberalistic freedom to emigrate that prevailed after 1800. A more practical outlook upon the conditions of the period was gaining a foothold. The idea spread among those governing the European states that emigration might help rid their countries of a constantly increasing group of poor, unemployed people, who were a burden to their countries economically, socially, and politically. That this idea was first worked out and converted into reality in England must have been a consequence of the special magnitude of the burden there. Industrial towns were crowded with unemployed masses kept barely above subsistence level by private charity (the scenery well known from Oliver Twist). The idea of a combined solution to this social problem of the home country and of the political problem of how to secure the territory acquired overseas as colonies was an obvious one, and hardly a new one in the nineteenth century. It had been practised during the previous century in the form of large-scale export of labor to the American colonies from Liverpool. But after 1814, this policy was taken up again on a grander scale, the instrument being an offer to poor people of cheap transportation across the seas. In many ways this so-called "assisted passage" became the nuclear weapon of imperialism, a social policy with wide implications. By 1819 Parliament had already voted a large appropriation for free transportation of emigrants to the Cape Colony. The idea was adopted by private parties (including a Mr. Wakefield) who saw this as a cheap solution to the problem of poor relief. During the decade 1836–1846, parishes contributed approximately £80,000, which was used for the shipping of about 14,000 poor Englishmen across the seas. The movement gained even larger dimensions after 1840 when a special ministry, the Colonial Land and Emigration Department, was established. This department was instrumental in sending 339,000 voluntary emigrants to Australia and other parts of the British colonial empire between 1849 and 1869. During this time, £4.9 million was spent on passage assistance, etc., 89% of which was paid by the authorities—an immense sum of money that no doubt was returned with interest and compound interest, too!

The idea of using freedom of emigration as a means of getting rid of "surplus" people was taken to its logical extreme in England during the nineteenth century: As an anticrime measure, criminals were sent to America, a more voluntary arrangement than the actual deportation of convicts to Australia at the beginning of the century. In August 1871, an act was passed "for the more effectual prevention of crime," under which sentences in certain cases might be tempered or even remitted if the criminal promised to emigrate, particularly to Canada or the United States. According to a American report, this caused the number of prisoners in English prisons to fall from about 20,000 in 1870 to less than 12,000 in 1891.

In the beginning, at least, this systematic, government-subsidized emigration remained a purely British phenomenon. True, the Austro-Hungarian government started a similar project in 1903, with emigrants being recruited by the thousands in the Slavic and Magyar territories; but in this case there was no political thought of colonization. On the contrary, it was stipulated at first that the emigrants were to keep their Austro-Hungarian citizenship and preferably return with the money they made.

In Denmark, as was almost predictable, ideas such as Wakefield's failed to take root. The government remained passive in connection with emigration. The surprising thing in working with the Danish source material is the paucity of commentary on emigration by contemporaries, even during the peak years in the 1880s when roughly 10,000 Danes left the country each year. But the very obvious thought of ridding society of destitute citizens, who might burden a parish for years and years, by buying them a ticket to America was current in Denmark at least as early as 1864. In February of that year, while war was raging in Denmark, the Danish resident at Washington, V. R. Raasløff (later minister of war), was called in to the secretary of state, Seward. The latter pointed out to Raasløff a report received from the consul at Elsinore according to which Danish parishes were shipping troublesome persons "on a large scale" to the United States. Much evidence indicates that the practice was not ended despite this complaint from the highest quarters. In general the American authorities found it extremely difficult to control the extent to which European countries solved their poor relief problems in this manner. The relief official of any parish might hand over a ticket to America to the most hopeless drunkard of his district, and only if the emigrant was too outspoken about the origin of his passage money when he reached, for instance, the authorities at Castle Garden, would the truth be discovered.

However, in some parishes the local authorities were so law-abiding as to inquire of higher authorities whether the method was legal, and from these cases one gets a clear impression of the wavering practice of the Danish administration. In 1873 the Town Council of Store Hedinge asked the Foreign Ministry if they might ship P. C. Gjessel, a journeyman baker, to the United States at the expense of the town, as he would otherwise have to be sent to the workhouse. The Ministry found it an excellent idea and even assisted insofar as the consul-general in New York was ordered to hand over to the baker 25 kroner on his arrival. Even as late as 1897 a similar case occurred: This time it was the poor-relief authorities who asked, and the same Ministry again provided help. But on the other hand, when local authorities applied to the Ministry of Justice for advice the answer was a flat refusal, "as it cannot be considered a form of relief to send paupers away." In 1882 this ruling was announced publicly for the second time: "On the occasion of a report to the effect that the poor relief funds of a certain parish have financed in several cases the transportation of paupers and others to America, it is decided that pursuant to an Act dated 1756 such use is not legal." A third publication of the decision was found necessary in November 1889, when the Town Council of Køge was found to have sent a drunkard to Buenos Aires.

But emigration was not only useful in reducing expenditure for poor relief—crimes of various types could be dealt with by the same measure. The Copenhagen police employed this method from at least 1865, as is documented in the reports of Døllner, the consul-general in New York, who warned against doing it too openly. Døllner wrote that when a criminal was pardoned it was unnecessary to write "in return for emigration to America"; merely "in return for leaving the country" would suffice. "That is exactly what we do," the Ministry of Justice answered, "but the newspapers disclose the true facts."

Døllner's warnings were of no avail. During the summer of 1868 the first official complaint came from Yeaman, the American ambassador at Copenhagen. A thief, Ole Sørenson, had been shipped to New York (he was also suspected of murder), and there was no hiding the fact that the police had arranged the removal of this unsavory character. The Ole Sørenson case seems to have caused some commotion in the United States and was said to have been the occasion for a memorandum from the president of the United States to Congress in which he recommended the passing of an act prohibiting immigration of convicts. However, President Andrew Johnson had little support in Congress at the time, and the bill did not pass until 1875. In spite of the complaint the police clearly continued to use this method to weed out the Copenhagen criminal world, and some evidence indicates that it was by no means a small-scale operation.

This situation lasted for only a few years. In May of 1874, the Castle Garden authorities carried out a thorough inspection when the ship "Washington" arrived with emigrants from Denmark and Sweden. Among them were discovered no less than six Copenhagen offenders, dispatched by the police. Now the American government took up the matter seriously. A sharp note in which the case was called "an unusual and unfriendly act" was delivered to P. Vedel, the permanent under-secretary of state for foreign affairs, and the Danish resident at Washington was called to account by the secretary of state. The Copenhagen police chief, Crone, tried to clear himself by referring to a special fund appropriated by the Copenhagen town authorities for that very purpose, and furthermore maintained that all six had served their sentences and left voluntarily. But it is obvious that Crone found the method quite proper, as old offenders would have a chance of improving their moral and economic situation in the United States, where they were not stigmatized by their prison record. However, the head official of the Danish Ministry of Justice, Ricard, says clearly that he disapproved of this point of view, and particularly of the fact that, despite warnings during the previous years, the police had failed to see to it that these practices were hidden more carefully from the American authorities. Thus the checks which the offenders received on departure (the six persons in question in 1874 each got $7.50 by way of initial capital) were stamped and signed by the police. Danish Minister of Justice C. F. Klein decided that the answer to the American government ought to contain both an apology and an attempt to play down the importance of the entire matter. Furthermore, the chief of police was to be exhorted to refrain from assisting any more offenders to emigrate. P. Vedel drafted an answer along these lines.

But the chief did not stop. He merely changed methods so that at least ostensibly the ticket would be paid for not by the police, but by relatives or other private persons with an interest in the offender. And as cases from 1882 and 1887 proved, prisoners were still released on condition that they left for America. In 1882, when the person in question was a swindler from Oldrup in Jutland, the American chargé d'affaires succeeded in preventing his departure. More serious was the affair in 1887, when a Mr. Riemenschneider earned 6 years' imprisonment by producing printing blocks for 1000 kroner notes. Before beginning to serve his term, he was offered the alternative of emigration and chose that. An accomplice of his preferred prison. But still the police had not learned their lesson. Every detail of Riemenschneider's departure was printed in *Morgenbladet,* the liberal Copenhagen paper, and on his arrival in New York the *New York Times* discussed the case in acrimonious terms.

During the 1890s the Society for the Welfare of Offenders seems to have taken it upon itself to arrange quietly for convicts' passage, but on one occasion rumors reached the public and were seized upon as a sensation by the American press. It caused a good deal of commotion when the Danish master thief Wirle was dispatched to the United States in 1894: A San Francisco newspaper ran the story with the headline "An-archist coming!" Once more the American ambassador at Copenhagen de-livered a protest.

One quaint episode from 1885 shows how poor communication could be between different departments of the police—the left hand did not always know what the right hand was doing. In the spring of 1885, a glove-maker named Hurwitz emigrated. At Stettin he lodged a pompous complaint with the Danish consul about the treatment he had been sub-jected to as a result of unsatisfactory traveling facilities. As usual, the police started an inquiry and charged the emigration agent with violation of the law about transportation of emigrants. However, when it came out during the investigation that the passage money necessary to get Hurwitz out of the way had been provided by the inspector of the Second District of the Copenhagen police, the emigration police immediately piped down and shelved the matter.

"Export" of paupers and convicts was no Danish or English specialty. As early as 1868 the American authorities were aware that the same practice was employed by Westphalia and Bavaria, and during the follow-ing years cases occurred in Sweden, Norway, and France. How large a number of paupers and old offenders were exported from Denmark is naturally unknown; all that is important here is to establish that European governments and authorities were of the opinion that mass emigration might be an advantage in ridding their countries of undesirable and "surplus" elements.

The best evidence of the view that the Danish authorities valued the social benefits of emigration shows up perhaps in connection with com-pulsory military service, which was introduced during the peak emigration years. The Military Service Act of March 6, 1869 (Sections 50 and 51) did state that it was punishable to leave the country without permission before draft age. But in 1887, when the First Conscription District sought in subdued terms to introduce a requirement that every emigrant state his conscription register number on his contract of emigration, the police commissioner refused point blank, giving as his reason that this was "liable to cause, compared with the present freedom in this field, con-siderable trouble to the emigrants, who would not get used to this restriction."

Further evidence of the sympathetic attitude toward emigration is found in the legislation that was passed in the course of the nineteenth century by all European countries to protect emigrants before and during the dangerous passage across the ocean. In this respect as in many others, England led the way, in perfect accordance with the general British under-standing of the political implications of emigration. This protective legislation is of general importance, because in many ways it created a precedent for the large complex of nineteenth-century British legislation passed to protect simple people from the callous institutions of industrialism and capitalism. Thus the social welfare concept, a phenomenon central to modern history that has developed during this century, can be traced back to the first British Emigration Act of 1803. The Passengers Act of 1803, which made provisions concerning the maximum number of passengers in relation to the size of the ship, was carried by a number of private members of Parliament; but it was without real importance because it provided neither a controlling authority nor any possibility of prosecution in the case of offence. Thus it was characteristic of both the 1803 Passengers Act and its subsequent amendments in 1828, 1834, and 1852—and of the first factory legislation from the same period—that they were humanitarian manifestations rather than actual protective measures. The sentiment behind this legislation was aptly expressed in the words, "Why should we deny our fellow citizens the protection and security which slaves have recently been guaranteed by law?"

In the course of the 1850s, a large number of European countries followed the British example. First came several German states where emigration was at an unusually high level at that time. As far as we know, Prussia came first with a directive in April, 1850; then followed Mecklenburg–Schwerin, Hesse, Saxony, and Hamburg. The legislation in force in Hamburg and Bremen was of fundamental importance, since practically the entire German emigration went by way of one of those two ports. In the 1860s, the Scandinavian countries followed suit—Norway by an ordinance on July 23, 1863 (to which was added a provisional order on April 6, 1867), and Sweden by the acts of August 6, 1864 (amended in February, 1869). A fault common to the emigration legislation before 1880 was that practically all of it dealt only with problems in connection with the passage, i.e., accommodation and provisions on board the vessels sailing between Europe and the overseas destinations. Legislation was indeed badly needed on these matters, as shipowners, particularly during the sailing ship era, had exploited defenceless emigrants in the most grievous manner—by filling the vessels until the passengers were crowded like sardines in a tin, underfeeding them, and neglecting the most elementary sanitary facilities, with the result that epidemics spread like wildfire in the packed quarters. But it is characteristic, at least of the Scandinavian countries, that emigrants were protected only to a very small degree against the exploitative recruitment practices and the lures laid by agents, despite the fact that it was the increasing information on these abuses that caused the question of legislation to be taken up in Denmark.

Quite apart from the impetus that may have come from Norwegian and

Swedish legislation in this field, the immediate initiative that led to an emigration act for Denmark had two sources. One was Døllner, the Danish consul-general in New York, who in several reports from 1865 had described the misery of Danish emigrants when they arrived at Castle Garden. The other was Captain Wilhelm Sommer, himself an emigration agent. In 1866–1867, he published several pamphlets earnestly requesting legislation in this field. But both Sommer and Crone, the chief of police whose opinion was asked about the need for protective measures, were noticeably more uneasy about the confidence tricks employed in the recruitment of simple peasants and townspeople than about the dangers these people had to face during the passage. Thus Crone writes about "the incredible recklessness with which especially the common man places himself in the hands of any agent." Still, the Danish Transportation of Emigrants Act of May 1, 1868, as its title correctly indicates, deals with practically nothing but protection during passage. It is true that the agents were bound both by their need to obtain a license to operate and by the requirement of an endorsement from the police on every single emigration contract. But an agent's responsibility was limited only to ensuring that sufficient accommodation and provisions were on board.

A tentative effort to control the agents' rather callous methods of recruiting potential emigrants was made in the March 25, 1872 amendment to the transportation act. But this attempt proved ineffective in contrast to the energy with which the agents pursued their business. The prevailing liberal principles only allowed legislation to intervene with emigration to a very limited degree; theoretically it did not concern the state that individual citizens left the country. But the citizens had a right to expect the state to offer them protection against physical injury during the transportation from the country. In this respect, Danish emigration legislation did not differ from that of other European countries.

The Emigration Act of 1868, with the amendments of 1872, remained in force unaltered until 1914. After 1914 the passive, protective emigration policy was followed by a more active government intervention into both the volume and directions of emigration. This new example of state paternalism was introduced in Europe in the 1880s, but first reached Denmark after World War I. Switzerland pioneered in the new active trend in emigration legislation, and passed legislation in 1888 that placed emigration questions in the hands of the Council of the Confederation, a provision that gave this Council the possibility of pursuing either a restrictive policy or of directing emigration toward definite colonization projects. Ostensibly the purpose of the new measures was protection, but in actual fact emigration had been made a matter of public policy.

In Germany the Swiss system was introduced with the national Emigration Act of 1897, which likewise placed the power with the highest authorities, the chancellor and the Federal Council together. The idea was that concessions would be granted only to agents and shipowners who held approved opinions about emigration policy—the purpose of this being the advancement of German colonial policy. Similar provisions were later introduced in Hungary, Austria, Italy, Spain, and Portugal.

The idea of an alteration of emigration policy first appeared in Denmark in the 1920s as a direct result of the recurrent economic crises that had produced serious unemployment, a problem for which the government, with its growing social consciousness, felt compelled to provide a solution. From the 1920s, writers in *Socialt Tidsskrift,* an influential Danish periodical concerned with social problems, wrote in favor of the creation of a Danish emigration commission similar to the German model. These views repeated an opinion stated as early as 1869 by C. St. A. Bille in *Dagbladet* that the fundamental fault of Danish emigration legislation was the lack of guidance offered to emigrants. In the 1920s, these ideas met with strong sympathy. In 1927 a commission was appointed, which worked out a bill that was immediately placed before the Rigsdag. Here the suggestion of the establishment of a commission for emigration with a staff of its own was found to be too expensive, and for two sessions the bill was shelved in a committee. Finally, in May of 1934 K. K. Steincke, then minister of social affairs, succeeded in getting the bill passed, though in a mutilated form and only because a definite plan for colonization existed which required an organization behind it.

Under the new act, a state Office of Emigration was set up to combine all functions related to emigration, i.e., supervision of agents, information activities and, most important, the execution of the much discussed colonization project. Venezuela was chosen as the goal, and about 450 Danish emigrants were dispatched after prolonged negotiations with the government of that country. The project was a pronounced failure. The emigration office also provided an information service by issuing pamphlets about the countries of immigration. Budget cuts in 1959 eliminated the emigration office as an independent institution.

From the preceding account, it should be clear that the attitude of the state toward emigration has passed through three stages: the restrictive stage before 1800, the protective phase (which was dominant during the period covered by this book), and lastly, the period of definite population policies, which began before 1900 in Europe as a whole but did not reach Denmark before the late 1920s.

It is characteristic for the liberalistic period, about 1800–1914, that it is extremely unusual to find discussions on the question of whether or not emigration is advantageous. When the emigration bills were presented in the Rigsdag in 1868 and 1872, virtually no opinions on questions of principle were put forward. Even the minister of justice himself was, as is typical for the period, rather hesitant about the general issues involved. In 1873 he wrote:

> Without feeling able to offer any very definite opinion as to whether large-scale emigration is an advantage or not, I am inclined to give an answer in the negative, and I am certainly convinced that there is every reason to take measures to the extent possible to prevent rash, insufficiently considered emigration which violates existing obligations.

In the same resolution, Ricard, the highest-ranking official in the Ministry of Justice, voiced his uncertainty on the subject, but referred to the head of the Office of Statistics as "supposedly of the opinion that emigration is a good thing." This man was the young statistician V. Falbe-Hansen (later a well-known conservative politician). Falbe-Hansen introduced a debate on emigration in the newly established Society for Political Economics that same year, 1873. He had recently returned from the United States and was enthusiastic about the refreshing delights of the New World. In an inspired speech, Falbe-Hansen praised mass emigration as a way of improving socioeconomic conditions in Denmark. "The main reason for the unsatisfactory conditions of the working classes is their excessive reproduction," he maintained. A thinning out of these classes would better the situation, and he was also strongly in favor of sending Danish convicts, prostitutes, agitators, and paupers to America. He concluded by suggesting the adoption of a resolution to the effect that the Society regarded large-scale emigration as a public benefit. However, his suggestion was evidently not carried. Thirty years later Adolph Jensen, also a newly appointed head of the Danish Office of Statistics, addressed a new meeting on emigration held in this same Society in December of 1903. Though his conclusions were to a degree similar to Falbe-Hansen's, Jensen presented a more balanced view which, because of its factual weight and its exceptionally intelligent reasoning, could not help but influence those who later dealt with this topic.

From the opposite political camp, that of the large Liberal–Agrarian Party (which had the majority in the Folketing), we find a single opinion printed in *Dansk Folketidende,* 1873, which illustrates the opposite point of view:

> As long as we have large stretches of land which might be made the object of more intensive cultivation, and as long as other

branches of trade might be developed much more, we must certainly deplore that the country should every year suffer such considerable losses of labor and capital.

Of course the Liberals used the topic as an admonition that society ought to be reformed, not in the interests of the favored few, but in those of the entire population. "Luckily," the writer goes on, "the rich are beginning to notice emigration because of a lack of manpower, but maybe the rich prefer this disadvantage to increasing discontent, and therefore perhaps even wish to promote emigration."

3

TRENDS IN THE LITERATURE ON THE BACKGROUND AND CAUSES OF MASS EMIGRATION

Since the turn of the century hundreds of large and small books have been published on mass emigration as a collective, social problem. One author after another has tried to tackle the cause of the phenomenon, its background, and its consequences by analyzing a limited part of the absolutely immense mass of raw source material concerning pre-World War I emigration. It is outside the scope of this book to deal with this literature; besides, several good surveys of it have appeared in recent years. Here only a few highlights will be presented, and only insofar as they touch on the line of thinking behind this book.

The first major European inquiry into emigration and its causes was made in Sweden where, at about the turn of the century, a powerful political movement arose which opposed the draining of labor resources. This prompted the Swedish government in 1907 to appoint a commission, "The Emigrationsutredning," which was to investigate the background of the emigration and its various aspects. Gustav Sundbärg, a dynamic character and an internationally recognized specialist in population statistics, was appointed to take charge. In the course of the next 5 years, he, together with a team of talented statisticians, compiled an incredibly comprehensive study which was published as a report that contained 892 pages and no less than 20 volumes of documents. This monumental work formed a European counterpart to the 21 volumes of the Dillingham report; both of them influenced political considerations as to whether overseas emigration should be stopped through legislative intervention.

Sundbärg's achievement still remains a cornerstone of European emigration research, an inexhaustible supply of statistical and nonstatistical materials concerning not only Sweden but the whole of Europe. His conclusions, on the other hand, must be regarded as obsolete. He had many peculiar opinions, especially about the character of his fellow countrymen. The influence of the Swedish national character, the "folk spirit," upon emigration is a theme on which Sundbärg formulated his own, frequently critical, views in the form of aphorisms, and which he published as an independent supplement. It was a most unusual supplement to accompany a government report. His conception of the Danes as compared to the Swedes finds amusing expression in terms that are sometimes flattering, sometimes anything but.

The background of Swedish mass emigration must be found in the structure of Swedish agriculture, concluded Sundbärg. He considered the influence of the towns and the entire set of problems relating to urbanization and internal migration of only secondary importance, and he touched only lightly on the idea that migration is the consequence of an interplay of forces in the country of emigration and in the country of immigration. In short, he saw emigration as a purely European question: The whole set of problems relating to push and pull effects in migration was unknown to Sundbärg, who lived in a period when research into economic cycles was still in an embryo stage. The voluminous arguments of the report and the amount of material embraced more or less took the breath away from further investigation in Sweden. Not until about 1960 was the study of emigration resumed as historical research at the universities of Lund and Uppsala. Work on questions leading out of Sundbärg's study was also pursued outside Sweden and Scandinavia, but to a very large extent was still based on the detailed Swedish raw material. Norwegian emigration, however, has been the object of a comprehensive monograph by Ingrid Semmingsen: *Vejen mot Vest I-II* (1942–1950), an extremely well-written and informative book.

World War I and the following years of financial crises accelerated the development of economic research, and at that time mass emigration came to be regarded as a factor in international economics. The issue was made the subject of research by large institutions, primarily by the National Bureau of Economic Research which, strongly supported by the newly established International Labour Organization (ILO), undertook to continue the collection of international emigration statistics initiated by Sundbärg. The result was two volumes called *International Migration* published in 1929 and 1931, the first containing a vast collection of statistical source material from countries all over the world, and the second brief interpretations of the material by experts from the various national regions. The section concerning the Scandinavian countries was written by Adolph Jensen, then head of the Office of Statistics in Denmark.

However, even before this collection of material was published, the first analysis that used rather more sophisticated statistical techniques had appeared. Then an American, Harry Jerome, published *Migration and Business Cycles* in 1926—one in a series of publications issued by the National Bureau of Economic Research. The violent fluctuations of the economic cycle since the 1920s had focused research on upward and downward economic movements, and Jerome's study of the correlation between business cycles and overseas migration was to constitute a "discovery" in the study of emigration that was decisive for the research done during the following decades.

Jerome's achievement in this field was to put a more precise formulation on the theory of push and pull in international migrations. Of course it had not been unknown before 1926 that these two factors were involved in causing mass emigration—i.e., that socioeconomic conditions in the country of emigration forced a group of young people to set out on a voyage across the ocean, and that the higher wage levels and the uncultivated areas beyond the sea exercised an attraction on Europe which drew the masses toward the new lands. Jerome took the opportunity to give a detailed description of the relationship between push and pull by comparing the strong fluctuations of the flow of emigrants from year to year with the fluctuations of the business cycles in Europe and America. He reached the conclusion that the fluctuations of the European market trend did not correspond nearly so well with the oscillations in emigration as did those of the American market trend. Apart from an approximately 1-year lag in emigration behind the upward and downward movements of the market, the two movements corresponded very closely. The conclusion must obviously be that the volume of emigration was governed primarily by economic conditions in the United States. When a boom was beginning to form in America, the rumor would begin to spread in Europe, and large numbers of emigrants would set out. When a depression followed with unemployment and falling wages, the stream of emigrants decreased, too. In other words, the pull was much stronger than the push.

Harry Jerome's demonstration of the fact that the volume of emigration before 1914 had been governed by the trend of the American market corresponds very well with the major occurrence in the field of population policy during the 1920s, the American restrictions on immigration. But his inquiry also seems to have been instrumental in bringing about a change in the method, and consequently also the direction, of migration research. Whereas it was formerly studied as a problem in political science and social policy, as a descriptive analysis employing statistics along the same lines as Sundbärg had followed in Sweden and Falbe-Hansen and Scharling in Denmark, emigration from this point on was regarded as a subject for economic analysis. General historical source material was pushed aside, while statistics (treated with all the most elaborate tools of modern economic theory) gained the foreground.

Dorothy Swaine Thomas, who was to develop Jerome's theory on the basis of Swedish material, offers a striking example of this shift. Her weighty book of 1941, *Social and Economic Aspects of Swedish Population Movements, 1750–1935,* has tables, diagrams, correlations, and analyses of regression on practically every one of its 478 pages, an impressive exploration reaching in depth into the statistics. The results confirmed Jerome's demonstration that the pull effect was stronger than the push effect. One of the new aspects of Thomas's study was that she distinguished between urban and rural emigration and between the economic cycles of the corresponding groups. This made it possible for her to make the reservation vis à vis Jerome that an industrial boom in Sweden and the consequent migration to the cities might contribute to a lessening of emigration. Thomas also investigated whether the variations in harvest yields in Sweden might have influenced the volume of emigration; but aside from the years of pronounced crop failure (1867–1869), she found no connection. A similar examination which I have done on the basis of Danish source material yielded an equally negative result. The explanation probably lies in the fact that the emigrants were not predominantly the farmers themselves, but their servants, whose wages need not have been directly dependent on the yield.

The pattern of the dynamics of mass emigration outlined by Jerome and Thomas was to be repeated in practically all subsequent works on this subject; and indeed it introduced a tidy order into the cause–effect relationship. The correlation between the fluctuations of emigration and those of the American market seemed a striking proof not to be easily refuted. At the same time, in many cases the relationship might be misunderstood, and push and pull might appear to be alternative solutions. But insofar as the motives of individual emigrants were concerned, the point was not that they made their decision to leave *either* because they were dissatisfied in Europe *or* because they felt attracted to America. It was a matter of *both* dissatisfaction *and* attraction, where the two ingredients, push and pull, were mixed in different proportions according to the fluctuations of the business cycles. For the more sophisticated economists and demographers, pure push–pull theory was an interesting creation, but not a final solution to the extremely complicated mechanisms behind the enormous migrations.

A problem which raised doubts about the true causal relationship between business cycles and emigration was the difficulty in establishing the exact order of sequence between these two factors during the few decisive months in the U.S.A. when a boom set in: Which came first, the increase in the flow of emigrants or the upward trend of the market? Measurement of the monthly flow of emigrants does not pose any problem apart from doubts as to the value of the source material. But what kind of figures will serve to measure the trends of the economy of a huge and richly diverse continent, where, moreover, statistical information was imperfectly kept? Should the unit of measurement be unemployment in the cities of the east coast or the price per bushel of wheat from the prairie?

Uncertainty next arises as to whether the flow of immigrants itself into the United States was a contributing factor in the barometric movements of the American economy, an idea that forms the basis for the next important work we will discuss—the contribution of Brinley Thomas. Thomas's development of the push–pull thesis goes so far as to almost refute the previous theory that the pull effect takes priority over the push effect. His works from 1951 and 1954 offer hitherto the most subtle, comprehensive, and also most disputed model of the dynamics of mass emigration. Hardly armchair reading for the layman, Thomas's studies open up wide perspectives not only for the study of migration but also for modern economic history in general.

Brinley Thomas's first achievement was to include a whole series of economic factors in his inquiry into cyclical fluctuations in order to provide a more exhaustive definition of business cycles. He made thorough use of railroad investments and indices of building activity, coal and steel production, and so forth. In the first paper, *Migration and the Rhythm of Economic Growth, 1830–1913,* Thomas demonstrated that in the early decades one could not ascertain a clear dominance on the part of the pull factor. But after the end of the Civil War, when investments in real estate and industry had helped business pick up, the pull effect did gain dominance. In his book of 1954, *Migration and Economic Growth: A Study of Great Britain and the Atlantic Economy,* Thomas put forward a further development of the theory of push–pull reciprocity. He constructed an ingenious model, based on information about the flow of capital between Britain and the United States, in which transfers of capital and migration of labor represented a kind of interaction across the ocean that he called the "Atlantic economy." The decisive factor in the cycle Thomas established was the direction of British investment, which changed according to where opportunities for profit lay. And investments pay the greatest returns where there is plenty of labor.

The first considerable immigration into the United States before the Civil War brought about an increase in building and railroad construction activities. British capital consequently lost no time acquiring a share in these enterprises and started to export iron and steel, while at the same time neglecting British domestic investments. The trends in construction activity indicate just this kind of interplay between the two countries. A downward movement in England (1871, 1892, and 1912) matched an upward one in the United States. The opposite was seen in 1877 and 1899: Emigration followed the flow of capital. When capital went to the United States, European emigration was stimulated by the resulting boom. Whenever investments from Britain stopped because a capital glut had developed in America and a "panic" subsequently occurred, immigration decreased accordingly.

To this rhythmic pattern Brinley Thomas linked the observation that the Atlantic economy also governed internal migration inside Britain. Whenever British investments shifted their direction into domestic building, mining, or industrial activities, the migrations changed their direction, too. In place of overseas migration we find a flow of migrants from rural to urban districts within Britain. To prove that this reciprocal action holds true not only in the case of Britain but in the whole of northwestern Europe, Thomas studied a province of Sweden—Västmannaland—and established that the same relationship exists there between internal and external migration.

There will be occasion later to question the material Thomas uses to establish the alternating rhythm between external and internal migration in Britain. His use of the Swedish source material also has been criticized because conditions in Västmannaland are special to that area, so that it cannot be considered representative of Swedish emigration as a whole. A more exhaustive inquiry into the alternation of these cycles is needed, and it might profitably be done in Sweden where a uniquely comprehensive material has been preserved for both internal and external migration. The Danish material is inadequate for this type of study.

The idea of introducing capital migration between Europe and the United States into the discussion of international population flow did not originate with Brinley Thomas. It had already been done fairly thoroughly by the Englishman, Julius Isaac, in his excellent and very informative book, *Economics of Migration* (1947). Admittedly Isaac does not enter directly into the argument about push and pull effects, but he does point out that capital export to the countries of immigration tends to encourage further emigration, whereas capital export from the New World to the Old—for instance in the form of interest payments or immigrants' remittances of money—might lessen the ability of a country to absorb more immigrants. Brinley Thomas's achievement was to dissolve the almost classical concept of push–pull that had arisen in the 1920s and had definitely outlived its time. It seemed too rigid and only led to a deadend, developing into endless discussions of cause and effect on the basis of altogether too flimsy raw materials.

The push and pull effects are not phenomena that pertain only to emigration: They may be applied to any kind of migration regardless of distance. When a new suburb of development houses is built today outside a city, one might equally well speak of push and pull in the eventual settlement of such a district. There is a push effect insofar as people find the noise and dirt of the central parts of the city repugnant and decide to move away from it. But there is a pull effect as well: This new area is attractive, and the developer will advertize to induce new inhabitants to move there. Will there also be some rhythm ruled by an economic cycle in the migration to these newly developed districts; and, if there is, what will that tell us about the connection between push and pull?

We have sketched an outline of modern research into emigration that shows how far an analysis of the cause and motives behind mass emigration has advanced since the time of Sundbärg. Economists have attained important and epoch-making results, but at the same time the historian cannot help sighing a little at the firm, sometimes even heavy-handed and generalizing way in which 52 million individual human lives have been dragged in and out of diagrams and tables, and have had motives for their momentous decision ascribed to them which they themselves very likely would have regarded without much understanding. When, in between working with so many figures, one stumbles onto actual documents from that time that shed light on the individual emigrant—his thoughts and sufferings before, during, and after the long voyage, however naïve and simple such thoughts may be—one realizes that mass emigration needs to be looked at from a personal as well as demographic and economic point of view. The historian can well profit from bearing in mind that the collective phenomenon is, after all, made up of individual cases, each one with its own history.

The following chapters recognize that the statistical method is an effective tool which enables one to penetrate the background and causes of emigration, but also that a purely historical examination must accompany a statistical treatment and supplement the results derived from the figures. Only a combination of these two methods will result in a historically correct and sufficiently cautious evaluation of this fascinating phenomenon.

An inspiring advocate of a similar point of view was Marcus Lee Hansen, who represented another, now discontinued line in the literature about emigration since World War I. Hansen, a second-generation Danish-American, was a professor at the University of Illinois. He died in 1938, only 45 years old. His publication was sparse, but it was imbued with a unique intelligence and mastery of the source material. Hansen's chief idea was that American historians ought to seek knowledge of American history in general—and of immigration in particular—through studies in Europe if they are to reach a true understanding of the development of their nation. He elaborated his views in an inspired survey of topics for research, *The History of American Immigration as a Field of Research* (1927)—a kind of appeal to historians to take up the study of overseas migration on the basis of the social, political, and economic conditions of the emigration countries. This appeal remained surprisingly unnoticed in the United States. On the other hand, it undoubtedly inspired European historians. The same can be said about his other sagacious articles on the same subject, which were first published after his death by Arthur M. Schlesinger. In particular, the first of these articles, "Migrations Old and New," should prove to be a source of inspiration to future students of migration.

Most in tune with Marcus Lee Hansen's approach is the Englishman Maldwyn A. Jones' book, *American Immigration* (1960), which is now a standard textbook at numerous American universities. A striking example of the narrowly American viewpoint is offered by another textbook, Carl N. Degler's *Out of Our Past: The Forces That Shaped Modern America* (1959).

4

DANISH EMIGRANTS—
BEFORE THEY LEFT

Before beginning discussion of the many aspects of Danish emigration it might be well to give a resumé of the main features of Danish domestic and foreign policy in the decades prior to 1914.

Politically Denmark's development has been determined by its geographic location between the European continent and the Scandinavian peninsula, between Germany and Scandinavia. For several centuries Sweden posed the greatest threat to Denmark, but the situation changed radically in the nineteenth century. Strong military powers eager to expand emerged in Germany and Russia, and presented a common danger to the Nordic countries. Prussia's interest in Schleswig–Holstein, and Russia's interest in Sweden then created a bond between the former Scandinavian rivals. German expansionism brought two defeats to Denmark in wars against Prussia and Austria, which reduced the Danish Crown's lands by 40%. The second defeat, in 1864, also brought with it disillusionment and loss of faith in the future, a state of mind that may have contributed considerably to emigration. Not a few of the discharged veterans from the second Schleswig war immediately afterward signed up with the Union

Army in the American Civil War. There appears to have been some form of recruitment activity, though this cannot be proved, nor can the number of these soldiers be ascertained.

In domestic politics the period after 1864 was also a time of disillusionment. Strong social tensions arose between an upper class of large estate owners who were politically and economically powerful, and the ordinary farmers, who, as a result of an improved educational system and the Grundtvigian folk high schools, had gained a political awareness. A class of slightly more well-to-do farmers, supported by the whole rural population, created the liberal party, Venstre, and Danish politics after 1866 became the scene of violent political battles over the establishment of parliamentary democracy. This political situation retarded important aspects of social and economic reforms needed to accompany the radical changes society underwent in this 30-year period, another circumstance that may well have contributed to decisions to emigrate.

Denmark's economy was based on grain crops to an unusually high degree even after 1850. Throughout nearly the whole of the nineteenth century, the structure of agricultural society was still characterized by the landowner's inherited rights over the peasant's land, even though these rights gradually were abolished. The reforms of the 1780s were only slowly carried out in the following century. At this time, when mechanization was unknown, the estates and larger farms were totally dependent on hired manual labor. To attract and keep workers, houses with small plots of land were built, and these small holdings formed the prototype for the great land division movement to be discussed in Chapter 11.

Though in many ways Denmark was different from its neighbors, in the main the social conditions of the nineteenth century were similar all over Europe. This is also the case with emigration—the motives for emigration discussed in the following pages were not peculiarly Danish phenomena, but describe most of the 50 million emigrants.

While emigration before 1800 was generally a result of influences from the top level of society, the reasons for emigration in the nineteenth and twentieth centuries must be sought at the "bottom" of the societies concerned: in a quiet economic and human process, which was unaffected by frontiers and which took place everywhere on the local level. To approach the problem of the nature of the process which released the great emigration, it is necessary to break down the figures of emigration for the largest units, the nations, into smaller units—regions, counties, and parishes. It then becomes clear that just as emigration varies considerably among countries, it also varies radically from one very small topographical unit to another. In other words, the process which sets emigration in motion acts with varying strength in different geographical areas. Topographical analysis of the emigration figures will demonstrate that it is in many ways arbitrary to speak of this nation's having a large emigration and that a small one. Only rarely does one find that emigration was spread evenly throughout the regions. America-fever can be located as spots on the map; and even examination of the smallest geographical unit, the parishes, does not produce an even distribution. Two neighboring parishes may exist where the one has a pattern of great mobility and the other practically none. At first glance this may appear to be a case of totally random distribution, but a closer look may well disclose a pattern that can provide a clue to its cause.

The existing statistics on Danish emigration have so far provided only a very crude picture of the geographical origins of most emigration overseas. The annual statistical summaries distinguished only between Jutland and eastern Denmark, and during the period under investigation even the definition of this division was changed. The Copenhagen police commissioner's reports, on the other hand, did distinguish between Copenhagen and the provinces. The computer processing of the Copenhagen material formed the basis of this study, and for the first time it has been possible to produce a quantitative picture of the topographical distribution of emigration in the period 1868–1900, a picture which can, despite certain reservations, be described as relatively exact.

In order to obtain a clear view of the distribution it will be practical, in the first instance, to ignore the chronological development and the yearly changes, and present a static view of the distribution of emigration among the Danish counties over all 32 years of the period. The total emigration figures are shown in Table 4.1.

TABLE 4.1

Distribution of Emigration by Main Regions, 1868–1900

	Counties	Regions
Copenhagen		31,799
Northern Zealand	11,892	
Southern Zealand	16,992	
Lolland-Falster	13,550	
Bornholm	5,055	
Zealand + islands		47,489
Funen		18,112
Eastern Jutland	28,646	
Northern Jutland	28,438	
Southwestern Jutland	10,582	
Total Jutland		67,666
All Denmark		165,066

It is apparent that Zealand, Funen, and the other islands minus Copenhagen had approximately the same number of emigrants as Jutland. All in all, two-fifths of the emigrants came from Jutland, another two-fifths from Funen, Lolland-Falster, Bornholm, and Zealand (excluding the city of Copenhagen), and the last one-fifth from Copenhagen itself. Out of every 100 emigrants who boarded ships for distant lands, 41 were from Jutland, 11 from Funen, 29 from Zealand and the smaller islands minus Copenhagen, and 19 from Copenhagen. The distribution is roughly that of the remaining population; according to the 1901 census 43% of the population lived in Jutland, a little more than 11% on Funen, 26% on Zealand and other small islands, and 20% in Copenhagen.

It is surprising to see the proportions represented by the main regions. The generally accepted belief has been that the bulk of the Danish emigration came from the part of Jutland that lies to the north of the Limfjord. Admittedly this area contributed in large measure to the total, but the unexpected discovery is that the figures for southern Zealand and Lolland-Falster exceed those for northern Jutland. It is striking how the figures increase steadily as one moves south in Zealand. Emigration from Jutland presents a far more scattered picture. In addition to the counties already mentioned in northern Jutland, very high figures are found in the eastern section of Jutland, whereas for Randers, Viborg, and Ringkøbing, which form a belt across the middle of Jutland, the figures are remarkably low.

The absolute emigration figures by counties give a picture of the numerical proportions among the different parts of the country, and also some impression of the places of origin of the Danes overseas. But since the sizes of the counties varied greatly, it is necessary to compare the emigration figures with the total population within each county in order to obtain a true picture of the extent to which emigration dominated this or that region.

Figure 4.1 shows, for the period in question, the number of emigrants per 1000 inhabitants, with the population of each county computed as an average of the 1870 and the 1901 census figures. The use of these population estimates makes a rough allowance for the substantial migrations among counties which occurred during that period. Thus when considering the relative intensity of emigration, Bornholm stands out as the region which suffered most from emigration; but when the figures are not rounded off, the difference between Bornholm at 138.9 and Lolland-Falster at 138.4 becomes minimal.

If Bornholm were placed correctly on the map—to the southeast of the rest of the country—the geographical pattern would emerge quite clearly. During the period in question, the impact of emigration was felt most in the southeastern part of Denmark. The difference between northern Jut-

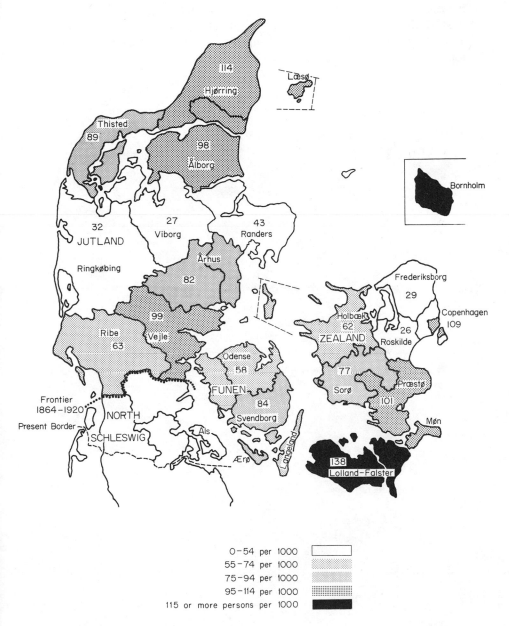

Figure 4.1 Emigration 1868–1900 per 1000 of population in the 19 Danish counties (average of census figures for 1870 and 1901).

land and southern Zealand becomes still sharper when emigration is seen in relation to total population. The map gives a general impression that intensity of emigration was centered in the northernmost and the southernmost sections of the country. The low intensity found in the center of Jutland emphasizes even more the impression that, with regard to emigration, Denmark was divided into two parts.

5

URBAN AND
RURAL EMIGRATION

Among the great epoch-making events which shaped the history of Denmark since the mid-nineteenth century, probably none happened so quietly' as the transformation of society caused by migration from rural to urban areas. A constant stream of families and individuals changed their surroundings—a tremendous event in the lives of those involved—but more or less imperceptible for society as a whole. This important alteration of the nation's demography went on in a period when the composition of the population was measured only once every 10 years—and long before the concept of regional planning had appeared. A trend toward migration to urban areas began to make itself felt from the mid-1840s, but first became widespread in the 1860s. This was hardly an isolated Danish phenomenon: The same thing occurred everywhere in Europe, developing along similar lines, and it must be viewed against a background comprising the breakthrough of liberalism, the industrial revolution, and the increasing birthrate in all countries. The relationships between urban and rural areas assume a central position in nineteenth-century history, and not least in a study of emigration. Internal and external migrations prior to 1914 constitute two sides of the same problem and should be studied together as far as possible. One of Brinley Thomas's achievements was the demonstration of this connection between internal and external migration, an issue previously only partly acknowledged by scholars. The cause, whether conscious or not, that made a young man leave for America did not differ much from the causes that led his next-door neighbor to move to the next town or to Copenhagen.

A discussion of the connections between internal migration and emigration will follow in Chapter 6. For the moment, our only purpose is to present a picture of the relationship between emigration from urban areas and purely rural emigration. At the beginning it is necessary to point out some of the pitfalls existing in the basic materials from which the statistics have been extracted. For example, it is imaginable that a young person from a rural district who wanted to emigrate might as a first step go to the nearest town in order to discuss the matter with the local emigration agent, and, convinced by the eloquence of the agent, sign a provisional contract that included the name of the town in the dating. In this way many emigrants could be erroneously counted as contributing to urban rather than to rural emigration.

In Sweden, studies have been made on this problem, i.e., whether the statements of emigrants agreed with the information available in the parish records as to their last place of residence. In Sweden, just as in Denmark, the contract was filled in by the agent. Though there was no police certification of the contracts in Sweden, the same information was contained in the passenger lists of the ships, and a duplicate of the list was sent to the police in the port of embarkation, usually Gothenburg. In a study of 401 emigrants from the period 1869–1873 entered in the Gothenburg records, it was found that 72% of the emigrants could be located with no difficulty in their home parish records. Another 10% could be located despite imperfect information, and only the remaining 18% had made distinctly erroneous statements (which includes those who had given the name of the nearest town instead of their home parish).

However, as already mentioned, the personal information the agents recorded about emigrants in Sweden was not subject to control by any authorities, as was the case in Denmark, so it seems reasonable to assume that the statements regarding residence in the Danish material will be more reliable than the Swedish. In this connection it interesting to note that in the Danish data that were computer processed for this study, there are only 408 persons out of a total of over 165,000 whose last place of residence could not be recorded for lack of information. This in itself is no evidence of the veracity of the statements, but it does seem to indicate that the system so accurately transmitted personal data that the major source of error must have been those emigrants who deliberately misstated their last places of residence in order to conceal their identities.

Inquiry into the reliability of the statements of residence is necessary, particularly because the statistical analysis shows, surprisingly, that Danish emigration originated in urban areas to a much larger extent than had previously been supposed. The distinction between rural and urban districts cannot be applied to the entire registered material of 172,000 emigrants. Two minor groups have to be omitted. One of these is the Mormons, all of whom are reported in the records as coming from the provincial town of the region. This is highly unlikely; more probably it indicates their religious community rather than their last residence. The other group comprises those emigrants who came from North Schleswig, where the indications of locality are highly doubtful.

There remain about 156,000 emigrants from the period 1868–1900: about 87,000 from the rural districts and 69,000 who listed Copenhagen or some other market town [1] as their last home. Though the rural residents were a clear majority in this period, the following 15 years saw a shift in the pattern. From 1900 to 1914, 47,000 out of a total of 90,000 adult emigrants (children are excluded from the distribution figures of the Annual Statistics) came from the towns, and only 43,000 from the countryside. Internal migration had created a new population distribution in the years preceding World War I. Unfortunately detailed analysis of the records after 1900 is not possible; however, it is feasible for the period 1868–1900. In the earlier period, the situation was such that out of every 100 emigrants, an average of 44 came from the capital or other towns, and 56 from rural districts. These overall totals conceal, however, great variations from one part of the country to another.

Once again the distinctive character of Bornholm shows up clearly in Table 5.1. As already mentioned, this Baltic island had the highest rate of emigration in the entire country; we can now see that the towns completely dominated the emigration from Bornholm far more so than was the case in the rest of the nation. With the single exception of Bornholm, all other regions show more rural than urban emigration, especially from Lolland-Falster, Funen, and the southwestern part of Jutland, a zone that comprises the whole of southern Denmark. In eastern Jutland, the urban areas played an important part in the emigration from the region, which is hardly surprising in view of the rapid expansion of these towns at that

---

[1] The term "købstad" means the greater towns dating from medieval times and having special rights. Denmark had about 50 more important towns of this sort.

TABLE 5.1

Distribution of Emigrants by Rural and Urban Areas (expressed in percentage)

	Towns	Rural districts	Totals
Zealand	22.9	77.1	100.0
Lolland-Falster	27.0	73.0	100.0
Bornholm	65.8	34.2	100.0
Funen	29.4	70.6	100.0
Eastern Jutland	43.4	56.6	100.0
Northern Jutland	26.9	73.1	100.0
Southwestern Jutland	29.7	70.3	100.0

time. The Århus district considered in isolation shows an almost equal division between rural and urban emigrants, with 48 out of every 100 coming from the towns.

So far we have disregarded chronological development in order to give the clearest possible picture of emigration as a whole. However, when studying the distribution of emigrants between the towns and the countryside, we are forced to take the variations over the years into account, as the ratio between rural and urban population in Denmark shifted considerably during the period. Figure 5.1 shows the annual volume of emigration from rural and urban districts, respectively. "Urban areas" include

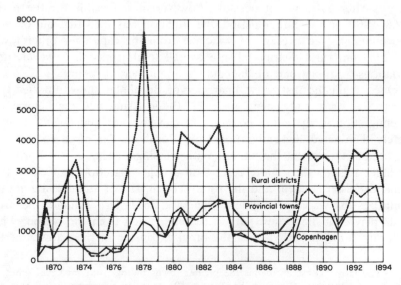

Figure 5.1 Emigration from Copenhagen, provincial towns, and rural districts, 1868-1914.

all Danish provincial towns and the metropolitan area of Copenhagen–Fredericksberg.

On the whole, the fluctuations in rural and urban emigration correspond to one other, and parallel the peak years that can be identified in emigration from practically every European country: the enormous wave in about 1882 and the ridge between 1887 and 1893.

In the early years, the curves move in a somewhat arbitrary fashion, but from about 1873–1874 the movement falls into a parallel pattern. Urban emigration reached its highest point during the earlier period in 1869–1872—the same 2 years in which Denmark, as well as the rest of Europe, experienced an economic boom. The peak of rural emigration, on the other hand, came in the following year, 1873, and from that time the level of rural emigration was for many years above that of urban emigration. The decisive peak in 1882, when Danish as well as Norwegian emigration reached its height, is remarkable for the steepness of the curve at that point. It is the one exception to an otherwise rather gradual curve, which suggests that one specific and powerful impetus might have led to this sudden rise in the rate of emigration.

It is quite obvious from Figure 5.1 that the peak of 1882 was distinctly an upsurge of rural emigration. The urban curve registers a rise too, but without approaching the peaks of either the previous or subsequent decades. The greater total for urban emigration from 1892–1914 than for the rural districts is probably due to the shift in population by internal migration in the decades after 1870. The urban population, which in 1870 made up 25% of the national total, had been growing during the last decades of the century until, according to the 1901 census, it reached 40% of the population. Inevitably this development influenced the emigration figures. The 1900–1914 period was characterized by two large waves of emigration, each 4 to 5 years in duration. The two plateaus are separated only by the extraordinary year 1908, when an acute economic crisis both in the United States and in Europe caused emigration from all of Europe to fall by as much as 50%, only to rise again the very next year.

The general decline in the emigration from rural districts and the corresponding rise from the towns reflects the continual and gradual growth of the towns at the expense of the rural areas, although this situation may be accentuated in the emigration records as a result of conditions of employment. While the rural districts experienced a loss of labor, unemployment difficulties in the towns accompanied urban migration. After the turn of the century Copenhagen experienced an industrial expansion so great that only a relatively few people thought of emigrating. But the provincial towns were still unable to absorb their share of the urban immigrants. Though these towns represented roughly 20% of the population in the period 1900–1914, 30% of emigrants originated there. Copenhagen was represented in the emigration figures in proportion to its share of the population: Both stood at about 20%. Another interesting feature in this connection is that although the rural population was 75% of the total in 1870 and was still more than 60% as late as 1900, rural areas contributed to emigration at a rate considerably below this average. In fact, on several occasions they were even below 50% of total emigration.

At this point it may be helpful to sketch roughly the trends in the rural–urban distribution of population compared with emigration. During the period 1870–1900, when an average of 31% of the population lived in the towns, 44% of emigration originated from the towns. In the following period, 1900–1914, the urban share of the total population increased to 40% while the urban share of emigration increased to no less than 52%. However, where a more detailed picture of emigration intensity is sought, it is pointless to use a population average that covers a long period of such crucial changes as the last three decades of the nineteenth century. The calculations of intensity appearing in Figure 5.2 are based on estimates of the population figures for each year between the censuses, both for the country as a whole and for each individual county, with a distinction made between rural districts and towns.

When we compare Figure 5.2 with Figure 5.1, which indicated emigra-

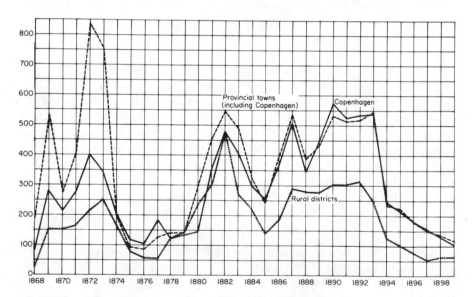

Figure 5.2 Annual emigration per 100,000 inhabitants in Denmark, 1868–1899 —urban and rural areas.

tion in absolute numbers, we find that the relationship between the curves for rural and urban emigration is inverted. The rate of urban emigration lies considerably above the rural rate, though the same general fluctuations are visible. The first years of each decade still can be identified as years of high emigration intensity, but the proportionate magnitude of the three peaks has altered. Particularly striking is the enormous peak formed by the urban rates for 1872 and 1873. Here, at the very beginning of the epoch of mass emigration, the Danish towns reached a level of emigration intensity that rivals the highest rates that Denmark's neighboring countries, Norway and Sweden, ever produced. It is not improbable that some connection exists between this wave of emigration from the towns and the agitation among workers, which led to the formation of the Danish labor party and its early political activity in 1872.

But in examining the graph more closely, it becomes obvious that the peak was not a peculiarly Copenhagen phenomenon. The Copenhagen curve moves in the same general direction as the total urban curve, but it fails to attain even half the intensity level of the curve that includes all urban areas. Consequently, if the capital is omitted from the calculation of intensity, the rate of emigration per 100,000 from the provincial towns in the peak year of 1872 turns out to be not 835 but 1220, i.e., 50% higher. In that one year, 12 out of every 1000 inhabitants of the Danish provincial towns left the country. As a basis for comparison, the highest rate of emigration noted for a single county in Sweden was 13.02 per 1000 inhabitants.

Not until 1885 did the intensity of emigration from Copenhagen reach that of provincial towns. Systematic omission of the Copenhagen figures would give a very different picture of the emigration intensity for these smaller towns—far higher than the rate indicated in Figure 5.2. As an example, let us look at the year 1882, one of the high-level years when the emigration intensity of the provincial towns was 619 per 100,000 inhabitants—a figure that falls to 546 when Copenhagen is included in the calculation. Since the metropolitan area and the provincial towns numbered about 290,000 and 298,000 inhabitants respectively, in that year, the effect of separating the Copenhagen figures should not be surprising.

The previous diagrams gave overall figures for the aggregates of rural and urban districts within the entire territory of Denmark. The figures of the individual counties show many variations from these nationwide averages. Even a sketch of the trends for the various provinces causes difficulties, as the differences between two neighboring counties may well be just as large as those between areas separated by several hundred miles. An example of the variations from county to county is illustrated in Figure

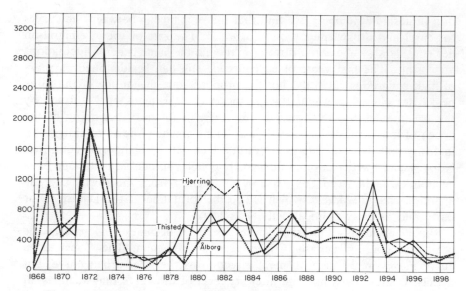

Figure 5.3 Emigration per 100,000 inhabitants in the cities of northern Jutland counties, 1868–1898.

5.3, which shows the intensity of emigration from three counties of northern Jutland: Thisted, Hjørring, and Ålborg.[2]

Apart from the peak at the beginning of the 1870s, it is difficult to identify general characteristics of the graph. The two small towns in Thisted county show the two highest annual rates of emigration intensity in all of Denmark: In 1872 and 1873, 2790 and 3170 per 100,000 inhabitants of these two towns emigrated, respectively. Hjørring and Ålborg give quite a different picture during these first years of the great emigration period. Here, especially in the towns of Hjørring county, there was a conspicuous boom in emigration as early as 1869, a phenomenon not registered in the towns of Thisted county. To a certain extent this early wave may have held the 1872–1873 rise at a relatively low level compared to that of Thisted. A really large wave of emigration may empty an area of potential emigrants for quite some time. The commotion caused by the departure of a large number of emigrants may even result in a kind of "anticipation"—i.e., some people might be swept along by the wave who might otherwise have left 1 or 2 years later. It seems unlikely that a peak like this could be repeated a few years later and reach the same level.

In actual fact this is all inference from very small figures, which are

---

[2] Denmark was divided into 22 "amter" counties, most often named after the main town in the area. After 1970 the number of counties was reduced to 14.

blown up because they are placed in relation to very limited populations. Caution must therefore be used in interpreting single leaps in the curve of intensity. At this level we ought not to look for causal explanations in the general economic situation. It is more plausible to see a sharp rise in local emigration as the result of the propaganda of a single energetic emigration agent, or a visit of a returned Danish-American. The influence of such factors on the curve of emigration will be discussed later.

The average for the whole country during the period 1868–1900 shows that the annual emigration per 100,000 inhabitants was 233. A distribution of these 233 emigrants per 100,000 inhabitants according to latest place of residence shows 342 per 100,000 inhabitants for the towns and 186 per 100,000 for the rural districts. Emigration intensity of the towns was very nearly double that of the rural areas.

We might very guardedly interpret the figures as showing that counties with many towns were better able to absorb influx from the surrounding regions than regions with few towns. Naturally there lies an economic aspect behind the demographic surface, because what we view as a county with many towns is of course a region of economic and industrial growth, and those with few towns will be regions where the towns are still dependent on their agrarian upland and consequently are stagnant.

A relatively much larger emigration from the towns than from rural districts is not a peculiarly Danish phenomenon. Norwegian and Swedish emigration exhibit this same feature. Sundbärg published material in his great report which makes it possible to make a direct comparison with the Danish intensity figures. The period covered is 1869–1897 and the Swedish figures are based on the registered emigration.

Figure 5.4 is a juxtaposition of Danish and Swedish emigration per 100,000 inhabitants from rural and urban areas. From this it may be seen clearly how much above the Danish level Swedish emigration intensity was—on an average it was twice as high. Surprisingly enough, the great wave of emigration that hit the Danish towns around 1872–1873 does not appear to have had a parallel in Sweden. Admittedly a very slight increase in Swedish emigration occurred in 1870–1872. But the main impression is that the Swedish high level from 1866–1869, at which time the emigration intensity of the rural districts was higher than that of the towns, was followed by a distinct decline that lasted until 1874. The unusually large emigration from Danish provincial towns in 1872–1873 appears to have been a phenomenon special to Denmark.

Other variations between the intensity curves of the two countries are of less importance. A few minor differences are worth noting—for one thing, the upward movement of the curve for Swedish towns about 1875, a time when Danish emigration was at an absolute minimum. Also the

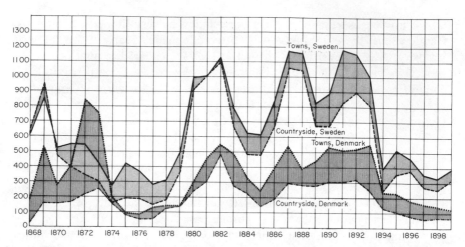

Figure 5.4   Emigration per 100,000 inhabitants in Denmark and Sweden, 1868–1899.

Swedish peak in the early 1880s stretches over the years 1879–1882, whereas in Denmark, and particularly in the rural districts, the peak is limited only to 1882. It is interesting to see that the strong decrease in emigration which began the dead period of the last half of the 1890s appeared in Sweden as early as 1891, but did not appear until 1894 in Denmark.

Although Figure 5.4 gives an impression of the variations in the annual oscillations of emigration from the two countries, it is only indirectly possible to see whether the same relationship exists between rural and urban emigration in Sweden as in Denmark; in other words, whether urban emigration is equally far above the rural emigration in both countries. A glance at the graph seems to suggest that the difference between the two curves for urban and rural emigration is somewhat greater in the case of Denmark than in the case of Sweden; a spot test confirms this impression.

In his statistical material, Sundbärg calculated that if, over the years 1891–1900, the Swedish rate of rural emigration per 100,000 inhabitants was put at 100, then the corresponding figure for urban emigration would be 128. If we make the same calculation for Denmark for the period 1890–1899, we find that for every 100 rural emigrants there would be 190 urban emigrants. The urban emigration is relatively the highest in Denmark; and there is nothing surprising in this, considering the very different distributions of population between rural and urban areas in the two countries. As early as 1800, the importance of the towns was much smaller in Sweden than in Denmark, and during the period of urbanization that accompanied the great increase in population, the Danish urban population remained at all times relatively much larger than that of Sweden. In 1900, 39% of the population lived in larger towns in Denmark, but in Sweden this was the case for only 22%.

6

EMIGRATION AND INTERNAL MIGRATION

It has been established that urban emigration was much stronger than rural. Furthermore, the comparison with Sweden demonstrates that the relationship between urban and rural emigration seems to be bound up with the urban structure of the individual country. Migration from rural to urban districts is itself a factor that may be decisive for the volume and distribution of emigration.

However, one might wonder if the urban emigration is really an independent factor with its own causes. How many of those who went overseas from the towns were genuine townspeople and not just people from the rural districts who passed through the towns on their way abroad?

Scholars who have worked with this problem previously have not been inclined to accept urban emigration as an independent factor. They have considered urban emigration as merely one stage in the emigration of rural people—a stay in the town before the actual departure from the country. Gustav Sundbärg (see Chapter 3) viewed the Swedish emigration as simply a question of rural land policy and did not accept the urban emigration as anything but a result of the social and economic tensions in the rural districts. Even though one part of Sundbärg's tabular material shows urban emigration intensity as higher than rural, the possibility of an interrelation between these facts is not discussed in his study. The preoccupation with rural land policy that colored the report throughout made Sundbärg and his associates overlook the particular problem posed by the towns.

Sundbärg's report was completed shortly before World War I; later Professor Ingrid Semmingsen discussed the problem in an article dated 1940, in which she made inquiry into the connections between migration to Oslo and Bergen from rural districts and the emigration from these towns during the period 1875–1885. Her results support Sundbärg's views. The number of persons emigrating from Oslo fluctuated greatly, whereas the migration to the town was a constant phenomenon independent of structural changes in the economy. Semmingsen viewed the large towns as a kind of population reservoir. When the migrants became too numerous, the towns were emptied of their surplus inhabitants through waves of emigration, merely to start filling up again with newcomers. But this reservoir contains nothing but rural population elements, and Ingrid Semmingsen maintained that even the emigrants who were born in town emigrated as a result of the agrarian conditions in Norway. Fundamentally she agrees with Sundbärg that the towns themselves were the creation of a surplus rural population, so that everything that happened in the towns was, in the last instance, caused by the agricultural conditions.

The crucial point in Ingrid Semmingsen's reasoning is the question of when a person who moves to town loses his "rural" character and becomes "urbanized." Of considerable interest in this connection is an inquiry undertaken at Uppsala by Fred Nilsson concerning emigration from Stockholm in 1880–1893. This work, part of a Ph.D. thesis on emigration from Stockholm, aims to answer the question Ingrid Semmingsen left open: How long a period did the emigrants from large towns actually spend in those towns before emigrating? Fred Nilsson investigated the background of a number of emigrants from Stockholm who were listed in the town archives, which contain information about the moves of every single emigrant before his departure abroad. Nilsson's study divided the emigrants into three groups according to the time they had spent in the capital before they left for America. One group consisted of persons who had arrived in Stockholm 1 year or less before departure, i.e., genuine emigrants in transit. Another group comprised those who stayed from 2 to 4 years, and a third group those who had been there for more than 5 years or even might have been born in Stockholm. The results of the study were surprising, for they showed that the transit traffic was much smaller than might have been expected. Out of 880 emigrants whose records were examined, only 27% were born in Stockholm; but the migrants to the city were not mainly people who had arrived only shortly before their departure, as Table 6.1 shows.

Almost 50% of the emigrants could be regarded as real citizens of Stockholm, since they had spent more than 5 years there, and only one-fifth were in transit from the rural districts. The distinctions chosen, 0–1, 2–4, and 5 years or more, seem acceptable. New residents, who had spent less than 1 year in a place, were unlikely to have had time to assimilate even had they tried. Differences between country people and town people were even greater than now, and most of the rural arrivals probably worked hard at adapting to their new surroundings. A superficial adaptation may have taken place within a short time, but probably several years were needed before the migrant could be considered "urbanized." A stay of more than 5 years in town would probably have eliminated any important influence from directly rural factors in the decision to emigrate.

But Fred Nilsson's study goes beyond this; he also categorized all emigrants born outside Stockholm according to the locality in Sweden from which they came, irrespective of the length of time they had spent in the capital. He found that a surprisingly small number came from Stockholm Län (the area surrounding Stockholm), and that large numbers came from regions which already showed a high emigration intensity. In following the routes of these emigrants from their birthplaces to Stockholm, one discovers that only a very small percentage moved directly from a rural district to the capital; the majority first moved to another town, spent some time there, and then moved on to Stockholm.

This phenomenon is not unknown in Denmark. Migration by stages—countryside to provincial town to capital—appears frequently from those census tables in which birthplace is related to domicile. But the outlines are blurred both in the case of internal migration and with the Danish emigration figures because we do not know the duration of the different stages of migration.

Fred Nilsson's work must be regarded as significant because it shows

TABLE 6.1

Emigrants' Length of Stay in Stockholm before Departure (expressed in percentage)

Number of years since arrival	Men	Women	Both sexes
Less than 2 years	20.3	19.5	19.9
2–4 years	33.4	36.2	34.8
5 years or more	46.3	44.3	45.3
Total	100.0	100.0	100.0

so clearly that urban emigration constitutes an independent phenomenon with its own set of problems. Even if the towns did form a kind of reservoir for a surplus rural population, Nilsson seems to have undermined the thesis launched by Sundbärg and Semmingsen that the towns were nothing but a transit point for emigrants en route from rural districts. The almost 80% of the town emigrants who originated in rural areas and stayed more than 2 years in the towns must have made a serious effort to adapt to the urban milieu and earn a living there. Urban emigration, in other words, must be able to give some indication of the capacity of industrialization to provide employment for the migrants to the cities. Research on the Stockholm region suggests a general pattern that may apply to other large towns such as Copenhagen.

In 1899 a government regulation was issued requiring emigrants to state birthplace as well as latest residence in the emigration contract. The idea of including this piece of information in the statistics must have already been old then; in the emigration register drafted and printed as early as 1869 the column for latest residence is headed: "Birthplace and last place of residence (if not the same)." From July 1, 1899, both birthplace and residence were actually entered in the register. A sketchy knowledge of the migrations of emigrants prior to their final departure for some foreign country is thus obtainable after 1900. A comparison of the two entries year by year would probably cause more confusion than enlightenment, so I have chosen to analyze a period of 5 years, 1910–1914, which covers almost 36,000 Danish emigrants, i.e., 23,000 men and 12,350 women. The distribution by last place of residence is shown in Table 6.2.

A comparison of the two distributions not only indicates the movements of the emigrants previous to their departures, but perhaps also gives a representative picture of the migration of the whole population, as the

TABLE 6.2

Emigrants Grouped According to Last Place of Residence and Birthplace, 1910–1914

	Last residence	Birthplace	Arrivals/ departures
Copenhagen	22.1	12.3	+9.8
Towns, east Denmark	9.4	8.9	+0.5
Towns, Jutland	21.5	16.4	+5.1
Rural east Denmark	16.5	18.8	−2.3
Rural Jutland	30.5	36.4	−5.9
Born abroad		7.2	−7.2
Total	100.0	100.0	+14.4

calculations are made for a group who, while still in Denmark, comprised about 1.5% of the entire population for the period in question. As might be expected, it was the capital which especially drew its migrants from the other parts of the country. Of the almost 8000 adult emigrants setting out from Copenhagen during this period, only 4400 were born there, whereas the rest, 3600, had moved to the capital at some time. What were the origins of these 3600 persons?

Most likely a considerable number were foreigners, particularly Swedish immigrants, who often settled in Copenhagen. Another group among these "new" Copenhageners probably came from the rural districts of the Zealand region, i.e., Zealand itself and the islands to the south. If we add the numerical difference between those born in east Denmark and those who actually emigrated from there $(18.8\% - 16.5\% = 2.3\%)$ to those born abroad, we get 9.5% which is strikingly close to the figure for migration into Copenhagen, 9.8%. The last 0.3% would have come from the peninsula of Jutland. For the towns of east Denmark, the figures for residence and birthplace more or less balance, which suggest that persons emigrating from these towns were also born there. As for Jutland, it seems that a considerable number of emigrants had previously made the migration from rural areas to the towns. Of the emigrants, 13,000 were born in the rural parts of Jutland, but only 11,000 were living there at the time of emigration, so 2000 must have been on the move even before going overseas. Just under 5900 were born in provincial towns, but over 7700 set out from these towns. Consequently 1800 persons must have moved there before emigrating, and it is a temptation to identify them with the 2000 from the rural districts. The last 200 must have crossed the Lillebælt or the Kattegat before setting out across the oceans.

Naturally a population of 2.6 million does not move according to a pattern as regular as that described here. As in an anthill, the paths of movement will have criss-crossed the country in all directions, even though mobility was more restricted than it is now. Still, the distribution shown in Table 6.2 gives a picture of migration which is not only plausible, but which agrees reasonably well with the census information from 1911.

Analysis of this census leads to the assumption that emigrants moved to Copenhagen less often than the rest of the population, while more of the emigrants moved from the rural districts to provincial towns and there made the decision to emigrate. Anyone who wanted to leave the country-side faced a choice he could make in stages—the first being whether to move from the countryside to a neighboring town. If he chose the town, as a large majority did, and still did not gain a foothold, there was a further possibility, Copenhagen or America. An increasing proportion decided on the second possibility at this point. For those who chose Copenhagen there was no further choice between two alternatives. The statistics show that the number of people who migrated back from Copenhagen to a town or rural district was very small.

But the statistics of mobility as a whole rest on a very uncertain basis, because, among other things, we do not know how many times a single person moved. It is perfectly possible for a resident of Copenhagen to have been born elsewhere and have moved to the city as an infant, so that to all intents and purposes he should count as a genuine Copenhagener. Mere moves cannot be read as a socioeconomic barometer. It is also likely that a person may have spent any number of years in a third location between two registered addresses. This would not appear either in the census, or in the emigration records of birthplace and last residence.

We shall have to resign ourselves to relying on a few fixed points and start from there. One such point is the statement of birthplace. Even if a certain number may have left their birthplace as babies, this criterion is still fundamental from a collective as well as from an individual point of view. A comparison of the statements of birthplace for the entire population and the statements given by the 36,000 emigrants (1910–1914) shows a pronounced difference, which substantiates the idea advanced early concerning the kind of choice facing the migrants—the choice between the next stage at home or emigration abroad (see Table 6.3).

The excess share of emigrants born in provincial towns compared with the whole population confirms the impression given by the emigration intensities of an earlier period: Emigration was concentrated in these towns. Market towns had the greatest difficulties in employing migrants—much greater than the capital. It seems both from the figures shown in Table 6.3 and from the relatively low emigration intensity of the capital that Copenhagen must have had a greater capacity for absorbing additional inhabitants, even if their number was much larger than the sum of migrants into the smaller towns. The higher degree of industrialization of the capital was presumably the reason for this. The labor market of

TABLE 6.3

Birthplaces of the Entire Population (1911) and of Emigrants from 1910–1914 (expressed in percentage)

	Entire population	Emigrants
Copenhagen	19.5	13.3
Provincial towns	19.9	27.2
Rural districts	60.6	59.5
Total	100.0	100.0

Copenhagen showed, as the business economists say, a greater elasticity than the rest of the country, probably as a result of difference in industrial investment.

One fixed point in the migration analyses of the censuses is the statement of net gain or net loss which tells, irrespective of migrations within the country, how many persons have changed their residence within each of the following groups: residents of the capital, the provincial towns, and the rural districts. The 1911 census shows an overall movement of about 8% among the population, whereas among the emigrants of the 1910–1914 period no less than 14.5% had changed residence before eventually departing. This seems to show that the mobility of future emigrants was almost double that of the population as a whole. It is hardly surprising that the person who would consider moving to New Zealand or America had previously found it easy to move from one part of Denmark to another. Emigrants may, on the whole, be viewed as people who found it difficult to adapt in their homeland. A few may have had a criminal past; but for the large majority the difficulties were probably the kind caused by social and economic conditions, problems which might vary from poor employment opportunities to a general feeling on the part of the individual that the prospects for the future were poor in Denmark, that hopes of advancement were nil. But, as we have seen earlier, the decision to emigrate was frequently the last resort after one or more migrations to new surroundings, where there should have been a chance of finding better conditions for employment and higher pay.

In this rather speculative demonstration of emigration by stages, from countryside to town to America, it may be refreshing to look at a real example—the fate of a family which was unusual in one respect, but otherwise quite representative of the mentality and behavior of the period.

When Niels Jensen Nielsen of Givskud west of Horsens was demobilized after the war of 1864, he married one Ane Katrine Ulriksen. The couple settled in Kolding and made a living out of some "small trading." Their income was small, and insufficient to support them and their first children. The whole family then moved back to Givskud where they took over the Nielsen family farm of 25 acres of moorland in return for keeping Nielsen's father as a pensioner. One of the children, now an elderly returned emigrant, Fred Hedebol, tells the story from there on:

> It came to quarrels between my parents . . . my father was fed up with life as a small farmer and wanted to emigrate. But my mother, who knew how fond the Nielsen family were of the bottle, feared moving to a strange country with the risk of being left alone to fend for her children. Finally when my grandfather died,

she let herself be persuaded into leaving. The little house and most of their belongings were sold, tickets were bought, and reluctantly she set out. The first stop was Vejle, and that was as far as they got. It so happened that they were met by the agent who had sold them their tickets. He explained that the berths he had booked for them had also been sold in some other town at the same time. Consequently my father and his family had to wait for the next ship to sail. Of course my father was furious, there he was with his whole family and with only the barest necessities in a small town where he had to find a place to stay for several weeks. At this point my mother intervened and seized the opportunity to change my father's mind, with the result that he told the agent to go to hell. The ticket money was refunded and we all settled in Vejle.

Of course the interrupted journey is something unusual, but otherwise there are many characteristic features: the father's hankering to migrate, the mother's conservative attitude, the miserable existence on the moorland farm followed by the move to Vejle. The sequel too was characteristic: One son, Peter Hedebol, went from the town to the capital (where he became a well-known mayor); another son emigrated to America. The parents remained in Vejle.

My father, who gradually realized that all he could expect was the miserable existence of a worker, felt that he had been cheated all his life. He had had his chance to see what America offered, and it had been wasted. Occasionally he felt bitter, and now and then friction would break out between my parents.

A connection has been demonstrated earlier between emigration and the concentration of urban areas in a county. Areas with rather large and expanding towns tended to have relatively lower intensity of emigration, whereas counties with idyllic little towns without any new factories or workshops usually produced a great number of emigrants. The phenomenon is bound up with the choice between the neighboring town or America. Wherever the town was big and expanding the choice was not difficult. If it was a small and stagnant place, on the other hand, the alternative of emigration was much more obvious and attractive. But did the young men and women of the rural districts who wanted to experience something new regard the neighboring town and America as real alternatives? The desire to leave the countryside might extend farther away than the next town, but still not quite as far away as America.

The official statistics offer very little assistance with the problem of internal migration, especially in the period before World War I. All we know is the situation every 10 years, and then only the rough lines of the overall movements between the major parts of the country. But the emigration statistics present us with a chance of viewing the fascinating problem of rural–urban migration from a new angle. As an example let us examine the densely populated area of southern Funen, and the relatively thinly populated Hjørring County, both regions that have a rather large emigration and that have been specially analyzed at the parish level here (see Figure 6.1).

The general impression the map gives of emigration distribution in northern Jutland is that it was rather evenly scattered over the entire area. Only the strip along the northeastern coast shows very low emigration relative to the population. The most interesting feature in this connection is the position of the towns and their surroundings. In this county there are

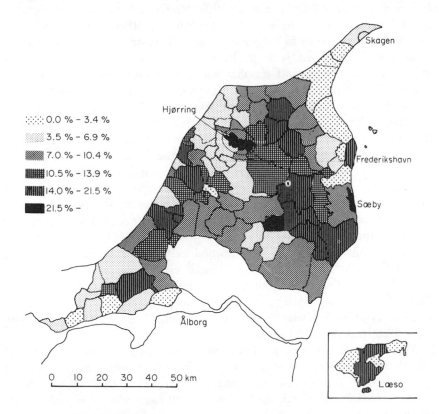

Figure 6.1 Hjørring county—emigration as a percentage of population (1880 census) in the period 1868–1899.

four market towns, Hjørring, Frederikshavn, Sæby, and Skagen. Skagen will not be included because it has little surrounding farmland.

These three towns experienced very different rates of growth during the period. The question here is whether the theory that expanding towns have low rates of emigration and stagnant towns high rates holds in the cases of these three towns.

The economic growth of Sæby was very slow compared with the average provincial town; and its emigration per 1000 inhabitants was indeed above that of most other towns, certainly far above that of Frederikshavn. This later town had undergone a most unusual expansion—the population had more than tripled in the course of 30 years, and as can be seen from the map, the rate of emigration was relatively low. But what about Hjørring, which had a considerable increase of population but also had a formidable emigration (the equivalent of 43% of the 1880 population emigrated during the period up to 1900)? The theory does not appear to work in this case. It is tempting to attribute this difference between Frederikshavn and Hjørring to different kinds of industrialization (here and in the following the term is used in its broadest sense). Because of the fishing and the local plants associated with it, Frederikshavn was able to absorb the influx of new people and on the whole to retain them also. Hjørring remained essentially a market town serving its agricultural surroundings, but without any industrial economic expansion. It therefore was difficult to support the migrants who added to its population. One small indication that this really was the situation is that the majority of the emigrants from the town of Hjørring had set out already during the first half of the period, i.e., between 1870 and 1885. In Frederikshavn it was the other way around—the majority of departures took place during the second half of the period. Industrialization must have been sufficient to keep down emigration before then. Furthermore, Figure 6.1 seems to give an indirect picture of the origins of the influx to the towns. We see that the emigration intensity is relatively low in areas immediately around the towns, but high in a zone farthest from the towns. This is clearest of all in the case of a belt of parishes running north–south halfway between Hjørring and Frederikshavn–Sæby, though the region along the coast of the North Sea south of Hjørring has similar areas from which 15–20% of the 1880 population emigrated.

The pattern which emerges from this map gives a clue to the nature of the alternatives—migration to town or migration overseas. In parishes very close to a town, people apparently preferred that as their goal. Frederikshavn is an island amid parishes with particularly low emigration; people within that ring moved to town or earned a living from its proximity. In the more distant villages, the conception of town life was hazier, and a larger part of these villagers preferred the great decision of overseas emigration. It should be noted, however, that a number of parishes with very high emigration rates, forming a north–south line on the map, had a particularly large increase of population during the period 1860–1880, compared with the surrounding areas. Even so, it seems from the location of parishes with high emigration intensity that it is possible to distinguish the so-called "urban sphere of influence." The most likely explanation why the southernmost parishes of the area had low intensity levels is that they were within the sphere of influence of Ålborg-Nørresundby, and emigration was directed southward toward the relatively highly industrialized towns on the Limfjord.

Railroads drew new lines through the landscape, and with them came about a new structure in migration. At railroad crossings, new towns sprang up. These station towns were an interesting phenomenon in the migration from country to town, because a considerable part of the influx went to this new type of town. Their population increased because of the railroads to an extent which made it difficult to distinguish between a small provincial town, a market town, and a large station town. An inquiry into this problem has been made for those areas in Jutland through which the railroads passed in the eastern and western parts of the peninsula. In the case of the eastern railroad, from 1860–1911 the station towns increased in population by 72% while other towns grew by only 11%. Along the western railroad, the difference is even more marked, with the rail connections increasing by 126% and towns without stations by only 46%.

One might suspect that migration to the station towns caused by railroad building after 1860 could have helped retard emigration. The trains placed the neighboring towns within reach of the rural population, thereby making internal migration a more feasible alternative to overseas emigration. If we include the station towns in the picture of urbanization, the difference between the Danish and the Swedish–Norwegian rate of urbanization becomes even more pronounced. The Swedish railroad network was by the turn of the century many kilometers longer than the Danish, but in relation to the total size of the country it was far more thinly spread. Consequently, the station town in Sweden plays a much less important role in the urbanization process than in Denmark. A likely explanation of the difference between the emigration intensity of Denmark and that of Norway and Sweden is that the rural populations of the other two Scandinavian countries did not possess the alternative to migration that existed in Denmark, i.e., migration to middle-sized towns within the country. Obviously this is not the sole explanation, but it is one that cannot be disregarded.

We have tried to demonstrate that emigration intensity is highest in areas farthest away from provincial towns, particularly those which show signs of industrial expansion. The migrants to these towns generally came from the surrounding areas. This is also implied in the theory of the urban sphere of influence, according to which migration from country to town is governed by the distance to town. The assumption here is that the horizon of the rural population at that time was so narrow that only rarely did people undertake moves over long distances, such as from one province to another. The distance over which urban influence is effective is believed to depend on the size of the town; but a more exhaustive examination of a larger region—the details of which are omitted here—shows that this is a theory which must be considered with reservation before it is accepted as a general rule.

The relationship between internal and overseas migrations has so far only been viewed in its geographical aspect, but the whole problem can be regarded from another and even more important angle, the temporal one— i.e., the question of whether internal and external migrations move in parallel fluctuations, or whether the flood of migrants in a certain period might remain within the boundaries of the country, and in other periods cross the borders and go overseas.

Here are some interesting perspectives that penetrate to the core of the issues raised by migration. Were internal mobility and emigration governed by more or less identical factors, or were they two mechanisms that alternated? No attempts at an answer will be made here—merely an indication of the problems the question raises. On the one hand, one might imagine that the urge for migration—the desire to break old ties or whatever it may be called—is something which arises in a population at certain times as a result of economic or social conditions. Migrants would then stream out of large areas both at home and abroad until new conditions slowed the exodus. In this case the pull effect might enter the picture as an important attraction, not unlike the lunar attraction that governs the ebb and flow of the tides.

The alternative is that during the nineteenth century there was permanent high mobility, primarily from the rural districts, but that this constant stream took different directions depending on the cycle in domestic and foreign economic conditions. It moved *either* toward the towns *or* across the ocean, according to conditions on either side of the Atlantic.

The latter viewpoint is the one adopted by Brinley Thomas (1954) in his book about migration and economic growth. During periods characterized by an ebb in the stream of emigrants to America, there should be an increase in internal migration to cities and towns. According to Thomas, the cause behind these fluctuations in the stream of people would be the changes in capital investment, domestic and overseas, which he sums up in the phrase "the Atlantic economy."

The counter-rhythm of internal and external migrations is demonstrated by Thomas partly by means of a table for England and Wales and partly by means of a table for Västmanland in Sweden. Table 6.4 gives Thomas's figures for English migration and emigration. For three of the seven decades between 1881 and 1901, Thomas's alternating rhythms of domestic and foreign migration really do appear. But outside of that period, it is difficult to find other relationships between the two columns of numbers. Thomas explains in a footnote that the internal migration shown represents the "net gain in towns and colliery districts." This implies that where emigration is included as a hidden element, the figures are for net gain. The great emigration wave of the 1880s will therefore be unavoidably registered in the net gain of the towns (i.e., the total increase of population minus the natural increase). The figure for the number of people who migrated to the towns will be lower because some townspeople emigrated and "concealed" a corresponding number of arrivals. It has indeed been stressed by A. K. Cairncross that a striking feature of the figures for English migration from rural areas is the uniformity during the entire period, while the figures for net migration to the towns vary radically. This suggests that the main flow of emigration came from the towns, but no definite solution can be derived from the available data, especially because the use of figures for whole decades must hide great variations.

Brinley Thomas's hypothesis can be tested on the Danish statistical records. At that time Copenhagen was a fairly large city and had considerable emigration; its population growth can thus be taken as a measure of the internal migration in Denmark. If one compares the net gain by decades with emigration for the whole nation, as Brinley Thomas has done, no correspondence is apparent. Luckily the sources include the capital's net population gain for each single year after 1880. Figure 6.2 compares this

TABLE 6.4

English Migration to Towns and Emigration Abroad (in thousands) [a]

	Migration to towns	Emigration
1841–1851	742	81
1851–1861	620	327
1861–1871	624	206
1871–1881	689	164
1881–1891	228	601
1891–1901	606	69
1901–1911	−207	501

[a] From Brinley Thomas, *Migration and Economic Growth* (Cambridge: Cambridge University Press) 1954, p. 124.

net population gain with emigration from all of Denmark. There actually appears to be an inverse relationship between the two curves for some of the years up to 1892, and somewhat less so in the period after 1900.

The graph contains the same fault as Brinley Thomas's statistics, i.e., that net emigration figures have been used. However, the Copenhagen sources differ from Brinley Thomas's English sources in degree of emigration intensity. In England, the intensity in the 1880s was as high as 2300 emigrants per 100,000, whereas in Copenhagen 571 was the high point. Thus the figures for emigration are hardly capable of significantly influencing the net population gain in Copenhagen. But the fourfold higher intensity in England would indicate that there emigration unavoidably influenced net population gain.

If the yearly emigration figures are added to the net population gain, a better though not complete impression of migration to Copenhagen is obtained. A graph based on these new figures still would not alter the

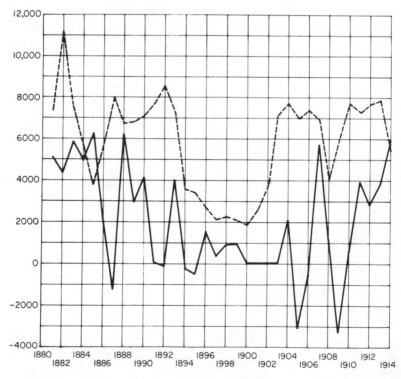

Figure 6.2 Net migration to Copenhagen compared to total emigration. The solid line represents net gain of Copenhagen population by migration; the dashed line represents total emigration.

course of the curve much since the fluctuations would remain virtually the same, though the whole curve is lifted by the higher numbers.

All in all, we are forced to conclude that Brinley Thomas's theory concerning an alternating rhythm between domestic and foreign migrations rests on a somewhat weak foundation on the English sources. Decade figures give an impression of such overly distinct variations that the results must be judged with caution. A detailed analysis such as that in Figure 6.2 shows that in the yearly fluctuations certain single years did exhibit Brinley Thomas's inverse rhythms, without, however, any overall obvious inverse correlation. The graph can also be read to substantiate another viewpoint, mentioned earlier, that domestic and overseas mobility rise and fall together. Mobility in this period falls into three phases: two of high mobility both to Copenhagen and abroad (1881–1893 and 1904–1914), and the decade-long period of inactivity between 1894 and 1903.

7

DISTRIBUTION OF EMIGRANTS ACCORDING TO AGE

In the search for causality in emigration the age distribution of the emigrants at the time of departure can give important clues. Generally two incentives, both opposite extremes, prompted people to emigrate: love of adventure on the one hand, and economic distress on the other. To these two extremes correspond two age groups: the very young between about 16 and 24, and an older group, above 40. In the latter category of men and women above 40, identification with their surroundings would probably be so complete that weighty reasons would be necessary to make them sell everything and set off to start from scratch in a new world. The older part of a population is far less mobile than the very young, who frequently have formed neither emotional nor economic ties, and have all their powers intact. As might well be expected, the young do form the most numerous group among emigrants.

On the other hand, it is likely that the majority of emigrants who returned came from the same group. These would be people who took a few "Wanderjahre" before coming home to settle down. With these things in mind we can operate with three groups at different stages of life, each of which entered upon emigration with different motives and expectations.

The earliest stage of life, childhood, is characterized by social passivity. Children among the emigrants were mere participants who followed along and presumably had no part in the decision of their parents to emigrate. The next stage, youth, is the most active, the most enterprising, and, as already mentioned, the group most independent of social and economic encumbrances. For them the process of decision making is relatively uncomplicated. The dividing line between this and the last group, that of the mature and the elderly, must probably be placed at the age of marriage, which, at the time we are considering here, occurred somewhat later than at present, the average age being about 30 years. The married group has all the economic and social ties that make breaking out of the old life so difficult, particularly if there are children. Since the practical aspects of emigration are so great, a strong push is needed to get people started, and inertia appears to be a greater force than energy. But when a family group of this kind does get started, there is a correspondingly smaller chance of return. Severe obstacles have to be overcome when a group like this emigrates, but the same obstacles would have to be overcome if they were to migrate back again collectively.

On the face of it, one would think that statements of age on the emigration contracts (from which they were transferred to the emigration registers) would be one of the most exact and therefore reliable types of information in this whole study. Everyone knows his own age, and it seems unlikely that even female coquetry would induce a person to give false information in the contract. However, an inspection of the whole source material (about 168,000 age statements from the period 1868–1900) indicates that even here there are pitfalls. The number of emigrants per year under the age of 1 year varies considerably from year to year. Among the emigrants of the period before 1900, there is an unusually large number under 1 year, and very few just 1 year old. Likewise the number of children at 10 and 11 years old is quite high, and the number of 12- and 13-year-olds correspondingly low. Social and demographic conditions cannot explain this peculiar phenomenon, but for the simple fact that emigrants lied to the agents about their children's ages when they bought the expensive tickets to distant countries.

Then, as now, fares depended on the age of the passenger: Children under 1 year were free, and those under 12 went for half fare. These age limits seem to have been universally accepted by all steamship lines during the entire period. It explains the high number of babies—very likely many were quite big for their age—and also the peculiar ratio of 11-year-olds to teenagers. The number of 12-year-olds is certainly understated as a result of false information. But a special factor may have actually reduced the number of 13-year-olds: One more year may have been spent at home before the important fourteenth birthday when they were confirmed, presented with a watch and an amber cigar-holder, and finished school. The false statements were caused by an understandable interest in saving costs, and they are not fatal to a general analysis of the ages of the emigrants.

A study of the age groups over 25 likewise reveals peculiarities, irregularities on a curve which indicate that a higher number of emigrants stated their ages as a rounded off number, 30, 40, 50, or 60 than as an odd number of years. The ages adjacent to the "round" ones are especially poorly represented. It is unlikely that people actually tended to decide to emigrate just as they became an even decade older. Many people in the nineteenth century were unsure of their exact age, and rounded it off to 40 from about the ages of 37 to 43. This phenomenon is known even today, particularly in underdeveloped countries. In George W. Barkley's book, *Techniques of Population Analysis,* there is a diagram based on the 1950 census in Venezuela, which exhibits exactly the same jumps at the points indicating the "round" ages. According to Barkley, this is the result of the questionnaire asking "How old are you?" A more exact request for day and year of birth would invariably have resulted in more exact answers. A date is a fixed thing to everyone, while age is a constantly changing number.

An analysis of the distribution of emigrants according to age (see Table 7.1) must start with a rough survey of the individual 5-year groups. Persons above the age of 40 have been arranged in 10-year groups.

The percentages show very clearly how skewed the age distribution is among emigrants. Almost 40% of them were in their twenties, and if the

TABLE 7.1

Age Distribution for All Emigrants, 1868–1900

Age	Actual figures	Percent	Age	Actual figures	Percent
0–4	17,297	10.1	35–39	7,896	4.6
5–9	8,568	5.0	40–49	8,681	5.0
10–14	8,397	4.9	50–59	5,609	3.2
15–19	26,867	15.6	60–69	1,915	1.1
20–24	43,841	25.5	70–	318	0.2
25–29	24,829	14.4	age not stated	4,299	2.5
30–34	13,556	7.9	Total	172,073	100.0

preceding 5-year group is included (the years from 14, the confirmation age, to 19, a group in which the majority are "independently deciding" emigrants), then more than 55%, or well over half the total number of emigrants were young people between 15 and 29. The difference between the 25–29-year-old group and the 30–34-year-old group is quite impressive: The former represent 14%, the latter 8%. Obviously a line of demarcation divides these two groups at approximately marrying age. Presumably the group of emigrants between 30 and 39 years must have been those who brought along the many infants and small children who comprised more than 10% of the entire number of emigrants. One remarkable thing, however, is the fact that the subsequent two 5-year groups (all children between 5 and 14) are so relatively sparsely represented. With the reservation in mind concerning the earlier mentioned errors in the statements of ages, the relation between the numbers of the youngest group and the two older groups suggests that parents or guardians tended to set out while the children were still very young, but were rather more hesitant from the time the children reached school age. Taking children out of school in order to emigrate was, as far as the best interests of the children were concerned, often a regretable step, since in most overseas countries, they would often never get a chance to return to school, partly because of language difficulties, and partly because of the lack of public schools as provided in Denmark. The pronounced jump between the two groups on either side of the confirmation age confirms the impression that this religious ceremony and the corresponding end-of-school age formed a threshold after which the young were allowed to decide their own futures. In some cases the "ticket to America" may have substituted for an education of some kind.

The previous chapter demonstrated the considerable difference between the emigration from the towns and that from the rural districts. By way of continuation, it may be of interest to find out how this difference looks for separate age groups. The rural emigration was made up of relatively younger people than was the urban emigration. Admittedly the rural emigration also included relatively more from the oldest groups. Probably these were grandparents emigrating to settle with their already emigrated children and their families. That this type of emigration is more common among the rural group than the urban is probably because the rural emigrants often became farmers abroad. On the farms they frequently had room for extra members of their families, whereas the urban emigrants tended to settle in overseas cities with cramped accommodations. Another difference between urban and rural emigration may be noted in connection with the two school-age groups, 5–9 and 10–14. Townspeople, for whom school education presumably played a rather more important part than for the rural population, brought fewer children in these age groups with them. But the true explanation is probably simply that, generally speaking, the rural population had more children than the urban population, 18% as opposed to 15–16%.

However, the important thing is that on the whole the urban emigrants made up their minds to go, and actually did set out, at a later point in life than did the rural people: 27% of the rural emigrants belonged to the age group 25–44 years, but 35% of the urban emigrants did. There is more than just ordinary statistical interest attached to this difference, and it can probably be taken as characteristic of the trend in migration in Denmark as a whole.

One might, for instance, interpret the figures as suggesting that emigration was more of an emergency measure to people living in the towns than to those from the country: It was more difficult to support a family in a town than in the rural districts. One ought to stress that the phenomenon is not special to the period treated here. Even nowadays there is a tendency among rural emigrants to set out at an earlier age than do people in towns, though the tendency was more pronounced before the turn of the century.

The higher average age among urban emigrants can also be taken as evidence of so-called emigration by stages. A young farmer, perhaps a son of a farmer or cottager who was for some reason not going to inherit his father's property, would move to some town in the hope of being able to make a living for himself there, for example, as an unskilled worker. He might marry and start a family; but gradually he would find out that it was very hard to support them all in a town during periods of unemployment, or when wages provided only a subsistence living for a family. Having gradually grown older, the man might think of emigrating to America, Canada, or possibly Australia, where he could get a homestead and thus return to his earlier agrarian life.

Although young people between the ages of 15 and 25 predominated in the masses of emigrants who were for a time the steerage passengers on all Atlantic steamers, all ages were represented, from the youngest to the oldest—even the age group "under 0 years" at the time of departure from Denmark. In the ship's doctors' casebooks there are constant entries of children born en route, emigrants born on the way across the ocean. The majority of these pregnant women were probably married, but there may have been a considerable number of unmarried young girls who had gotten into trouble and were therefore emigrating. Large emigration ships carrying between 200 and 1200 passengers contained, during a prolonged voyage, an entire, though small, "independent" population, experiencing births and deaths, just as on shore. From doctors' casebooks, we can see that most of the ships docked in America with a small surplus, i.e., the number of births more than made up for the number of deaths, unless it happened (which was not infrequent before 1870) that some epidemic disease broke out on board. Such a disease was likely to take a heavy toll among passengers so tightly huddled together.

Many emigrants brought along flocks of children; and especially during the early period before 1890, children were a dominant element on board the emigrant vessels. The proportion of children among the emigrants culminated concurrently with the culmination of Scandinavian emigration altogether, i.e., in the first half of the 1880s. During the following decades the number of children gradually declined, paralleling the trend among emigrants toward lower average ages and fewer married couples. The largest families came mostly from the rural districts despite the fact that adult rural emigrants had a lower average age than their fellow emigrants from the towns. A related factor is that the townspeople practiced a certain amount of birth control, which was practically unknown in the rural areas until after the turn of the century. Very poor housing conditions in the big towns and extensive unemployment forced people to consider the connection between living conditions and family size.

While the under-15 age group among emigrants decreased steadily after 1890, the 15–19 age group increased at the same time to such an extent that its share of the total number of migrants no less than doubled during the period 1866–1914. Obviously large-scale emigration was developing into a young people's movement. Though the increase among this group came largely from the rural districts and less from the towns, one should not disregard a factor of common importance to all—the draft to which all young men became liable at the age of 20.

The fact that rural emigrants were more numerous than urban seems to be connected with the development of the structure of Danish agriculture, including the political problem concerning the parceling out of land to small-holders. Broadly, one may say that when the young people from the rural areas emigrated in the last decades of the nineteenth century, this was closely bound up with the problem of whether these people would be able to set up for themselves by obtaining land of their own to cultivate. Admittedly the very young ones of 15–19 years were too young to farm independently, but they were perfectly well aware of the paths that lay open for them. For a young man of that age there were, in general, three possibilities: He might obtain some land of his own, however small a piece it might be; he might migrate to some town in Denmark; or he might as the last resort emigrate to some overseas country. Accordingly, the constant increase in the number of rural 15–19-year-old emigrants during the period would indicate a corresponding incease in the difficulty young people had in obtaining independent farms. The small decrease in the last years of the 1890s can give further support to this theory, as at this time the political questions about small-holders and their holdings were taken under consideration by the Danish parliament. As part of the negotiation policy conducted by the moderate left under Frede Boisen (a branch of the agrarian Venstre) after 1891, a proposal for distribution of small plots was pressed until it resulted in the first Small-Holders Act, in 1899. The whole problem will be treated in detail in Chapter 11.

The age at which most Danes acted on the idea of emigrating was between 20 and 24. Between 1868 and 1900, this age group consisted of about 44,000 persons and constituted more than one-fourth of the entire overseas emigration from Denmark. With this group, we do not see the same development as with the younger group from 15–19. The proportion of emigrants who were between 20 and 24 remained more or less constant at 25% during the whole period till the end of the century. One feature is common to the young age groups: They both made up a relatively high share of the emigration in the period 1875–1879, and a small share in the agrarian Venstre) after 1891, a proposal for distribution of small plots a time of economic prosperity combined with considerable emigration, while the years 1875–1879 are characterized by depression and very sparse emigration. The consequence of this seems to be a general rule that runs as follows: Slumps are characterized by the emigration of young people, while booms encourage the older age groups to set out. However, a study of the other age groups will reveal that the problem is more complicated than it seems at first glance. What primarily holds down the relative share of the younger age groups during a boom period is the increasing number of children. But the age groups over 24 seem to follow other rules.

Considerable interest is attached to the group aged 25–29, as it shows a substantial decrease in emigration during the period in question.

It is as though this group exchanged roles with the 15–19-year-old group during the years of the first boom, 1872–1873, and during the following years of depression, 1874–1879. A corresponding change can also be traced in the subsequent age groups, 30–34 and 35–39, both of which started with large proportions of the total, but gradually sank to a lower level during the following years. The main trend seems to confirm the theory that emigration during the 1870s had something of the character of an emergency solution; and, furthermore, emigration at this early time was a risky business—both maturity and courage were needed by a person setting out to overseas countries. Conditions in the countries of immigration were less well known and also more primitive than was the case in a later day; the earlier emigrants paved the way for later generations.

As a tentative explanation for the pronounced fluctuation of emigration,

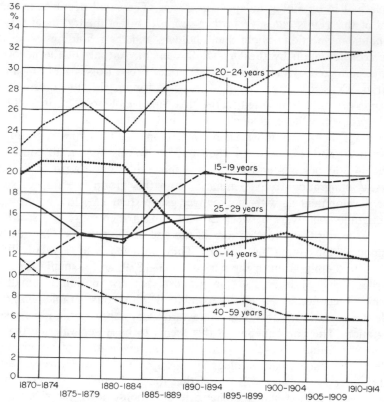

Figure 7.1 Age groups as a percentage of total emigrants, 1868–1914 at 5-year intervals.

it has been suggested that such movements might originate from variations in the European birthrate. It is a very obvious hypothesis that persons born in a year with a very high birthrate will find it difficult to support themselves when they have to make a living, and that there will be a tendency among such a generation to resort to emigration on a larger than average scale. The phenomenon called the "baby boom" of the years 1943–1945 was a well-known feature of the post-war period; and the nineteenth century cannot have been without similar circumstances.

Brinley Thomas (1954) has advocated the viewpoint that there is a pronounced correlation between birthrate and emigration, and by way of proof he used a diagram based on figures obtained from Sundbärg's tables (see Figure 7.2).

In my opinion Figure 7.2 must be described as an abuse of statistical materials—an abuse in two respects. First and foremost, because the two

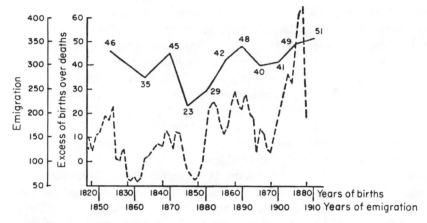

Figure 7.2 European natural increase and emigration, 1820–1910. The solid line represents quinquennial excess of births over deaths per 1000 of population; dashed line represents annual emigration from Europe per 100,000 of population. [From Brinley Thomas, *Migration and Economic Growth* (Cambridge: Cambridge University Press, 1954), p. 156.]

curves have been arranged with a lag of some 25–30 years between them, which serves to bring about the desired correlation. But who can say that the average age of the entire European emigrant population from 1820 to 1910 was 25 years? If we chose 22 years of age as the difference between birth and emigration age (which would give a more correct average), the curves would move in exactly the opposite rhythm. Second, we get a grossly distorted picture from using birthrate figures for the whole of Europe taken together. Birthrate is a factor that varies enormously from one country to another, even from one county to another. The local variations are sometimes greater than the fluctuations of emigration.

So, no adequate documentation has been produced to show a connection between birthrate and emigration, and inquiries into the Danish materials show that such a connection would be extremely difficult to establish. A calculation of emigration rates in relation to the numbers born in successive generations has been made on the basis of computer-processed material coupled with birth figures from 1840 on. An analysis of this kind would disclose if, for instance, the large numbers of people in the generation produced by higher birthrates of the second half of the 1850s would be more likely to emigrate later on than other generations. Nothing was found to suggest that this was the case.

The fact that the age distribution among emigrants is not identical with that of the population as a whole goes without saying. Emigration fever will strike hard in certain age groups between youth and the marriage age:

able-bodied people who are valuable from society's point of view. The percentage age composition of emigrants from 1868–1900 compared with that of the population of 1880 shows this great difference. The only age group with more or less the same proportion among emigrants as the population as a whole is the 30–40 group. Emigration must have served to hollow out the 20–24-year-old group and the ages on either side of it, which formed the socially most valuable part of the population. In many countries, such as Sweden, this circumstance caused many to voice the opinion that the wave of emigration ought to be stopped or at least restrained, as it drained society of the best of the labor force. In many parts of Europe, economic arguments were advanced about the cost to society from losing the labor of one person. An Austrian economist reached an astronomical figure for his estimate of society's loss by including in his calculation items such as food, clothing, and education for everyone who emigrated after the age of confirmation: He regarded these expenses as a social investment converted into a social waste, in that the investment paid no return to the home country, since it never benefitted from the labor of the emigrant in question.

The main trends in emigrant age composition are the same for all of northern Europe, even if there are occasional variations from one country to another. In Denmark, and to an even higher degree in Norway, emigration was concentrated around the age group 15–24 years. In Sweden, however, the distribution was much more evenly spread among all age groups.

8

MEN AND WOMEN AMONG THE EMIGRANTS

Crossing the oceans in order to build a new civilization west and south of the Old World was primarily a venture for men. So many women stayed home in the old country that toward the end of the nineteenth century there was widespread anxiety about the excess number of women that would result in Europe; in England this fear was strong enough to give birth to a special society, "The British Women's Emigration Association," whose purpose was to encourage the emigration of women in order to create a balance between the two sexes. The problem attracted public attention, even from people who were not personally concerned. Thus in the 1880s a German professor at Dorpat, Herr Rauber, claimed to have proved that the ancient legend about the Amazons really had its origin in government-inspired propaganda with the aim of encouraging the surplus of Greek women to emigrate and establish special women's societies in other parts of the world. Rauber's hypothesis probably cannot be described as anything but a fairy tale, but it must surely have been at least partly inspired by the emigration problems of the author's own time.

The greater proportion of men among the emigrants is one of the fundamental features of large-scale emigration. A mixture of general love of adventure and an urge to find better economic conditions may be considered characteristic of men. Women are conditioned to be more passive and are inclined to take a more reactive than an active attitude on questions of improved economic circumstances. Whatever the facts may be in this relationship, the unequal distribution of the sexes was treated as an important problem in the countries of immigration, especially in the United States. Women became scarce in American society, and the proportion of women declined steadily, paralleling the landing of millions of new emigrants, among whom the men formed an absolute majority. During the 30-year period from 1860 to 1890, the female proportion of the foreign-born population was reduced from 46.7 to 45.7%—seemingly an insignificant difference, but nevertheless a difference that made itself acutely felt in the life of the community. During the decades to come the difference was reduced a little, partly because the beginnings of emancipation in the countries of western Europe made the number of female emigrants rise—a result that we can see in Denmark, too.

It is well known that the years after the turn of the century saw a new wave of emigration to the United States, a wave which far surpassed the "old" wave from western Europe in number. In the mass emigration from Italy and the eastern countries of Europe, even fewer women participated, and the result was that by 1910 the female proportion of the American population had fallen to 43.6% from 46% in about 1900.

Danish-born Americans felt this scarcity, too. Very often the men found it difficult to find a Danish girl to marry; frequently they would fetch a wife from their own part of Denmark. The same thing was true with regard to help on the farms that these Danes established on the prairies. A Danish clergyman, Grove-Rasmussen, who traveled around the United States in 1870 in order to organize Danish congregations, recorded that he often heard complaints that Danish girls who had been brought over to work as servants with Danish emigrant families seldom stayed with these families more than a few months, as they tended to marry neighboring Danes very quickly. One Danish emigrant's wife explained that last time she had carefully specified that the servant she had sent for was to be both "old and ugly," as she hoped that this would guarantee her not having suitors, but even in this case in no more than 6 months the woman was engaged to marry. Gradually the disproportion between men and women in the countries of immigration was reduced as the immigrant children grew up. The disproportion did not exist among these boys and girls to the same degree; one would have thought that when a family was considering emigration it was of minor importance for the parents whether the children were boys or girls. But obviously it must have had some influence, for, compared with the population as a whole, the number of boys among the children was high; and there seems to have been some tendency to take special care of small girls that is reflected in the proportion of girls in the first three 5-year groups, i.e., 0–4 years, 5–9 years, and 10–14 years. There must also have been a desire to avoid exposing 10–14-year-old girls to the gales of the Atlantic and the hardships of pioneer life. They may have been left with relatives or friends, waiting until they were considered old enough to travel at the age of 15–16. Then they would set out to meet their parents, unless they had settled with foster parents and did not want to leave them.[1]

In the older age groups, as we have already explained, the discrepancy between the two sexes was far greater. For the entire Danish emigration in 1868–1900, the situation was this: Out of every 1000 emigrants, 614 were men and 386 women. This includes all age groups. But in consideration of the phenomenon from a social viewpoint the children must be eliminated, as they cannot be regarded as independent emigrants. When children have been deducted the figure changes to 367 women out of 1000 emigrants, i.e., one-third. Just as the countries of immigration acquired an unequal sex ratio because of this imbalance among immigrants, so did it have considerable repercussions in the countries of emigration. In Denmark, this was even more so than in many other countries because the situation there was particularly acute. The departure of 96,000 grown men and only 60,000 women noticeably disturbed the balance of the Danish population. Even before this, men had been in the minority in Denmark: In 1840, 494 persons out of every 1000 were males. But mass emigration caused this to drop to 491 in 1880, 487 in 1901, and to no more than 485 in 1911.

This quantitative imbalance may look small, but it was of great importance for the frequencies of marriage and birth. Many years passed before this lopsidedness was evened out. Before 1911 women outnumbered men by no less than 81,000; this means that there were 1061 women per 1000 men. After 30 years had passed, during which emigration subsided, a reasonable balance between men and women was attained. From 1911 to 1950, the number of women per 1000 men gradually fell from the 1061 cited to 1017, which is now regarded as equilibrium.

Emigration thus left an imprint on the structure of the population, but a more exact impression can be obtained through studies of the emigration statistics themselves. The number of women who emigrated from Copenhagen and the provincial towns was much higher than that of female

---

[1] In Finnish emigration the situation is, strangely enough, the opposite. Here the number of girls was larger than that of boys for groups under the age of 16.

emigrants from rural districts. For the whole period until 1900, the difference was one of 383 females per 1000 urban emigrants as against 352 females per 1000 rural emigrants. This makes a difference of almost 3% (with children altogether eliminated from the calculation). Seeing that two-thirds of the rural emigrants were men, one might expect a huge surplus of women to have formed in the rural districts over the years. However, this did not happen. About the turn of the century women were in the minority in the countryside; this was the result, among other things, of an interplay between internal and external migration, which in this as in so many other circumstances worked together and regulated things. The point is that whereas emigration removed far more men than women, far more women, on the other hand, migrated to the towns. In fact, so many women did so that the balance in the rural districts shifted to produce a slight majority of males.

The explanation of this cannot be found solely in the increasing difficulty for girls to find husbands in the countryside. Of greater weight was the question of occupational opportunities: the demand in towns for female servants for middle-class households and the fact that early Danish industrialism depended a great deal on female labor. The demand for unskilled male labor was far smaller while industry was still relatively primitive. This explains why emigration from the towns was so large, especially male emigration.

That women predominate in internal migration, at least in the "footloose" age groups, is not a phenomenon unique to the period before 1914. We can see it even now, demonstrated by the 1950 census, for instance; and it is also the case in Norway.

In age groups where emigration is highest, the proportion of females is the lowest. It is relatively small in the case of rural districts where the young girls had the possibility of staying as dairy maids or milk maids, or, as was more common, moving to town to enter domestic service. In the age groups between 30 and 40, the women make up a larger share of the emigrants, because this is the married woman's group. And, finally, when we approach the pensioners' age groups, we find the proportion of women rising to reach a majority. This of course agrees with the ratio in the population as a whole, in which the average duration of a woman's life is quite noticeably longer than a man's. Nevertheless, over the age of 60, men are still a majority, even if a small one, among emigrants from rural districts. The reason may be that for settlers on the prairies, an old grandfather might be able to give more help in house building or ploughing than an elderly female relative.

From 1868 to 1914, a rather characteristic development took place in practically all age groups—namely, that women became gradually more numerous in both relative and absolute terms. This was particularly the case during the last years of the 1880s and the 1890s. Early in this chapter it was suggested that the increasing number of women may have been a consequence of the emancipation of women, the idea being that a steadily increasing number of women felt free and independent enough to make the decisive step of overseas emigration. But we should also point out that as the foreign-born population of the United States grew, there was an increasing demand for helpers, servants, and possibly wives. This demand produced a considerable drain on the home country's resources of young women as the emigrants gradually established themselves with farms or in towns. This created a pull factor in the emigration process on which Søren Kjær, a Danish politician of the period, expressed his opinions. He visited the United States in 1887, and on his return wrote in *Randers Dagblad:*

> The demand for Scandinavian girls, particularly Danish ones, is enormous. Mr. Lambke, New York, told me that I was welcome to send 3000 girls any day I pleased. Inside a few days he would promise to get them all work at a beginner's wage of 7 to 12 dollars. Girls who are skillful at housework and dairywork might obtain 25 dollars. Working in the fields is unknown for women in the States.

If one distributes the increasing number of girl/woman emigrants from Denmark according to the localities they came from, one will find that a surprisingly large part of the emigrants after 1890 came from the towns —and not the smallest ones. As already mentioned, women formed a majority among the persons migrating from rural to urban districts. A result of this tendency was saturation of the demand for female labor in towns, particularly since industry was going through a period of rapid mechanization that brought about a change from female to male predominance among the workers employed. There was more increase in emigration among young girls of 15–19 than among the somewhat older ones, 20–24 years. Probably the very young ones were less frequently fettered by emotional ties, and unmarried and unengaged as they were, could better travel freely than their older sisters. In a subsequent section we shall deal more thoroughly with changes in the age of marriage in the years before 1914.

A calculation of the average age, at the point of departure, of the thousands of emigrants is a practically impossible task by means of pencil and paper; but with the help of a computer it can be done quite easily. Among the interesting results is the characteristic difference between men and women in this respect.

The youngest segment of the emigrants, children, must be regarded as irrelevant in this connection, so everyone under the age of 15 has been withdrawn from the material before this tabulation was made. Table 8.1 shows the result for the whole of Denmark, for the period 1868–1899.

The average naturally rises somewhat above 20 with the elimination of children under 15, though the most common age of emigrants was about 20. But women generally were some 2 years older than men at the point of departure. Furthermore, we can establish that the average age of urban emigrants of both sexes is about 1 year above that of rural emigrants. Both facts fit in with the general impression obtained so far, and agree with the interplay between emigration and internal migrations. The emigration from the towns was largely made up of persons who had previously migrated from a rural origin to a town and had spent some time there—the reason for their higher age at the time of departure.

But the average age was not the same in the 1910s as in the 1870s. It declined gradually in the years approaching World War I. Women who set out from the rural districts to America in the 1860s were thus at an average of 30–31 years, but in the 1890s were only about 27 years old. In one part of Denmark, the island of Bornholm, where fishing and sailing dominated employment opportunities, the urge to migrate came over the people at an early age; the average age for adult men from there was under 22 years.

The question of the very great differences between the numbers of male and female emigrants deserves a special analysis, as this is probably a means of penetrating those social conditions in the country of origin which governed the push factor in large-scale emigration. The problem stands out in sharp relief if a comparison is made between the Danish records and the figures for the rest of Scandinavia. It will be obvious that despite certain uniform movements over the years, there are considerable differences from one country to another. Figure 8.1, which is borrowed from the report of the Scandinavian History Conference (1971), makes this quite clear.

Two features of Figure 8.1 are remarkable. One is the fact that the emigrations of all the countries show two main movements: a downward

TABLE 8.1

Average Ages on Departure for Male and Female Emigrants over the Age of 15 (1868–1899)

	Towns	Rural districts
Men	26.9 years	25.9 years
Women	28.5 years	27.8 years

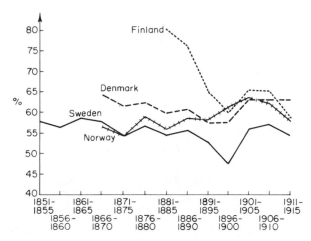

Figure 8.1 Men as a percentage of total number of emigrants from each of the Scandinavian countries, 1871–1915.

trend in the proportion of men toward the turn of the century, and a steep rise thereafter during the boom that started in 1903 and ended with the crisis in 1908. Second, it is notable that Sweden has much more equilibrium in the distribution between the sexes, far closer to half and half, than either Denmark or especially Finland.

Another striking feature is the fact that the two "old" countries of emigration, Sweden and Norway, from which the flow to the United States was already considerable as early as the 1840s, are at more or less the same level in the 1870s and 1880s, whereas the curves for the two "new" countries, Finland and Denmark, start remarkably high, and fall off gradually to the level of the other countries. On this basis one may advance a general hypothesis to the effect that all national emigrations pass through various phases, beginning with a pioneer emigration consisting mainly of men. This earliest group settles and begins gradually to act as a pull factor by fetching women (wives), helpers, and friends across the ocean. Many important features of European large-scale emigration might be explained if this could be confirmed with more comprehensive international material; for instance, certain aspects of the fluctuations and particularly the changes in the structure of emigration over time. As far as Denmark and Finland go, the facts are clear. As for Sweden, there is also a demonstrably marked predominance of men during the first phase (1851–1855). But this seems not to be the case in Norway, where individual spot inquiries into the earliest material show a clear tendency towards family emigration, with an equal distribution between men and women.

While the development in 1870–1900 seems to reflect a gradual change in the structure of emigration from the individual countries, it is hard to understand why the entire process seems to start all over again after 1900. Once more the male element becomes predominant in all three Scandinavian countries and women drop to one-third—and that in spite of the fact that the pioneer period was finished years earlier. So far there is no explanation of this.

There is, however, another interesting feature about Figure 8.1 that we are able to explain, namely, the difference between Denmark and Sweden. When the entire period 1868–1900 is regarded as one, the difference is considerable. In Denmark, for the 15–19 age group, for every 100 men who emigrated only 54 women did so; but in Sweden the corresponding figure was 94 women. During one single period, the last 5 years before the turn of the century, the number of emigrating Swedish women from all age groups was indeed larger than the number of men. Furthermore, we find that the emigration of women from Sweden reached its greatest density in the towns. As early as 1886, women constituted a majority among the emigrants from towns.

When this is viewed in connection with the previously mentioned fact that women formed a majority in internal migration, the relation between the distribution of sexes in Denmark and Sweden must imply that migrant women had been unable to find work in the towns. Industrialization advanced at a slower pace in Sweden than in Denmark and was obviously unable to absorb excess labor. The slower rate of industrialization is certainly one important reason why emigration from Sweden was so much greater than from Denmark. If the Danish women had participated in emigration to the same extent as did Swedish women, the total Danish emigration would have reached the same level as that from Sweden.

A large majority of Swedish emigrants departed from Gothenburg. But a substantial number traveled via Copenhagen, buying their tickets from some Danish emigration agent. This practice was widespread in 1869–1871 and especially in the 1880s. Thus 42,828 Swedish emigrants traveled via Copenhagen during the period 1881–1900. The strange thing about this group was that the number of young men compared with women was surprisingly large: 67 men per 100 Swedish emigrants—about the same ratio between the sexes as in the overall group of Danish emigrants.

The large flow of Swedish men to Copenhagen emigration agents had one very concrete explanation: Copenhagen was the port of embarkation for the more or less "secret" Swedish emigration and especially for young men who wanted to evade military service. In 1887 the Swedish ambassador lodged a complaint with the Danish foreign minister claiming that the Danish police did nothing to stop Swedish emigrants who were running away from their military service; on the contrary, they allowed Danish emigration agents to advertise in Swedish newspapers that emigrants departing from Copenhagen were not obliged to show "prästbetyg," a permit from the vicar to leave the parish. The minister straightforwardly rejected the complaint after a recommendation from the chief of emigration police who wrote:

> Why should we stop these conscripts? The Swedish emigration via Copenhagen is an extremely profitable business for this city. If it was stopped both local agents and the capital as a whole would suffer a considerable financial loss. If these conscripts are to be stopped the job should certainly be the responsibility of the Swedish police.

Undaunted by the Swedish complaints, the Danish agents continued to advertise. It is a well-known fact that letters of advertisement (in closed envelopes) were systematically sent by the thousands to Swedish towns and rural areas, bearing in large type the legend "prästbetyg not necessary." In 1910 another complaint came from the Swedish ambassador, but the answer seems to have been much the same on that occasion. The following year newspapers in the southern part of Sweden printed several articles in which the practice of the agents was severely criticized—a reaction that was probably of more avail than the ambassador's complaints.

Previously in this chapter it was mentioned that the proportion of women in emigration was susceptible to the fluctuations in the business cycles. This formed a pattern from which we can probably deduce a general model for sex distribution in emigration, to the effect that the emigration of women is more constant than that of men: The relative number of women rises in periods of low emigration and falls in periods of increasing emigration activity. In essence, when a new wave of emigration begins, the men lead the way as pioneers, and only when the wave has reached its peak does the female emigration come in, helping to make the decline less precipitous.

The fact that the men formed the vanguard of every wave of emigration at least during the first decades of the large-scale emigration, and then later made room for the women is quite clear from Figure 8.2, which shows the fluctuations of the total Danish emigration year by year until 1914, with an added curve showing the annual percentage of men in the emigration.

In the case of the two earliest high points of emigration, 1872–1873 and 1881–1883, the figure shows clearly that men are in the majority from the beginning of a rise; the predominance then decreases. A somewhat weakened expression of the same phenomenon is found in the peak

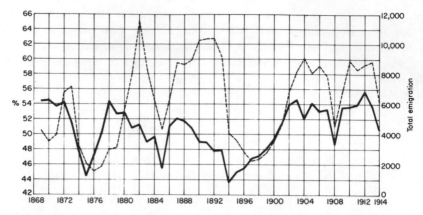

Figure 8.2 Total annual Danish emigration, 1869–1914 (represented by dashed line) and percentage of men in annual emigration (represented by solid line).

after 1886 and again in 1903–1907. Also notable is the way the proportion of women parallels the sudden fall in emigration in 1885. A more nearly equal emigration by both sexes would, of course, have given the emigration curve a completely different look, with steep rises and falls. This is the case in Sweden, where the distances between peaks and valleys are much greater because women played a much more important part in emigration than they did in Denmark. The fact that the curve of a country's total emigration is shaped, among other things, by the different emigration behavior of men and women should serve as a warning against drawing conclusions too freely about pull and push in emigration on the basis of the annual fluctuations.

9

FAMILIES OR INDIVIDUALS
IN EMIGRATION?

The emigration of adult women must, as previously mentioned, be regarded as two problems, each with its own background: (1) unmarried women who want work—a group of emigrants who are, from a social point of view, little different from the male emigrants; and (2) the somewhat older age group—married women who follow their husbands, if not at the same time, then later. The characteristics of these two groups indicate the difference between two fundamentally separate types of emigration, another of the structural problems concerning emigration which gives rise to interesting observations about emigration as a social phenomenon.

The decision behind the break with the home area is more difficult and serious in the case of a whole family than for a single, independent person. Furthermore it is much more complicated for a family to get a foothold in the country of immigration; and of course raising the money for the tickets is a huge problem for a whole family. If we leave out all cases in which the decision to emigrate was made in the United States, i.e., where emigrants were brought over by means of prepaid tickets, it is possible to see from the lapse of time and from the topographical distribution of family emigration in proportion to the emigration of individual persons whether emigration was chiefly a manifestation of a general tendency to migrate, pervasive among the younger age groups, or whether it was a consequence of social distress sufficient at a certain time and place to make families set out in considerable numbers.

With certain reservations it is possible to say that 21% of the adult male emigrants and 37% of the female emigrants traveled in family groups. The problem is whether this Danish situation corresponds with the picture in the other Scandinavian countries, particularly in Sweden (see Table 9.1). Professor Sten Carlsson described the Swedish situation in his paper, "From Family Emigration to Individual Emigration," in the Festschrift dedicated to William Moberg.

The comparison covers roughly the same period and shows, very clearly, important aspects of the difference between Danish and Swedish emigration. In Sweden more unmarried women were emigrants than was the case in Denmark, while on the other hand, genuine family emigration was relatively more weakly represented, or so it seems. The large number of women in the Swedish emigration confirms the impression given in the previous chapter, but the ratio of married to unmarried is a surprise. A percentage distribution as is used in this table is tricky because a shift in one direction will affect the proportions with respect to the other factors. So, when the proportion of unmarried women is so large in Sweden the ratio of married women must inevitably fall correspondingly.

However, if one goes back to the early period of Swedish emigration, one will find that most of the emigration consisted of families. From the decade 1851–1860, the earliest period from which we have usable information, a cargo of 100 Swedish emigrants would be composed of 60 parents and children and only 40 single emigrants—27 men and 13 women. From this early time we have no statistical information about

TABLE 9.1

Danish and Swedish Emigration According to Familial Position (in percentage)

	Denmark 1868–1900	Sweden 1871–1900
Unmarried men	41	36
Unmarried women	19	30
Married men	11	9
Married women	11	8
Children	18	17
Total	100%	100%

family emigration from Denmark. But Danish figures for the period after 1868 show clearly that Danish emigration, just like the Swedish, started with a particularly large share of families with children, an element which was gradually reduced in the course of the period until 1900 (see Table 9.2). In the 1870s close to 50% of Danish emigrants were members of a family group, while in the 1890s the percentage of families had been reduced to about 25. The trend is unmistakable and in complete accordance with the main tendency as described in the chapter on age distribution, where it was found that the groups ages 25–40 decreased in this period. By means of these figures we are able to make a new and more exact comparison with the structure of Swedish emigration.

We see that family emigration from Denmark was slightly above the Swedish figures during the two earliest decades, which were characterized by extensive emigration, whereas the ratio fell below the Swedish average during the last decade. Both countries show the same main tendency of a rapidly diminishing family emigration toward the present.

It seems that we are beginning to trace the outline of a general rule that large-scale emigration from every country will pass through a sequence of phases, irrespective of the time at which emigration starts. We get the impression that in the 1870s Denmark was, so far as family emigration goes, at a point which corresponded to that reached in Sweden as early as the 1850s and 1860s.

Unfortunately it is impossible to make actual comparisons between Denmark and Norway for any period of reasonable length. The marital status of Norwegian emigrants was not registered until 1888. For the decade 1891–1900, figures seem to indicate an even lower rate of family emigration from Norway, but as children were omitted from the records a direct comparison between this country and Sweden and Denmark is impossible. A constantly falling rate of family emigration can be traced, however, by another measure: the proportion of children in the total of emigrants, assuming that number of emigrating children per couple was the same throughout the period. Family emigration seems to have decreased at an even faster rate than in the other two Scandinavian coun-

TABLE 9.2

Percentage of Married Couples and Children in Total Danish and Swedish Emigration

Years	Sweden	Denmark
1871–1880	42.2	43.0
1881–1890	36.9	38.3
1891–1900	29.4	29.0

tries. By 1900 it was at a level which was about one-third of the 1871 level, and it continued to fall steadily after 1900. However, it should be noted that during the two periods of high emigration rates for Norway, 1881–1885 and 1901–1905, the proportion of children, too, temporarily increased—an indication of increasing family emigration during these periods.

But it is risky to draw conclusions about family emigration directly from the proportion of children in the total. This is confirmed by a study of the Swedish material, which reveals that the number of adult married persons did not decrease nearly so abruptly as that of children. While children were more numerous in the families during the decades before 1890, this situation changed after 1890, so that the number of married persons then exceeds that of their own children. In short: The emigrants took a constantly smaller number of children with them abroad.

Unfortunately, corresponding calculations cannot be made for Denmark after 1900. The only thing we can tell is that, although the proportion of children among Danish emigrants was decreasing after the turn of the century, this certainly did not happen at the same speed as in Norway. The situation seems to have been more or less the same in Sweden as in Denmark, so that Norway was exceptional in this respect.

The fall in family emigration and the rise in the emigration of individual young people is one of the more clear-cut features of the trend in large-scale emigration before 1900. The explanation (also described earlier) is that after the middle of the 1880s, emigration was no longer a remedy against, or a way out of, an actual social and economic emergency in Europe. After 1885 industrialism was better able to support the constant influx of people to the towns. But there was another factor across the ocean which must be taken into consideration. In 1890 a statement was made by the American Bureau of the Census that the era of the Homestead Legislation was now past—no more free land was available in the United States. The last free sections of land in Montana, Idaho, and North Dakota were being brought under cultivation, and in the future new immigrants would be forced to buy land in the open market. This was a decisive point and some years later inspired the historian, F. J. Turner, to develop his famous frontier thesis.

A connection between the 1890 declaration and the decrease in family emigration from the Scandinavian countries obviously suggests itself, since families were the groups most likely to seek homesteads. A family unit preferred to remain stationary, and only with some difficulty adapted to the changing places of employment so frequently the fate of industrial and agricultural laborers. Homesteaders settled as farmers and depended on the labor of the entire family. But as it became gradually more difficult

to obtain free homesteads (and the difficulties started before 1890), capital became necessary to purchase already cultivated land, and this made
the whole idea of emigration problematic.

This trend toward a decreasing number of children per emigrating married couple indicates an increase in the number of young childless couples
among the emigrants. Another possibility is that before the turn of the
century a large number of engaged couples emigrated together with the
aim of earning enough money to marry abroad. After 1900 improvement
in the economic conditions of the middle classes, together with the constantly falling marital age, resulted in such young people marrying before
they left Europe. For a young couple in the nineteenth century, marriage
was much more of an economic problem than in the mid-twentieth century.
This economic hindrance could not in many cases be overcome until the
couple had reached a rather advanced age. Among young people of the
underprivileged classes in the rural areas, a sine qua non of marriage was
the possibility of obtaining a plot of land, however small. Economically
it was an extremely risky thing for agricultural servants to marry. It was
understood that young men and women who worked as servants or farmhands lived on the premises; and generally wages were so low that the
purchase of a house was out of the question. Married agricultural laborers
with landless cottages had no prospect of escaping from the miserable
rural lower-class milieu. Emigration offered these young couples a way out.
Provided they could raise the necessary funds to finance the voyage, emigration could get them a homestead on the prairie.

The volume of emigration undertaken with this kind of background cannot be gauged directly from the emigration statistics. The married couples-
to-be are hidden among the large number of single men and women who
formed the majority of emigrants. But all the same there are traces of
these "postponed marriages" in the normal Danish marriage statistics. In
1864, when the Danish soldiers were at the front, the number of weddings
fell; but during the following years the number rose again to a level of
approximately 8.5 marriages per 1000 population, the same level as before
the war. During the period 1868–1872, however, the rate was as low as
7.3, the decrease obviously coinciding with the first important wave of
emigration. During the depression period in the 1870s, 1874–1878, the
rate of marriages rose to its old level of 8.5; and during the great period
of emigration in the 1880s it fell once more to the 7.0 per 1000 level.
Especially striking are the figures for the period 1886–1892. Here there
are very low rates of weddings in a period where family emigration constituted a particularly large part of an already swollen emigration. The
fact that the end of the 1890s, a low tide in emigration, has correspondingly high figures for marriages gives a final touch to the picture. Admit-

tedly, the great periods of emigration occur in periods that coincide with peaks of the Danish business cycles, so that the fluctuations of the marriage statistics may be influenced by economic conditions; but there can hardly be any doubt that the postponement of weddings by emigrants had an effect on the Danish statistics.

Another influence on the number of marriages is the fact that the marital age was constantly falling toward the turn of the century—for women as well as for men. Around the middle of the nineteenth century the average age for grooms was about 31.6 years, for brides about 28.6 years. Both are surprisingly high seen through modern eyes, the 1960 averages being 26 and 23 respectively. To a certain extent the explanation lies in economic conditions—in the question of whether the man would be able to support a family—but changes in ethics may also have been of importance. It is certainly a fact that during the second half of the nineteenth century the marrying ages fell, for men to 29 years and for women to 26. This downward trend can reasonably be regarded as a consequence of the improvement of wages which the lower classes enjoyed in this period.

Men were able to support families at ever earlier ages. A study of the emigration registers reveals the surprising fact that there was a considerable number of married couples where the wife was older than her husband, and also couples who, in view of the ages of their children, must have been very young at the time of marriage.

This phenomenon of young engaged couples traveling overseas with the intention of getting married, and our hypothesis that the emigrating families were to be found among the group constituting the youngest slice of the marriage-age statistics both raise the problem whether some small part of the emigration may have been prompted by the hope of getting married at an earlier point than would have been economically feasible had the parties not emigrated. (See Figure 9.1.) Another characteristic that these two things have in common is that they cannot be illustrated by means of statistical data.

The adult section of the family group, the husbands and wives, must be found in the age groups over 25 years, to judge by the marriage age statistics. A comparison between the emigrant total belonging to this age group and the number of family adults will show that they are almost identical, a fact that must mean that the number of single emigrants from this age group was quite small.

A problem of considerable interest in connection with family emigration is its relation to the fluctuations of the business cycles: in other words, the question whether family emigration had the same rhythm as that of single persons, and consequently helped to make the peaks of the emigra-

1872

Den

danske Pige,

eller:

Jens, der vilde reise til Amerika.

Kjøbenhavn 1872.

Forlagt af, samt trykt hos Behrends Enke, Gothersgade 81.

Figure 9.1 Numerous broadsheet ballads sold on the streets of Danish towns convey the stormy feelings aroused by the decision to emigrate. In this naive ballad from 1872, Jens, who wants to be rich in a hurry, implores his Danish girlfriend— apparently in vain—to go with him to America. (From the Royal Library, Copenhagen.)

tion curves even higher; or whether families, as was the case with female emigration, showed a lag that had a leveling effect on the curves by making the peaks flatter. Figure 9.2 shows family emigration as a percentage of the total emigration; that is, the annual number of members of family groups out of 100 emigrants. For comparison, the graph also has a curve indicating the total emigration in actual figures. The graph gives a somewhat blurred picture because of the sudden fall in family emigration in the period after 1881. But so far as the earlier part of the period is concerned, there seems to be an interplay of considerable interest.

In the cases of the first emigration waves, 1869 and 1872–1873, it is quite obvious that family emigration was dropping during the peak period, but increased afterward. What we have here must be the lag which occurs because married men depart alone and then send for their families a few months or a year later. During the depression in the second half of the 1870s, family emigration understandably decreased; during periods of unemployment and similar troubles it is difficult for a family group to raise

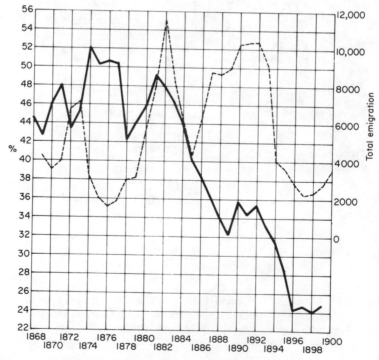

Figure 9.2 Family emigration as a percentage of the annual emigration, 1868–1900. Family emigration is represented by a solid line; total emigration is represented by a dashed line.

the funds to escape their misery. But, for the great boom in 1882, the graph shows the curious—and opposite—phenomenon of family emigration leading the way and culminating 1 year before the actual high point in 1882. It is difficult to give a demonstrable reason for this development, but it seems reasonable to see a connection with the economic crisis that culminated at about the new year, 1878, and then developed into a prosperous period about 1880. But it is curious, nevertheless, that the peak of family emigration occurred as early as in 1881. Furthermore, the 1882 peak seems to have had no lag for wives and children, so this wave must have consisted mostly of the very young.

That family emigration decreased in the 1880s and following years is probably connected with the improvement in employment, particularly in the towns, a consequence of the breakthrough of industrialism. The fall in family emigration can be seen as the forerunner of the general low tide in emigration in the second half of the 1890s. The period 1895–1900 differs fundamentally from the previous period by having a particularly low emigration simultaneously with economic conditions that must be described as an intensive boom, especially for the towns. Moreover, during the first years of the period, the farmers recovered from the crisis that had plagued the end of the 1880s. The total impression is that whereas emigration in the 1870s and 1880s moved with the fluctuations in business cycles, it fell out of step during the 1890s. This is another instance of something which we have previously observed: that emigration assumed a different character after 1885. The age composition changed; women attained a more prominent place; and family emigration was reduced to a factor of minor importance.

Emigration is built of a series of individual decisions to make a change of course. The number of persons reaching such decisions determines the volume of the emigration. But the volume is also determined by the extent to which the decision is made by heads of families. If family emigration catches on emigration will swell because every single decision to depart concerns several persons. If we can assume that the fathers of the families made the decision alone, we find that some 17,000 heads of families determined the fate of about 61,000 Danish emigrants. In other words, 11% decided on behalf of 40% of the entire group of emigrants.

When we study family structure, an interesting phenomenon comes to light that illustrates the close connection between short- and long-range migrations. Migration statistics for Sweden demonstrate opposite trends in the Swedish migrations to America and to Denmark/Norway, respectively with regard to family structure.

While the family was of steadily decreasing importance in overseas migration, its importance in short-distance migration increased inversely.

On a graph, the curves of the two movements would intersect at right angles. In emigration to America, the family percentage started at 42; in migration to Denmark (from Sweden) it was 22%. By 1920 this ratio had reversed itself: Families now represented 25% of those who set out for America, but 43% of those moving to Denmark. This is probably connected with the fact that immigration of single women into Denmark was decreasing after 1890. What was left was an immigration of men—to a large extent craftsmen, such as tailors. It is reasonable to surmise that the rise in families in this emigration resulted from the decrease in the tramp traveling custom of journeymen, again a consequence of adjustment to industrialism. The opposite rhythms of the two kinds of emigration from Sweden are of interest, not merely because they give a picture of the Swedish emigration to Denmark which no Danish statistics can give; but also because here is a suggestion of a pattern which may have held for Danish emigration to other European countries. Unfortunately our knowledge of such migrations is very meager.

The sizes of the Danish emigrant families naturally varied a great deal. About 15% of the family groups comprised six or more persons. If the fathers of such large families had not in many cases found the difficulty of raising funds for all the tickets insuperable, the proportion of this kind of emigrant would probably have been much larger.

Very often children who had reached confirmation age were allowed to decide for themselves whether to accompany their families. Some of these young people also emigrated, and their decisions may have influenced the entire family's decision. A case in point is the following story of a family that left for the United States in March, 1872, including all five sons.

The background is as follows: In the summer of 1871 the family, who were living on the island of Møn, received a visit from two persons recently back from the United States. The visitors gave an ecstatic description of the wonders of America. The father of the family had for years been thinking of emigrating, while the mother had been stubbornly against the idea. The morning after this visit the eldest son, aged 14, told his parents firmly, "As soon as I have been confirmed I shall go to America." This made a strong impression on the mother, who then became convinced of the need for the whole family to leave together. If she refused to go she would have to face the risk of being left alone in Denmark with a dissatisfied husband, and all her children in America.

This story is known to us from preserved contemporary letters, and it throws light on several important incentives to emigration, as well as fitting in well with the statistical data presented in this study. The longing to go abroad on the part of the young son is a characteristic feature reflected in the age distribution of the emigration statistics. The father's positive attitude and the mother's equally negative one are both psychologically well founded, and they agree with the unequal distribution of men and women in Danish emigration. Finally, it is striking how the returned Danish-Americans, the so-called Yankees, provided the final push which set the family moving.

In this period the number of children in the average marriage was much larger than is the case now. On a basis of statistical data from Copenhagen it has been shown that among domestic and other servants, who formed a considerable part of the emigrants, 32% of married couples had 5–8 children, and 12% 9–12 children. There was even greater fertility among craftsmen; more than 50% of the married couples had more than 5 children, and as many as 14% had 9–12 children. Rural laborers had the highest average number of children: In 1901 the figure was 430 per 100 couples. By comparison, the figures for emigrants were relatively low; but they cannot be completely wrong, for the corresponding figures for Sweden were about 2 children per married woman, with a rising trend toward the turn of the century and a falling one afterward.

A family who purchased tickets to America and departed with a very large number of children and an even greater number of trunks and bundles, and then arrived without any housing or employment must have been a common phenomenon. Such a family would face extremely difficult circumstances during their first winter in the new country, unless they were unusually well off. In many cases families set out with a knowledge about this or that county in the Midwest where good homesteads were available. But before they had their land ploughed and until they had gathered the first crops, the family had to live—to have a roof over their heads and food to eat. This made it more practical for the head of the family to set out alone first and then to send for his wife and children. Actually this happened in a surprisingly small number of cases. Out of more than 17,000 Danish families registered between 1868 and 1900, only a few over 5400 were wives traveling alone with their children. It was obviously not the practice in the earlier period of mass emigration for the man to get himself established before sending for his wife and children; but that procedure became more common after 1880, particularly during the period 1890–1894. There seems to have been a certain backlog accumulated of husbands who had departed during the boom period 1880–1889 and had hesitated to send for their wives and family.

In the "classic period" of large-scale emigration before approximately 1890, a large majority of a year's emigrants departed during the early months of the year, March and April. Families with both parents tended to go a little later, in April through May; but for wives traveling alone with their children, the time of departure was generally much later, usually late summer. Of the total number of families, some 20% set out in the period of July through September, but the corresponding percentage for wives with children was 34. This seems to indicate that it was common for the men to set out early, for instance in the beginning of March, so that they might have some 5–6 months in which to get established abroad.

10

THE OCCUPATIONS
OF THE EMIGRANTS

Attempts to classify the statements of occupation given by members of an entire society into a reasonably simple and uniform pattern have always posed one of the major difficulties of social statistics. It is really necessary to cut some corners in order to fit a huge, heterogeneous material into a few groups; and the general results obtained will be of uncertain value, insofar as the classification into occupational groups must in many cases be based on a subjective evaluation. One of the sources of inaccuracy which must be taken into consideration is the fact that a person will, when stating his occupation, frequently be tempted to misrepresent his job a little to make it sound more grand.

The information about occupations given in this book may convey an impression of being limited to a relatively narrow range; but this fact more than anything else shows that emigration was actually an "infection" that attacked only certain strata of European society. The occupational range of the emigrants was much more limited than that of society as a whole. If the number of trades represented on board an emigration vessel was not very large, they were certainly the most common ones in the countries that the emigrants had left.

Let us watch all the different occupations file past up the gangway of an emigrant ship. In this chapter the trades of emigrants are summarized in a number of main groups, each of which is again divided into special subgroups. A listing of all 99 occupational groups would be of little interest, as the number of persons registered in certain groups is very small. This is the reason why several occupations have been grouped together in some cases. The figures given cover the entire period 1868–1900, and the total number of registered emigrants from this period. Thus are included persons from North Schleswig, who emigrated via Denmark, and the group of Mormons, which brings the total to over 172,000 persons. For each main group we list first the absolute number and then the percentage of total emigration accounted for by the group in question. We start with the most important Danish occupation—agriculture—and within this the subgroup of independent farmers (see Table 10.1).

Figure 10.1 Ready for sailing! A well-known scene in European harbors before 1914 as thousands of emigrants crowded into the narrow steerage areas of the steamers and left home and family for good. Here we see Copenhagen harbor from which the Tingvalla Line carried Danish and Swedish emigrants on a direct route to New York each week. (Woodcut by Knud Gamborg from *Illustreret Tidende,* 1882, p. 371.)

TABLE 10.1

Farmers among Danish Emigrants, 1868–1900

Type of farmer	Number	Percentage of total emigration
Landed proprietors (large estates)	78	0.0
Owner–farmers	387	0.2
Smallholders	3271	1.9
Other independent farmers (millers, gardeners, etc.)	70	0.0
Total of independent landowners	3806	2.1

Considering the percentage of the entire Danish population which lived by farming before 1901, the number of emigrant landowners is very small. In 1901, the total number of agricultural properties of all sizes was rather more than 250,000; and during our period many of these will have had more than one owner. The very small share of this sector in emigration goes a long way to explain the volume and the composition of the Danish overseas emigration as compared to that of other countries. Further details will be given later to illustrate this problem.

However, certain things lead us to believe that the figures may well be a little too low. One individual piece of information indicates that during the years around 1868 emigration of independent landowners was not in-considerable. The statement in question comes from the report of an emigration agent to the Ministry of Justice, and says, among other things:

> Everywhere I have been, I have been sorry to find the population, particularly the lower classes, small-holders and cottagers, and unfortunately even a large number of farmers, seized with what can only be described as emigration mania brought about by traveling agents and returned emigrants.

The situation is probably this: The occupational label of "farmer" (landmand), which was so common before 1872, comprises an unknown number of independent small-holders, owner–farmers, and tenants; but as this uncertainty has relevance only for these 4 years out of 32, it cannot drastically change the relative proportions of independent owners to laborers and servants in agriculture.

That there are 78 emigrants recorded from the close to 2100 large landed estates in Denmark should probably not be taken at face value. Very likely some of these large landowners were only making a visit to the United States, for example, and had every intention of returning to Denmark. But the figure may also cover a number of bankrupts, who were hoping to reestablish themselves on the prairies. A curious detail is that one-third of the large landowners state that Copenhagen was their last residence.

By 1901, 26–30% of all landowners in Denmark belonged to the group called owner–farmers, but among emigrants this class represents a much smaller share. The majority of the 387 emigrating owner–farmers, i.e., 225, came from Jutland, and one-fourth of them from the three counties north of the Limfjord. One notable aspect of these farmers is the late date at which this group joined the large-scale emigration. Between 1868 and 1879, the total of emigrating owner–farmers was 9, not even 1 per year. But then suddenly in 1880, the figure rose to 51—32 from Jutland and the rest from eastern Denmark. In the sequence of business cycles, the year 1880 forms a transitional period between the depression of the late 1870s and the boom of the early 1880s. The agricultural crisis around 1889–1890 was reflected in emigration from Jutland more than from any other part of the country.

But all in all, the number of independent farmers who emigrated was very small, and looks even smaller when compared with the number of their laborers and servants who emigrated during the same period: 45,656 comprising 27.6% of the total emigration. As the total emigration from the rural areas amounted to a little over 84,000 persons, it is quite clear that the majority of them were laborers and servants of some kind—in fact, 57%. It may be, however, that the figure for servants from the rural districts is really a little higher, about 62%, since a number of persons grouped as "maids" were counted together with other groups of women, while they really should have been regarded as agricultural servants.

With a total emigration of rural servants amounting to 52,000—an annual average of 1625 out of an agricultural laboring and servants class averaging 176,700—we get an emigration intensity of 920 out of 100,000 servants per year, obviously a very high emigration frequency. Before entering into an analysis of town occupations, one small group of statistically negligible weight should be mentioned: sailors and fishermen (see Table 10.2). Fishing and sailing offered a living to rather less than 3% of the population. The emigration from these trades is considerably lower than from the population as a whole.

As for the sailors, the majority came from east Denmark: only 224 from Jutland out of nearly 1000. As might have been expected, Svendborg County (southern Funen) and Bornholm are very strongly represented in this sector. The particular branch of shipping that is based on small craft saw a prosperous period in the nineteenth century, centered in the islands

TABLE 10.2

Emigrating Fishermen and Sailors

	Number	Percentage of total emigration
Fishermen	730	0.4
Sailors	969	0.6
Total	1699	1.0

south of Funen. But even before the turn of the century this trade had begun to yield to the quicker and cheaper steamships. It seems as though sailors tended to emigrate when they saw fit, irrespective of the fluctuations in business cycles. Very likely a large number of them escaped the official statistics. They were employed on board overseas freighters and left the ship when they found a promising place. For Norway, the number of sailors believed to have emigrated in this way between 1870 and 1914 is estimated at 51,000. About 23,000 returned after a period, however.

The next group of emigrants to be discussed is skilled laborers, with craftsmen dominating (see Table 10.3). One dilemma was whether to count the individual emigrating craftsman as a master craftsman or a journeyman. Only craftsmen described as masters have been classified as independent; otherwise they have been listed as journeymen. This procedure has undoubtedly reduced the number of independent craftsmen, particularly if they came from rural areas, where it was common that independent craftsmen did not use the title of master.

TABLE 10.3

Emigrant Skilled Workers from Industry and Crafts

Type of worker	Number	Percentage of total emigration
Independent, crafts	415	0.2
Independent, commerce	1,386	0.8
Professions	155	0.1
Students	331	0.2
Clerks	1,568	0.9
Shop assistants	1,852	1.1
Other white collar	3,298	1.9
Journeymen	18,914	11.0
Apprentices	288	0.2
Total in commerce and industry	28,207	16.4

Commerce, industry, and crafts all increased in importance during the period after 1870, concurrently with the development of industrialism. In 1870 these trades comprised about 32% of the population, and in 1901 a little more than 40%. However, these figures are not immediately comparable with the 16.4% given in Table 10.3 as representing these trades in emigration. The population figures include unskilled workers and servants. If we deduct these groups, we find that commerce and trades make up a share of the emigration proportionate with that of the population.

In the trades discussed here, Copenhagen has a dominating position. Of the master craftsmen, 40% came from the capital; so did more than 50% of the independent tradesmen and as many as 70% of the office employees. Emigration did not become widespread in any group of independent tradesmen until the middle of the 1880s. Thus we find that 40% of them departed in the period 1887–1893, and that they followed the trend characteristic of the rest of the emigration. No particularly numerous emigration from urban trades is traceable in the period 1876–1879, when all must have suffered from a severe depression.

The picture is more or less the same for office workers and civil servants. A certain number of "black sheep" probably fell into this group; persons dispatched to America by their families, in the hope of saving face under the threat of discovered embezzlement or other such unpleasantness. Studies of emigration invariably disclose cases of this kind, and many of them, too. But that is a type of emigration which for obvious reasons is difficult to document statistically. The probability that the method enjoyed fairly widespread acceptance is indicated by knowledge that even the public authorities used it extensively at an earlier time. But the flock of black sheep can never have been overwhelmingly large, particularly not in this period of large-scale emigration, which can be explained by unmistakable features in the socioeconomic background.

During the last few years Swedish scholars have worked their way into something approaching an answer to the vital question of the intellectual make-up of the many millions of emigrants. Was it, generally speaking, those who had the lowest intelligence who emigrated to America and Australia, those who could not hold their own in Europe—black sheep who were perhaps forced to resort to illegal measures in order to survive in the competition? The reason that Sweden is the only country in Europe able to provide any kind of evidence in this respect is to be found in the dominant position of the Swedish vicars in society. One of the duties of a vicar was the arrangement of the annual "examination" concerning the intellectual status of his parishioners—their qualifications in reading and writing together with their general knowledge and understanding. Alongside every name in his church register he then made a mark, and the result is that there exists from as early as the eighteenth century a relatively uniform assessment of the intellectual level of the Swedish population. A comparison of those Swedes, rural as well as urban people, who emigrated later on, with those who remained in Sweden, reveals that everywhere, irrespective of the corner of the country chosen, emigrants generally made higher marks than the rest of the population. They were brighter in school, had a wider picture of the world, and were the kind of persons to whom it would occur to leave their habitual surroundings. It is equally clear that the persons who contributed to migration within Sweden, from village to town, were also placed intellectually above those who never left the place where they were born. But the actual emigrants abroad seem to have had the highest intellectual level; a fact that says something about the loss to their native country that large-scale emigration caused, and which also contributes to an understanding of the immense economic expansion that occurred in the major countries of immigration, especially in the United States.

A particularly interesting problem is the emigration of journeymen, a social class which was traditionally characterized by pronounced wanderlust. It is not hard to imagine that itinerant journeymen might travel across the Atlantic just as well as to southern Germany and Switzerland. The craft trades, which had enjoyed centuries of protected existence with monopolistic rights and restricted recruitment, were, after 1864, in a period of crisis caused partly by the introduction of freedom of trade under 1857 legislation that came into force in 1862, and partly by the increasing volume of industrial production that invariably brought about serious difficulties in the corresponding branches of craft production.

As a class, craftsmen had traditionally been the most internationally oriented in the country. From about 1600, it had been customary for young journeymen to gain additional education by spending some years traveling in European countries before they became master artisans and set up on their own. In the nineteenth century, these itinerant craftsmen still played an important part, but gradually the system changed character. Decisive in this respect was the abolishment of compulsory guild membership after 1862. Until then a traveling journeyman could always depend on help from the local guild wherever he went; but after that he was left to fend for himself in finding housing and work. Admittedly journeymen continued to travel after 1862, even if on a reduced scale, but probably only unemployed journeymen did so, in search of work. The considerable numbers of such unemployed craftsmen without fixed addresses developed into a social problem, which was probably not without influence on early Danish socialism. Craftsmen were among the most important participants in the First International in Denmark, and the disturbances around 1872. Apart from the unrest in Copenhagen there were complaints from many provincial towns about itinerant journeymen who were accused of begging and of creating disturbances in the streets. The result was that after 1875 a number of societies were established in order to care for these migrants. Hostels were opened for journeymen in various towns so that they need not resort to begging. A parallel development took place in the case of unskilled, unemployed migrant workers; Trade unions began building hostels for them after 1885, because the journeymen's institutions would not take in unskilled workers.

Fortunately it is possible to get some statistical impression of the volume of these migrations. Every journeyman was obliged to have an artisan's record book, and in every town where he stayed for over 24 hours he had to have his presence in the town recorded in this book by the local authorities. This registration was officially recorded, since a small duty was levied on it until 1875. The number of registrations is not necessarily identical with the number of traveling journeymen, since the same man might pass through a town many times. In many cases the journeymen never even reached as far south as Hamburg, but nevertheless the registrations do give an impression of migrations from year to year.

The results are directly relevant to the question of overseas migration, because they allow one to see whether craftsmen emigrated for the same reasons and in the same rhythm as they traveled around Europe—in other words, whether a craftsman's move to America had the same character as the travels of an itinerant journeyman. Figure 10.2 shows both the annual migrations of journeymen within Denmark and the annual direct emigration of journeymen during the same years. The registration figures used are from the town of Odense, which was specifically chosen for the purpose because there is an uninterrupted series of figures available for that town for the entire period. Such figures as can be obtained from other towns show the same movements as those given here.

The migrations of journeymen within Denmark clearly reflect that they are migrations toward localities where work might be obtained. Activity was at a peak in all the years when times were bad and unemployment high, and fell correspondingly in boom years which provided employment opportunities without any need for migration. The years 1872–1873 mark one of the most pronounced booms, an offshoot of the Gründer period that lasted until some time in 1874 before the tide turned in the towns. The year 1880 marks the end of the 1870s depression and the beginning of a new upward movement that was to last, as far as the towns were concerned, until some time in the 1890s. The craftsmen's migrations were obviously dependent on the business cycles. Was this also true of internal

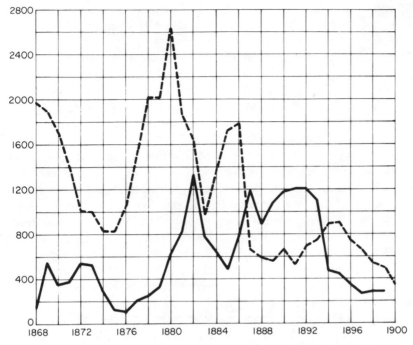

Figure 10.2 Internal migration by journeymen and emigration of journeymen. Journeymen–emigrants are represented by a solid line; migrating journeymen registered when passing Odense are represented by a dashed line.

migration as a whole? When journeymen left the towns with their knap-sacks, they would meet on the roads rural migrants on their way toward the towns.

But why does emigration follow not the same movements, but a rhythm quite opposite to that of the internal migrations? The question opens up wide perspectives, but raises problems, too. It seems as though the curve confirms Brinley Thomas's theory about the contrary rhythms of external and internal migrations. But the Danish material as well as the English is too incomplete to provide a foundation for a firm opinion.

Closest at hand is the explanation that capital was necessary for emi-gration, both for the crossing itself and for a start abroad, whereas when a craftsman traveled in the customary way it cost him practically nothing and might even prove a source of income to a lucky man. The chances of saving the amount necessary for emigration were best during good times when wages were at their highest. But one cannot, on the other hand, dismiss the possibility that the two curves may be mutually depend-ent on each other in such a way that internal migration was periodically reduced because craftsmen chose overseas emigration instead, particularly so in periods when money was more abundant and rumors of emigration were current among people in town and country.

Another notable thing about the craftsmen's emigration curve is the way in which it differs from the curve of all Danish emigration during the same period. The summit of craftsmen's emigration was clearly in the period 1887–1892, whereas the 1882 peak of the aggregate emigration was less important in their case. It is equally striking that in the earliest emigration boom, that of 1869 and 1872–1873, which was dominated particularly by emigrants from the provincial towns, the crafts play a very insignificant part. This was the time when most was heard about unrest among the members of the crafts in connection with the emergence of socialism. Could this be the reason behind the very limited emigration?

Emigration naturally varied from one craft to another. Some trades were almost completely obliterated by the competition from industrial production. One such trade was file cutting, which was still represented by 40 journeymen in Copenhagen in 1882. By 1892 this number was reduced to 15, the rest having emigrated because the files they made had gone out of use or had been replaced by machine-made articles. Millers were among the groups who suffered most from the development of steam power. According to *Møllertidende,* a periodical for millers, journeymen millers emigrated in such great numbers that an actual scarcity of labor resulted in Denmark. That the tendency to emigrate preceded the decline in the demand for skilled labor in this case was due to the very low pay and the unreasonably long hours characteristic of this trade. One case is known of labor conflicts which led directly to emigration. When the master cabinetmakers of Copenhagen started a system of blacklisting journeymen who were not wanted in the trade and were to be refused work by the masters, many of these proscribed journeymen were forced to emigrate to America as the only way out of their troubles. The affair was an offshoot of the advance of socialism: Several of those on the blacklist were socialist leaders.

Out of all the many crafts it has been possible, in this analysis, to distinguish only six of the largest for separate examination, while file cutters and other specialized trades have had to be lumped together in one large group. But for these six groups, i.e., bricklayers, joiners, carpenters, house painters, smiths, and bakers, we get figures that are fairly representative of the trends in different trades over the whole range of craft production. These six trades account for 10,145 craftsmen; that is, well over one-half the total of about 18,000 emigrant craftsmen. All six trades are among the largest, and particularly striking is the large number of smiths among the emigrants. This must surely result from the difficulties in adjustment that they faced in connection with industrialization. A comparison between the emigration figures and the actual number of persons employed in the various trades according to the 1880 census provided a measure of emigration intensity to serve as a yardstick (see Table 10.4).

The table clearly confirms the crisis in the smith's trade associated with industrialization in the towns. In the rural districts it had been possible for smiths to settle and do business even before the Trade Act of 1862 came into force, so no marked changes would have been felt there. A division of this craft between urban areas (including Copenhagen) and rural areas shows that the emigration of smiths was a distinctly urban phenomenon. The total number of members of this trade in Copenhagen and the other towns in 1880 was 3179. Of the emigrants, some 1800 smiths came from the towns. In other words, by the 1880 yardstick, the emigration ratio was no less than 56 per 100. But, for the rural areas, the corresponding figure was as low as 17 per 100. The majority of emigrating smiths came from provincial towns, not from Copenhagen. In eastern Denmark there was a total of 718 independent and assistant smiths in the provincial towns in 1880; 500 smiths emigrated during the period in question, i.e., an intensity of about 70 per 100. For Jutland the corresponding figure is as high as 75 per 100, whereas the Copenhagen ratio is about 45 per 100. These figures show that, in this field as in many others, the provincial towns offered their inhabitants insufficient means of support, while industry in Copenhagen was better able to employ the smiths, even though they belonged to one of the earliest trades to be affected by industrialization: iron founding.

Apart from bakers and smiths, all the crafts discussed here belong to the building trades, which clearly do not have such a high emigration frequency. But the same situation holds as in the case of the smiths—that the ratios for the rural districts are considerably lower than those for the

TABLE 10.4

Emigrants per 1000 Craftsmen in Six Selected Trades, 1868–1900

Craft	Total number in each trade (1880)	Emigrants 1868–1900	Emigrants per 1000 craftsmen of that type
Bricklayers	9,248	1,220	132
Joiners	11,074	2,116	191
Carpenters	8,846	1,907	216
House painters	3,450	815	236
Smiths	11,962	3,253	272
Bakers	3,637	832	229

urban areas. Thus the rate of emigration for bricklayers by the 1880 measue was 19 per 100; but for the rural areas alone the figure was only 10 per 100. And in Copenhagen, where the bricklayers were enjoying the boom caused by speculative building in the new suburban areas that were developed to provide housing for migrants to the capital, the number of emigrating bricklayers was much smaller.

Emigration intensity among house painters was relatively high (about 24 per 100). This was an almost exclusively urban trade, whereas in the country painting was regarded as work which anyone could do for himself. The number of painters in urban areas was 2300, and in all rural areas only 1100. The corresponding emigration ratios were 28 and 15 per 100 respectively.

A considerable number of the craftsmen, about 16%, were married men who emigrated with wife and family. But the variations from one trade to another were quite substantial. More than any other trade the bricklayers tended to travel as a family. Of the bricklayers, 22% were married, compared with 21% of carpenters, 18% of the joiners, and only 13% of smiths and bakers. Furthermore there is a distinct geographical difference. It is quite clear that especially craftsmen from Jutland were married men traveling with wife and children. Among bricklayers from Jutland, more than 25% had wives and families with them, whereas the percentage was only 19 among their eastern Danish colleagues. If we assume that family emigration is more a reflection of social distress than is the emigration of single persons, these figures again show that Copenhagen was able to provide a living for its inhabitants to a degree that towns in Jutland could not.

However one should not make too much of the fact that the number of emigrating craftsmen from Copenhagen who traveled with their families was smaller than among those from the provinces. Figures of this kind may give a distorted view insofar as the father of the family can have set out ahead of the others.

The craftsmen were aged on the average between 25 and 28 years at the time of departure. The average age varied from one part of the country to another, the variations being quite distinct, though not very great. Of the urban emigrants, those from Copenhagen were the oldest, and those from the smaller towns the youngest of all. In a number of areas the craftsmen were older than their opposite numbers from the provincial towns at the time of setting out for America. The rural craftsmen seem to have been slower to take the step of emigration, inclined to arrive at their decision later in life than was common among urban craftsmen. But it is also probably true that they did not generally have difficulties of the same dimensions with which to contend. In the country, industry was not at first so much of a menace holding out the prospect of unemployment. That threat did not materialize there until later, as a secondary consequence of industrialism. It was caused by mass-produced wares from the towns penetrating into rural areas, among them factory-made horseshoes which replaced the product made by the village blacksmith.

Before we leave the subject of crafts altogether, two small groups akin to the crafts should be mentioned. These were two relatively recent trades that offered good chances of employment both in Denmark and in America: dairy work and photography. The two were represented by 744 and 126 emigrants, respectively. For a dairyman trained in Denmark a move overseas, to the United States for example, was a potentially lucrative undertaking. The dairy system launched by the farmers' cooperative movement in Denmark was at that time unique in the whole world. Admittedly cattle raising as practiced in both North and South America was not primarily intended as milk production, but in the areas near large towns dairies were a necessity, and at that time these people, the technologists of their time, had their chance.[1] The advisory pamphlets handed out to emigrants in the 1870s warned them not to expect immediate employment in the fields for which they were trained. They should be prepared to accept the first available jobs, however hard and poorly paid, and then later look for work in their own trades. But it appears that dairymen were actually encouraged to come to a particular place and help to establish dairies. The 744 dairymen may be the nineteenth century equivalent of the modern phenomenon called the "brain drain." According to the 1890 census, the total number of dairymen in Denmark was 2560, of which 1150 were head dairymen and the rest assistants. Considering their relatively small total number, an emigration of 744 in the course of the last 32 years before the turn of the century is quite impressive, although it is true that many of them may have returned to Denmark after starting one or more dairies abroad.

The world was probably not as wide open to the photographers as it was to dairymen. These small-town operators, who depicted our grandparents and greatgrandparents with one hand resting on a broken Greek column against a background of painted idyllic landscape, met harsh competition in the United States, where techniques were more advanced than in Denmark. Although only 126 emigrated, this was quite a large emigration in relation to the number of Danish photographers in 1890, when the entire country could muster no more than 600 altogether.

A large group of unskilled workers, which one ought perhaps to call

---

[1] In Chicago, Danish dairies were of considerable importance. The first Danish milk store was opened there in 1871.

"workers of unspecified types," as Sundbärg did in the Swedish emigration statistics, emigrated between 1868 and 1900 (see Table 10.5). Many of them belonged to the very groups of the population that had first tried their luck in a town or the capital before deciding to set out for America. In the chapter about migration between rural and urban areas, we saw that migration to towns, as opposed to overseas emigration, showed a considerable majority of women migrants. Among the group of emigrants treated here—workers from urban areas—the picture is the same: The emigrants include a large number of women, young females who had left the country to become parlor maids or cooks in prosperous homes. The stream to Copenhagen was particularly strong, partly because it came from two sources—from the countryside outside the capital and across the Sound from southern Sweden. In 1892 a Copenhagen cook received an average monthly pay of 15 crowns, a parlor maid 13 crowns, and a maid-of-all-work 12. By way of comparison we might note that the pay of a journeyman craftsman of the same period was 50–75 crowns.

A consideration of this wage level and the problem of periods of unemployment might lead one to think that emigration could be interpreted as a reaction to these conditions. Indeed there is support for this view in an analysis of the combined emigration of men and women from Copenhagen. Until the mid-1880s, a larger percentage of the emigrating men than women came from the capital; but then the relationship changed, and the difference became steadily greater up to 1914. The evidence given by the statistics seems to be that from the middle of the 1880s, a glut in the female labor market developed in Copenhagen. This impression is confirmed by the fact that the Swedish statistics show a marked decline in the emigration of women to Denmark from the late 1880s. After the turn of the century this migration was minimal: A rumor that no work was to be found in Copenhagen would stop the influx of young girls to the Danish capital and even turn the stream so that a considerable number would migrate from the overcrowded area to the United States where the chances

TABLE 10.5

Emigration of Unskilled Workers from Towns, 1860–1900

Type of worker	Number	Percentage of total emigration
Urban workers and servants	15,076	8.8
Domestic workers	930	0.5
Female domestic workers	12,168	7.1
Total	28,174	16.4

of a job and of marriage were infinitely better. A quite recent inquiry into the Swedish emigration to Chicago shows that the same tendency toward a female predominance in the migration to the towns can be found in the migration to the United States (Beibom, 1972). Among the Swedish population in Chicago—some 18,000 persons in the 1880s—the women constituted a clear minority.

It seems as if the relatively large overseas emigration of female servants resulted in a balance in the labor supply and demand. It may even have caused demand to exceed supply. After 1892, the earliest year for which there is information on wages, a remarkable rise in wages took place for this class of the population. The monthly pay received by a maid-of-all-work rose from the 12 crowns of 1892 to 16 crowns by 1901 and as much as 20 crowns in 1910. That increase of about 66% was probably not outdone in any other sector of the Copenhagen labor market. Side by side with this, the number of servants decreased steadily. At the beginning of the nineteenth century, the number of domestic servants had been very large indeed; more than 13% of the total population of Copenhagen were then servants. By the middle of the century the figure was only 9% and in the 1870s it was still 8–9%. By 1880 it was down to 6%, a level that remained constant for the rest of the century. For Copenhagen no figures exist to show the sex ratio among servants, but it seems likely that the major part of the reduction occurred in the male group. Footmen, coachmen, doormen, caretakers, etc., were the first to go, while the maids in the kitchen and scullery were still a necessity, and cheaper than the men.

No doubt the drop in the number of servants reflected a flight from this kind of work, rather than economy measures on the part of the middle classes. There was an increasing disinclination to belong to the servant class, on both social and economic grounds. In both respects they were an outcast group without parallel in Danish society. The Copenhagen middle classes, who had been the instigators of the liberal constitution of 1849, gave a clear expression of the contemporary view of servants when they withheld their right to vote without causing any strong protests. Servants without a household of their own—and it was on exactly that point that they differed from other workers—did not obtain the vote until 1915. The reason why the disenfranchisement of servants was without political dynamite may be that domestic servants in the traditional sense were a constantly diminishing group toward the turn of the century. From about 1905, when the constitution was taken up for revision, the issue was insignificant in the debate. The flight from the servant class into the working class was a phenomenon particularly characteristic of the urban areas.

From the 1870s, the workers in the towns organized in trade unions with the purpose of preparing for the big struggle against the employers.

The weapon of the workers was the strike, but as the following story shows, emigration could be an alternative to continuing the struggle. In a Copenhagen newspaper there appeared on July 6, 1905 an advertisement which ran: "Two tickets to America for sale." The police authorities found this kind of agent's activities rather peculiar, and inquired with the editor who had inserted the advertisement. The owners of the tickets turned out to be two Copenhagen industrial workers who, prompted by dissatisfaction with their pay, had decided to emigrate to the United States. However, since they had bought the tickets, their employer had consented to wage increases large enough that the two men now wanted to abandon their plan. They wanted to sell the tickets, presumably because the agent had refused to take them back. Whether they succeeded is not known.

In the preceding pages emigration of certain main groups was described; these were further divided into subgroups. To sum up, the position of the principal trades, disregarding all the subgroups, is reviewed in Table 10.6. Dependents are excluded, since their numbers are relevant for questions concerning family status of emigrants but not for the occupational distribution as such.

Table 10.6 gives clear evidence that Danish overseas emigration was not a phenomenon that selected people at random among the social classes. It was obviously a movement that primarily affected what the socialists called the proletariat. The higher social classes were only peripherally touched by emigration fever, an infection that spread mainly where there was social tension or outright distress. Out of 110,000 emigrants, more than two-thirds (69%) belonged to the class of workers and servants. If, for a moment, we disregard the fact that a new generation took over

TABLE 10.6

Emigration, 1868–1900, for Principal Occupations

Trade	Number	Percentage of total emigration
Independent farmers	3,806	3.4
Rural laborers	47,656	43.2
Shipping and fishing	1,699	1.5
Commerce and professions	8,590	7.8
Craftsmen including apprentices	20,487	18.5
Domestic and industrial workers (urban)	28,174	25.6
Total	110,412	100.0

during the course of the period in question, we can say that out of every 1000 servants and workers, roughly 200 would have emigrated before 1901. A drain of almost 76,000 workers from a small country such as Denmark must unavoidably leave a mark on working and wage conditions in the country.

But en route from 1868 to 1914, interesting changes took place in the relative positions of the main occupational groups. These reflect economic developments in Denmark during this period, and especially the reactions of the various social classes to urbanization and industrialization.

In Figure 10.3, showing the occupational distribution of male emigrants over the age of 15, the only groups shown are, for the sake of clarity, the three principal ones: workers, craftsmen, and independent farmers. I decided to present the distribution in percentages (each group as a proportion of all trades).

It is hardly possible in this graph to see any reaction to the agricultural crisis of 1884–1894, even though it seems from other evidence to have had a very severe impact on small farmers and small-holders. After the turn of the century the proportion of independent farmers rises again materially. This may be due to the fact that a slightly different criterion is then used in connection with the classification; but a genuine rise is not unlikely, especially when the large-scale emigration to Canada in these years is taken into account. However, the most important result that can be deduced from the curves of the diagram concerns the relation between workers and craftsmen. It is obvious that there is, from about 1870, a

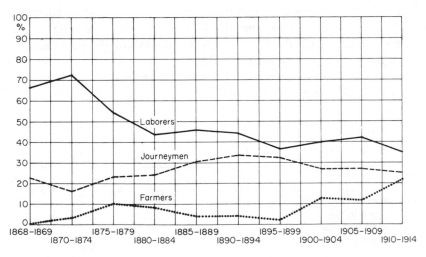

Figure 10.3 Principal occupational groups of male emigrants over 15 years of age, in percentage of totals.

gradual convergence of the two lines, which ends with their almost touch-
ing at about the turn of the century. This trend illustrates the fact mentioned earlier that conditions for craftsmen deteriorated steadily in the
years up to 1914. Craftsmen found it increasingly difficult to get established as independent masters since their prices could not compete with
those of factory goods; and except in the case of a few trades such as
carpentry and joinery, they could not get jobs in industry where unskilled
workers were preferred for wage reasons. Here too is a plausible explanation for why the curve for industrial and domestic workers shows a decline:
Their labor was wanted by the factories, and their harsh social and economic conditions were gradually easing. No distinction is made in the
diagram between urban and rural workers. If that had been possible such
curves would probably have shown the development even more clearly.

   To attempt a comparison between the occupational structure of the
Danish emigration and that of other European countries is an extremely
risky affair. This is so partly because foreign countries have their own
economic conditions; partly because a translation of the various designa-
tions of occupational groups leads to inescapable difficulties; and because,
on top of that, the systems used by statisticians for their counts and censuses have varied so greatly from one country to another and from one
decade to another. A comparison between England and Denmark, for
instance, would not lead to anything. Only 8% of the English population
were employed in agriculture about 1900, whereas the corresponding figure for Denmark was 49%. Similar disparities would exist in a comparison
between Norway and Denmark, as fishing was the livelihood of a considerable part of the Norwegian population. But in the case of Sweden there
are strong similarities. Both countries had a very high percentage of persons employed in agriculture. A rough distribution of the populations of
these two countries can be seen in Table 10.7.

   Armed with knowledge of the difference in the industrial structure of
the populations, one is far better able to make a comparison between the

TABLE 10.7

Occupational Distribution of the Population for Denmark and Sweden in 1901 (in percentage)

Industry	Denmark	Sweden
Agriculture and fishing	48	50
Industry and mining	25	21
Commerce and transport	12	7
All other industries	15	22
Total	100.0	100.0

emigration from the two countries. An adaptation and combination of the main groups of the occupational systems of the two countries enables us to present some fundamental facts on the different emigration patterns.

The first fact that stands out is that emigration cut surprisingly little into the Danish farming class compared to what happened in Sweden. The higher share of farmers in Swedish emigration is evidence of the severe crisis in Swedish agriculture during the nineteenth century. The pressures were obviously sufficient to make it seem attractive to owners of cultivated land, buildings, tools, etc., to give up all in exchange for a piece of uncultivated prairie without buildings, implements, or stock. Conversely, the fact that only 4% of all emigrants from Denmark were farmers of any kind must indicate that Danish landowners, regardless of the size of their properties, were not eager to exchange them for other, even larger, holdings in the New World.

The reason for this fundamental difference must be sought in the differences in the development of the agricultural structure of the two countries, and particularly in the gradual changes in the size of holdings. The trends in the parceling out of land in the two countries seem to have moved in opposite directions. Already, before 1800, Sweden showed a pronounced fragmentation of holdings, known as "hemmansklyvning," which resulted in farms proper being replaced to a large extent by a huge number of tiny lots on which part of the servant class was settled.[2] This trend lasted into the nineteenth century and culminated about 1860, when the number of these pitifully small holdings ("torp") was about 100,000. From then on the tide turned. After 1870 the number of these very small holdings decreased, while the number of farms increased and so did the number of laborers without land. Presumably the immediate cause of the change was the great Swedish agricultural crisis in the late 1860s, when the farming population was on the verge of starvation. One of the main causes of the crisis originated in the very country to which so many of the farmers emigrated, America. After the Civil War, large-scale exports of grain from America made European grain prices fall. It is not surprising that conditions of crisis arose from the subdivision of land referred to earlier, when one notes how incredibly small Swedish holdings were in the entire period —even by comparison with conditions in Denmark where intensive farming also made a marked reduction of the size of holdings possible.

After the agricultural reform legislation of the late eighteenth century, land was parceled out in Denmark too, but not to an extent that bears any comparison with the situation in Sweden up to 1870. Also, the size

---

[2] The origin of this situation was a system of inheritance: Farms were divided into as many parts as there were sons.

of the average holding remained far above the Swedish norm. An order of 1819 by the Danish government restrained the tendency to subdivide farms, and this was partly the reason why the medium-sized farm was still the predominant element in the 1880s. Farmers still owned 75% of the agricultural land. The grain crisis of the 1860s was felt in Denmark just as in Sweden, of course, but in Denmark it was possible to parry its effects by means of a large-scale readjustment to dairy farming, and the increasing subdivision of holdings was consonant with this more intensive type of farming. Although the subdividing of the land into smaller holdings was stagnant for a period in the 1880s, the trend otherwise continued apace by contrast with the situation in Sweden, where small-holders abandoned grain farming and to a large extent emigrated to America. Their plots were combined into larger units to counteract the falling grain prices.

It seems that we can draw the same conclusions as a Swedish scholar did in the 1910s, that "conditions for the farming population have taken a more favorable development in Denmark as well as in Finland during the last generation than in Sweden." The Danish agricultural structure was such that once a person had been lucky enough to obtain a piece of land, large or small, he was provided for, though changing economic conditions might reduce yields to a minimum. Yields remained large enough at least to make it rare for a farmer to sell all and emigrate to 160 stubborn acres on the wild prairie.

11

AGRICULTURAL STRUCTURE
AND EMIGRATION

Until the beginning of the nineteenth century, Denmark was an agricultural country to such an extent that many events and trends in the political and social history of the country were basically caused by structural changes in the agricultural sector. To simplify matters, one might say the development of Danish agriculture after the middle of the nineteenth century was governed by three principal factors: the consequences of the agricultural reform legislation in the last decades of the eighteenth century, the large demographic expansion after 1800, and the marketing conditions for agricultural products, at home as well as abroad. All of these three factors were of such decisive importance as a background for the large migration out of rural areas that each deserves separate treatment.

The agricultural reforms after 1770 set in motion a very extensive development. The translation of the reforms from paper to reality took several generations; and gradually they took on new shapes, adapting to changes produced by demographic expansion. One thing of overwhelming importance was what we might call the spiritual effect of the reforms—the change in outlook which they caused. The emancipation of the farming class initiated by members of the land aristocracy and civil servants was the first stage of a development that made a large part of the population socially and politically conscious, although this awakening came very slowly and at the beginning only affected the more well-to-do farmers. But this development of the farmers into a political group, the establishment of organizations like Bondevennerne (The Peasants' Friends) and the Liberal (farmers') party, are all just one aspect of the emancipation of the farmers caused by the agricultural reforms. The other side was a gradually growing realization that there were possibilities in life outside the village and the social circumstances into which an individual had been born and reared. What could be called a "social buoyancy"—an ambition for better living conditions—developed in the rural population. It made itself felt in many ways, but common to them all was a striving toward one aim: a larger degree of independence. It was not merely a wish to become wealthy, but also a drive toward independence, even if this might lead to economic sacrifices. More than anything else, social buoyancy found expression in the constantly increasing migration rates. Here the reforms had opened up a possibility that had been more or less closed in the past. It is not just coincidence that the abolition of peasant bondage came to be seen by posterity as a symbol of the whole, many-sided work of reform, though it was in fact not the most epoch-making part of the legislation. More than half a century passed from the abolition of peasant bondage until the great migration from countryside to town became a phenomenon of real importance.

It seems that a period of slow intellectual maturation was necessary before the movement began. The time shortly after the middle of the nineteenth century, when migration started in earnest, seems to have been a period without changes in agriculture sufficient to explain the phenomenon. It looks as if one or two generations had to come and go before the notion of the right to move freely was generally accepted. The following may serve as an illustration of the point, even though it comes from a country far removed from Denmark. After the end of the American Civil War in 1865, the black population of the South was liberated, and blacks became free to move from the places where they lived. But mobility among the former black slaves remained extremely limited during the following decades. Only very few left the cotton districts. However, in the years just before and after World War I the black population of the South suddenly began to move, and hundreds of thousands moved to the large industrial towns of the North: Chicago, Detroit, Pittsburgh, and others. It is true that a tangled complex of causes was involved, and one of the important factors was the process of industrialization and the consequent "pull" on labor. But the impression remains that a period of adaptation is needed before a movement—in this case migration—gains momentum.

What is true of internal migration must also be true of the large wave of emigration from Europe, and consequently also from Denmark from about 1868. Here another factor comes into play: the demographic expansion mentioned earlier. In connection with emigration, it was a question of whether the country itself had an outlet for surplus population from its rural areas. This demographic expansion, which started in the second half of the eighteenth century, and which gathered momentum after the middle of the nineteenth century has already been discussed, so at this point only its effect on the rural population will be described. During the period before 1860, when migration out of the agricultural areas was still extremely limited, the effects of the expansion would naturally be the creation of a pent-up population surplus. At the time when large-scale migration began, the previous balance between the four main social groups of the rural population—the great landowners, the farmers, the small-holders, and the servants and laborers—had been disturbed, and a corresponding lack of proportion in the distribution of the available arable land between the groups had arisen. The general trend was one of a constant increase in the number of the landless proletariat, who were forced to find a livelihood either as day laborers with their own domestic establishments, or as domestic servants boarding and lodging with others. The direction this development would take was to depend on how far the landowning classes were inclined toward parceling out the land, either as a means of providing inheritance shares for several sons from a single farm, or in order to set up small-holdings with the purpose of retaining the local labor in the district. The agricultural class of domestic servants and laborers (in Danish called "tyende") led miserable lives in the nineteenth century. The Servants Act of 1854, and the fact that these people did not obtain the vote under the 1849 constitution, were both clear signs of social discrimination.[1] The main features of the 1854 act were distinctly designed to protect the employers. The entire system involving a servant's conduct book and compulsory registration with the local authorities was even at that time seen as degrading. The protection that the law afforded rural servants in return was modest; and was even more so in practice since the employers and the authorities were often social equals, while the distance between an ordinary servant and a public official was immense. The contemporary public realized the degrading position held by servants, politically as well

---

[1] Men who did not have independent households did however obtain the vote before 1915.

as socially, in consequence of the 1854 act. The case for moderating the most humiliating provisions became a theme repeatedly raised in the Rigsdag during the years to come.

It was characteristic of the debate during the entire period from the 1860s to the 1880s, when the legislation on the subject was taken up for discussion again, that even the Liberal party, the farmers' party, showed no real interest in taking the sting out of the social problem associated with domestic service. By and large, the liberals saw eye to eye with the conservatives regarding the protection given to the employers by the law as right and proper, and the result was that the 1854 act stayed in force unaltered in the main until it was replaced by the Employment of Assistants Act (Medhjælperloven) of 1921. It is true that the Liberal party was an agrarian party, but it did not represent all social interests within agriculture. A similar attitude can be detected in the earliest approaches to a small-holders' legislation in the late 1880s.

Another factor in addition to the law helped keep the domestic servants as a group at a very low social level: their wages. The pay of an adult male farmhand in about 1870 was approximately 100–150 crowns per year, a very low wage considering the fact that the average annual consumption of an agricultural laborer's family was estimated at the same time at about 230 crowns.[2] True, there was a slow but sure increase in the real income of rural laborers from about 1870, which can be shown as a curve with a very steep rise until about 1887, then a slight fall to 1880, followed by a steady rise again until World War I. This increase was a direct consequence of migration away from agriculture. Of course there was during the same period an increase in urban workers' incomes too; but that was a result of organized trade union pressure. Rural laborers at that time had no kind of organization; they merely left the "trade" if they found it unsatisfactory, and improved wages were therefore necessary in order to retain the labor force.

The first rise in wages, in 1872–1873, may have had some connection with the general social unrest, which found expression among the urban workers in the first socialist attempts at activism. That very same year complaints from the landowners' organizations began to appear in periodicals and books that servants were leaving their posts before their time. These complaints were to be repeated over and over again during the following decades. A sample examination of the so-called police documents in the judicial series of the district archives shows that such complaints were not unfounded. Especially in 1872–1873, but to some extent

---

[2] The 1880 rate of exchange was 1 dollar equalling 3.60 Danish crowns. One crown equalled about 30 cents.

also in 1874, one finds letter after letter from both large and small land-owners reporting runaway servants. The letters appear to have been duly entered in the police report, then shelved. The district authorities were well aware that it would be useless to start a search, as the servants in all likelihood would be on their way to America.

The major readjustment in agriculture after 1880, when grain produc-tion was heavily reduced in favor of livestock farming during the course of a few years, proved of decisive importance for the rural population. It is true that the cultivation of beets for winter fodder and the milking of cows required both more labor and smaller farms; one might therefore think that when this readjustment took place simultaneously with a large-scale migration of servants and day laborers to town, the result would be to speed up the process of subdividing farms and parceling out the land. However, it is hardly possible to produce statistical proof of this. But the reduced supply of labor does seem, on the other hand, to have been a main factor contributing to a considerable increase in efficiency. Thus a well-known agronomist, Christian Sonne, wrote in 1915 that the reason Danish agriculture managed to survive the labor-demanding shift in pro-duction was its use of equipment—centrifuges and harvesters, for example, among other methods of mechanization.

There is little doubt, however, that improved wages were not the best way to keep servants and day laborers on the farms. The social ambition of young people in domestic service and of the older ones who were day laborers was to become independent, to obtain their own plot of land to cultivate. The prospect of an entire life spent in domestic service was certainly not attractive for a generation with social buoyancy. A person who within a certain period of years after his confirmation had not yet succeeded in getting land of his own (and what could one expect to get at an annual pay of 200–300 crowns?) would be very likely to leave the countryside either for a town or for America.

But in the earliest part of the period there was still free land to be had in Denmark, just as there was overseas. The reclamation of the moorlands in Jutland was just then beginning, and as a part of this effort farms were parceled out that could absorb some of the surplus landless population. The reclamation process undoubtedly had an effect on emigration, a fact touched on in characteristic terms in a pamphlet published in 1866 called, "What is the reason for the present high prices of landed properties?" The author, A. Jacobsen, wrote:

> The emigration period has not yet begun in Denmark, because even if there are too many people here and there in East Denmark, there is certainly room for them in Jutland. Danes need not go to

America . . . There is certainly a great deal of work to be done
in Jutland, but I do not think that a man from the islands of East
Denmark has sufficient stamina, frugality and thrift to dig himself
into the moorland. This is a job for the Jute.

It seems as though Jacobsen was right. The reclamation did hold back
the inclination to emigrate, and the new inhabitants of the moors were
chiefly recruited from the peninsula itself. The emigration of people in
rural service from the moorland regions of central and western Jutland,
Viborg, and Ringkøbing counties did not really start until after 1884.
Before that time they made up as little as 1–2% of the entire emigration
of servants. After 1887 their share of the annual emigration from rural
areas was about 5–6%. During the earlier half of the period, eastern Denmark was predominant in the emigration of members of the rural service
class, while Jutland was the source of the majority of emigrants during
the latter half, after 1884. No doubt part of the reason for this lies in the
reclamation of the moors. Emigration from Jutland did not reach the
level of that of eastern Denmark until all new holdings had been taken
up for cultivation.

If we compare the geographical distribution of emigrating servants with
the data showing where in Denmark the land was richest, gave the best
yield per acre, and hence cost the most, we find, surprisingly, that the
largest number of emigrating servants came from areas with the best soil
(see Table 11.1).

The ranking may have changed a little from one year to the next, but
not much. It can surely not be pure coincidence that the highest emigration intensity is found on Langeland, that Lolland-Falster and Bornholm
were second and third, and that at the same time farm servants' emigration reached very high figures in these very areas. The implication of
these facts can be read as: Where land prices are the highest and a laborer's
chance of ever being able to buy a plot of his own consequently extremely
small, there is likely to be found the greatest inclination to emigrate.

TABLE 11.1

Yield in Crowns per tønde[a] Cultivated Land, 1880

Langeland	167	Fyn	142
Falster	153	Bornholm	142
Sjaelland	148	Jutland	99
Lolland	144		

[a] A very old Danish unit of area, originally the area of land which could yield one barrel
of rye or barley, later fixed to be equal to 1.36 acre.

But on the other hand, where the soil was best, large landed properties predominated. Was there then a connection between the emigration of farm servants and estate employment of large groups of laborers, characterized according to one author, Warming, by "low moral conduct" among male farmhands who could not find other employment? Warming adds that "the situation was made even worse by so many being together on one place." The parts of the country with high emigration intensity also exhibited a marked concentration of manors and other large estates. In Lolland-Falster, for instance, 25% of the land was held by very large estates, while the number of large properties in eastern and northern Jutland was much smaller. On Bornholm the situation was different. Here, working conditions in both urban and rural areas were completely unstable as a result of a considerable immigration of Swedes. When the ships with Swedish farm hands docked, the farmers turned up with their carriages and picked out of the miserable crowds what workers they wanted, and then paid them wages far below the level normal for the local inhabitants.

A letter from Bornholm, written in the autumn of 1872, gives a vivid picture of the agricultural conditions on that island:

> The Bornholm farmers pay their small-holding laborers much too poorly in relation to the prices of necessities. But the huge number of immigrating Swedes rules out a rise in wages. An ordinary laborer who is not a craftsman has often only the choice between America or the poorhouse.

Even if the large estates predominated in areas with a large emigration of farm servants, the connection between the two factors is not quite clear. Firmer ground is to be found in looking at the opposite end of the range of property size: the number of small-holdings and the increase in that number. A considerable number of plots under two hectares were parceled out, and this meant that about 30,000 new holdings were established after 1873. The rhythm of the process varied much from one part of the country to another as well as over the years. The main trend of the development was that such holdings became steadily smaller. During the period between the counts of agricultural holdings in 1873 and 1895, the share of the very smallest holdings in the total number of small-holdings increased from 20 to 30%, while the other group decreased correspondingly. At the same time the number of landless cottages decreased, but at a very slow pace. Such miserable laborers' cottages with no arable land attached were much more common in Jutland than in eastern Denmark.

However, the size of small-holdings was not decisive for the matter of keeping the rural laborers on the land. Of far greater importance was the question of whether land distribution developed at a pace that could keep up with the increase in the rural population. An excellent survey of the development of Danish agriculture, published in 1907 by the Danish Statistical Department, makes it possible to calculate the rhythm of this process between the three agricultural surveys of 1873, 1885, and 1895, i.e., prior to enactment of the small-holders' legislation. If we disregard west Jutland, where the reclamation of moorland comes into play, the figures show that the parceling out of land for small-holdings was slowing down in all parts of the country from the 1870s or at least from 1885. In some parts we even find an actual drop in the number of small-holdings, and a not inconsiderable one. This was the case, for instance, in Lolland-Falster, where the cultivation of sugar beets played a part in this development; and in eastern Jutland, where the attraction exercised by the developing towns was presumably strong enough to outweigh even the prospect of obtaining land. We can say that in the most densely populated rural areas distribution of land generally had come to a stop at around 1873.

Before drawing any conclusions from this, one must face another central problem: Was this phenomenon a cause or a consequence of these migrations to both the towns and to America? On the one hand it may be argued that the discontinuation of land distribution was the cause, a viewpoint we put forward earlier in this study: that the reduced chances for rural servants to obtain their own holdings contributed to both migrations. But it is also possible to make the opposite assumption: that parceling out stopped because young agricultural workers left the scene and there was insufficient manpower to man new holdings. However, the general impression of conditions in the rural districts, together with the fact that the number of emigrating landowners was extremely small, weighs against the latter explanation. The demand among rural servants and day laborers for independent property was undoubtedly very great, and those who were disappointed on that score would be inclined to leave the countryside, since the future in store for them as permanent servants was anything but attractive.

Before looking more closely into this aspect of the development, we should remember that an inquiry into the changes in agricultural life, i.e., the changes in types of farms and small-holdings, will invariably lead to the conclusion that the discontinuation of parceling the land can also be regarded from a third point of view, the political. A study of the trend in the development of large estates in Denmark after 1850 shows that there was here a movement that was exactly congruent with the general political trend in this period: the advance of the great landowners as a dominant political group, defenders of their own rights and those of the crown. Between 1850 and 1860, there was a reduction in the land hold-ings of the large estates. But from 1860 on there was a very marked tendency to amalgamate the larger holdings that was especially striking in the case of very large estates. This trend coincides with the first political victory of the landed interest, the revised constitution of 1866. The rate of land amalgamation on the very large estates increased between 1873 and 1885, a period that can well be called the golden age of the great landowners in Danish political life. From 1885, when a protracted and crucial political crisis began, and during the following 10 years, this devel-opment slackened considerably. The number of new large estates fell; and during the following period, 1895–1905, there was a definite decline, particularly in Jutland, in the holdings of large landowners. The golden age was clearly past.

As for the small-holders, the trend was more or less in inverse propor-tion with this development. There was a noticeable increase in the number of small-holdings in the 1860s, a trend that slowed during the 1870s and came to an almost complete stop after 1885. Is there a connection here? A large number of small-holdings were parceled out of the large estates, which were particularly dependent on the retention of the local labor force. But during the period of intense conflict between the ruling conservative landowners' party and the liberal opposition party, there was widespread terrorizing of day laborers and small-holders to prevent them from voting Liberal. The possibility of political motives in the parceling out of land from large estates cannot be overlooked in this period of severe political tensions.

The region of Lolland-Falster was characterized by quite special condi-tions. The unusually large emigration from this part of the country was centered in the rural areas, and drew its strength in turn from the rural servants and day laborers. What was the reason for the extra large stream of emigrants from these two sizable islands south of Zealand—a region that was not exceptionally densely populated and whose rich soil offered every possibility of a livelihood for its inhabitants? The population surplus in Lolland-Falster was not unusually large during the period before the beginning of the emigration; the surplus there was a good deal smaller than that in the northern part of Jutland, but somewhat above that of east Denmark other than Bornholm. Lolland-Falster was in much the same kind of geographical position as the other emigration-prone areas, Born-holm and Langeland. All were relatively isolated islands far from any large expanding towns. The towns of the islands themselves were small and unimportant, not at all attractive to people with the itch to move to new surroundings.

The most striking thing, however, was the connection between the cultivation of the sugar beet and migration. The two began at approximately the same time, i.e., in the early 1870s. The prime prerequisite of the introduction of the sugar beet in this area was probably the predominance of large estates, the owners of which knew of the riches that had come to the large estates of Prussia and Mecklenburg through the cultivation of sugar beets. In 1872, three brothers founded a sugar factory in Lolland, and another factory was started at the same time in Funen. Both of these establishments suffered a sad fate, partly because the state immediately placed a protective duty on their production, partly because of the falling market after 1873. Last, but not least, was the lack of interest on the part of the farmers in taking up the cultivation of the sugar beet. The advantage of sugar beets was that they improved the soil; and it was envisaged, moreover, that the waste product—the mash—could be used as fodder for cattle. The production started in 1872 was probably a premature endeavor: The changeover of agriculture to animal products had not come yet, and the farmers consequently had no use for the mash for larger herds.

The transformation of agriculture came after 1880, and with it came the spread of sugar beet production in the region. But a major difficulty from the start was a scarcity of labor to do the work of thinning out and weeding the beet fields, and that is the point where sugar beet cultivation and emigration connect with each other. As early as the beginning of the 1870s it was impossible to find enough laborers locally to do this work, and from about 1874 the device adopted was calling in foreign workers, at first from Sweden. These seasonal laborers, the majority of whom were women, stayed in the sugar beet areas from the beginning of May until November 20th. A very efficient system was used to recruit such labor, despite the fact that the period in question was prior to the establishment of public employment bureaus. The Swedish "sugar beet girls" continued to dominate this field until late in the 1890s, even after the importation of Polish laborers that had started early in that decade. In 1899 there were still 480 Swedish women, compared with only 82 Polish women, working on land belonging to the sugar factories. But at about the same time, the Swedish sugar factories in Scania began to expand their area of cultivation and drew off local labor that had previously gone to Denmark. After the turn of the century, the importation of Poles rose enormously, together with increasing production. In 1909 alone, for instance, 8600 Poles came, the great majority of them women. Normally they arrived in groups of between 20 and 50, each group with its own "Aufseher," a German labor agent who had recruited them in Poland and was responsible for them in Denmark. A description of one of these groups and their leader has it that he was usually seen walking backward in front of a long row of women, leaning on a strong oaken stick and constantly repeating the words, "forward, forward."

The systematic importation of rural labor from regions where the social situation was even more desperate than in Denmark was an interesting phenomenon. It is relevant in the present connection, too, as it may help explain the exceptional intensity of the migration from the beet-growing areas. At first glance it appears that the condition of the rural laborers in Denmark could not have been so bad if it was necessary to import such large contingents of foreign labor. There was obviously a large, unsatisfied demand for servants and farm hands. But it is not as simple as that. Weeding, which made up by far the largest part of the work the foreign laborers did, was very seasonal, and was unable to support anyone during the winter; the rural laborers had to live in the winter, too. Still more important was the fact that it was distinctly considered women's work. One author, Christian Sonne, wrote about this point:

> Permanently employed laborers will nowadays normally be offended if they are ordered to take part in that kind of work . . . and they really have a right to feel that way. It is definitely not men's work. The bent working posture necessary for effective execution of the work is hardly acceptable to men. They regard themselves as unfit for it, maintaining, as I have frequently heard it expressed myself, that they lack an extra hinge in their backs which women are supposed to have.

Beet cultivation, a highly industrialized form of agriculture, thus tended to give the male labor force a push. Frequently male servants and day laborers would find it difficult to find local work apart from purely factory jobs in the sugar works. Furthermore, and even worse for them, the importation of labor was liable to depress the level of wages. This was a point that began to evoke political interest, especially just after the turn of the century. The large landowners and the sugar factories claimed that the Poles received exactly the same pay as Danish labor, and that they were consequently not depressing wages. But the Social Democrats took up the issue and demanded measures against the exploitation of the workers. The stir caused by the Polish labor question brought about the 1908 act on supervision of foreign laborers, which was designed to protect immigrants in much the same spirit as the act to protect emigrants some 40 years earlier.

It is difficult to say for sure whether wage conditions may have been the force behind the great emigration of farm servants from the sugar beet regions. Certain facts, however, seem to speak rather clearly in favor of this possibility, particularly insofar as men's wages are concerned. Inquiries were made by the Statistical Department, in the years 1872, 1892, and 1897, into the wages paid to rural laborers and farm servants all over the country. These results provide us with a very interesting picture of the variations from one part of the country to another.

Table 11.2 offers many suggestions about the emigration propensity of rural servants and its causes as well as its effects. As far as the sugar beet cultivation is concerned, it is striking that neither in Funen nor in Lolland-Falster did the male laborers enjoy anything like a full share in the general increase in wages. In the case of Funen, the general wage level at the beginning of the period was above the national average; so the result was that despite the slow rate of increase there, Funen laborers received wages that were more or less the national average at the end of the period. It therefore seems reasonable to conclude that there must be a connection between the low Lolland-Falster wages (well below those of all other regions by the end of the period) and emigration from there, in which the male element was clearly dominant.

The most conspicuous section of the table, however, is the right-hand column, which shows the very pronounced increase in wages for women in eastern Denmark. It seems beyond doubt that what we see here reflects the consequences of the internal migration in which women, as already mentioned, were predominant. Female farm servants played an important part in the changeover to dairy farming, since dairy maids were indispensable to every farm with more than 10 cows. Male farmhands were

TABLE 11.2

Percentage Increase in Wages of Rural Laborers and Farm Servants, 1872–1897

Region	Men	Women
Zealand	78.4	108.6
Bornholm	85.0	180.7
Lolland-Falster	54.1	145.9
Funen	52.4	110.5
Eastern Jutland	85.1	82.2
Northern Jutland	99.1	92.1
Southwestern Jutland	84.1	82.4
Average percentage all of Denmark	79.4	102 9

gradually replaced by reapers and harvesters, but mechanization of milking did not occur until about 50 years later. The wage table shows that it was on this score that the farmers were forced to make the greatest efforts to hold on to the labor force, particularly in Zealand where the magnetic attraction of Copenhagen was a constant threat. Jutland does not show the same pattern of development; there the rising curves of men's and women's wages are parallel. If anything, the increases in women's wages lag behind those for men. Nevertheless, the percentage of women among the unmarried emigrating farm servants was a little higher from eastern Denmark than from Jutland (26.3% as opposed to 24.8%).

One curious detail is the extraordinarily large increase of wages in Bornholm. One would have expected the immigration from Sweden to keep the wages there at a minimum; but emigration may have had a substantial effect nevertheless. Conversely, the unusually high laborers' wages of southwest Jutland (a region where the soil was lean and the wages were the highest in the country) may partly explain why emigration from this part of the country was so modest.

From this analysis, we may conclude that two factors, the discontinuation of parceling out the land for small-holdings and the variations in the wages of rural labor both served as a "push" toward emigration.

12

EMIGRATION FOR POLITICAL
OR RELIGIOUS REASONS

While the large emigrations of the seventeenth and eighteenth centuries were mostly initiated as a result of quite concrete religious or political motives, nineteenth- and twentieth-century emigrations generally had no political or religious motivation behind them. The emigration was characterized by a long series of individual resolves made on the basis of economic grounds. Striving toward happiness, or a better standard of living, greater independence, acknowledgment of individuality—all these factors made up a mass movement devoid of any political program. Of course, the emigrants were a host of dissatisfied persons, dissatisfied with their social status, wages, and prospects. But their protest against society was not organized; it was not emigration by design as had been the case with the English dissenters, for example.

However, the economic motives are not the dominant ones for all the emigrants in the great wave after 1830. Here and there were to be found small streams of political or religious ferment that moved out to the coasts and across the seas. Even in Denmark there were examples of organized emigration projects, though the number of people in each was usually very small. The present chapter deals with these movements: first the political ones, and then the religious.

By the terms of the Peace of Vienna in 1864, Denmark surrendered the duchies of Schleswig and Holstein to Prussia and Austria. The minority with Danish sympathies living south of the new Kongeå border lost their Danish citizenship then, which means that emigration from this group does not, strictly speaking, belong in this inquiry. However, the Danish minority of the population of North Schleswig played such an important role in Danish history during the years after 1864 that it would be pedantic to exclude even a short summary of the emigration from there. Emigration from this area, as we shall see, assumed enormous proportions and was to a large extent channeled through Denmark.

The region between the present frontier and the 1864 border had a population of over 150,000 persons, of whom the people in rural areas were Danish-speaking. A difficult period began for this group, particularly so after 1866, when Prussia assumed sole administration of the duchies under the Peace of Prague. From the very beginning, the Danish population felt that Prussia had no intention of respecting national minorities. Administrative measures were taken in order to advance a determined policy of Germanization. The Danish minority tried to counteract such steps with passive resistance. During the first decade they placed considerable trust in the expectation that the border would be moved in accordance with Section Five of the Peace of Prague, 1866, which allowed a plebiscite. But in 1879, this hope was frustrated by the agreement of Prussia and Austria to delete this part of the treaty.

One problem in particular caused troubles between the Danish minority and the Danish government in Copenhagen on the one hand and the German authorities on the other: the issue of option. As in many other peace treaties, the Vienna treaty provided that the inhabitants of the ceded territory had the right to opt for Denmark, i.e., to choose Danish citizenship instead of German. There were many North Schleswigers who availed themselves of this right for either national or emotional reasons, and also as a means of escaping German military service. According to the Danish censuses, it was relatively few who preferred to go north and settle in Denmark.

Most North Schleswigers went south to Hamburg and from there to America. Actual emigration figures for the four counties with the Danish majority population are only known from the period 1882–1886. At that time the collection of such statistics was prohibited by the authorities, presumably in order not to tempt others to follow. However after North Schleswig reunited with Denmark in 1920, an estimate was made of its population development, and it showed clearly that the emigration had been extensive. The emigration surplus, i.e., the difference between the excess of births and the actual increase in the population of the region, indicated a considerable emigration. Table 12.1 illustrates the development, in 5-year periods, in accordance with the German censuses.

Here is a clear case of population flight, with emigration before 1900 having been proportionally much above that from Denmark and occasionally even above that from Sweden and Norway.[1] This was a flight which truly dug into the population, taking away far more than the excess of births could replace. Though the motive for this emigration may have been primarily political, it is impossible to completely ignore the economic element. Economic conditions of the region suffered from the new border after 1864. The towns lost the possibility of industrial expansion, partly as a result of diminished agricultural surroundings, and partly from the competition of industry in Holstein and Germany. And the Danish type of agriculture practiced in North Schleswig was forced to compete with the more efficiently run large estates of the central and southern parts of the duchy. Toward the end of the 1890s, emigration dropped, although it was a period of economic boom.

During the same years the German authorities carried on a severe persecution of the Danish minority—a new German population was moved up to the border area in order to carry through a Germanization. But at

TABLE 12.1

Emigration from North Schleswig, 1867–1910

	Emigration surplus	Population average	Estimated annual emigration per 100,000
1867–1871	4,900	155,000	316
1871–1875	7,000	153,400	455
1875–1880	6,700	155,500	430
1880–1885	14,500	150,800	917
1885–1890	9,400	145,200	646
1890–1895	6,900	143,400	481
1895–1900	4,900	146,000	336
1900–1905	4,200	151,000	279
1905–1910	900	160,000	56
Total	59,400		

[1] Compare these intensity figures with other European countries as indicated in Table 1.2.

that time most of the younger generation of Danish-minded people had already moved away to America.

There can be little doubt that emigration from North Schleswig was politically motivated. Similar extraordinarily large emigrations can be detected in the other German states annexed by Prussia in the course of the 1860s, such as Hesse-Nassau and Hanover. If we add up the emigration figures for these three conquered territories, the total comprises more than two-fifths of the total Prussian emigration, despite the fact that the population of the three provinces amounted to no more than one-fifth that of Prussia. Another remarkable detail in this connection is that all the three territories mentioned had extremely low birth and marriage rates compared with other parts of Germany: The birthrate was about 32 per 1000 inhabitants annually compared with 42 per 1000 in western Prussia. But this particular demographic feature existed in the period before annexation, too.

A year-by-year comparison between the Danish North Schleswig figures and the corresponding figures for Denmark shows more or less the same variations, except that there is in the Schleswig figures a slow scaling down after 1883, which corresponds to the similar development in German emigration in general. Even the peaks of 1872 and 1882 appear in the same proportion, the earlier one being higher than the later.

Occupational variations among the North Schleswig emigrants showed an even greater predominance of agrarians than in Denmark. This was a natural consequence of the Danish minority south of the border being predominantly farmers. The number of independent landowners was just as small as among the Danish emigrants. The majority were young, unmarried farmer's sons, rural laborers, and servants. It was difficult for rural laborers to find work in Denmark. Young North Schleswigers came from relatively well-to-do backgrounds. In contrast to the poor Swedish and Polish laborers, they did not view Denmark as an attractive place to work. Consequently they preferred to go to the New World. Moreover, quite a few of them had fled German military service. These young men ran the risk that the Danish government would be forced to hand them over to German authorities as deserters, in accordance with the agreement on the exchange of offenders.

Overseas emigration was business, too, and might involve considerable profit. Where emigrants exerted pressure to leave, shipowners' agents gathered to fish in troubled waters. This caused a national problem: Should Danish emigration agents be allowed to work south of the border? Nothing seems to have been done to prevent their activities until 1884, when the Germans adopted a more strict course. But the agents advertised in North

Schleswig newspapers, and very likely had subagents among the Danish minority.

However, in 1884, the traffic was declared illegal. The German ambassador in Copenhagen approached the Danish government with a strong warning against Danish agents recruiting emigrants in Schleswig. The Danish government feared the consequences, and an inquiry into the matter was held in Copenhagen City Court. The episode was probably the reason why this small branch of Danish overseas emigration did not rise in 1889–1892 like the rest of the Danish emigration.

The change in the nature of Danish emigration during the second half of the 1860s has been mentioned previously. Before the American Civil War, the majority of the emigrants from Sweden, Denmark, and Norway had been involved in group emigration. Various leaders of an idealistic cast traveled the country, inviting people to join in the establishment of colonies in the Middle West; some of these men also had a personal economic interest in promoting emigration. The agrarian politician, Rasmus Sørensen, was the first and most important one in Denmark. When the political movement toward a more liberal government seemed to have run aground after 1845, Rasmus Sørensen's plans for an organized emigration to America ripened. The general upheaval in the spring of 1848 anticipated the project; and the plans were first carried out in 1852 when Sørensen, now a member of the Folketing, became impatient with the rate of political progress. During the following years he became what might be called an idealistic emigration agent who traveled everywhere in the country; he was reputed to have been involved in the emigration of some 500 Danes to the United States. However, Sørensen died in 1865, at a time when the conditions for large-scale emigration had not yet developed. The Civil War had ended, but its aftermath was still paralyzing the American economy, and steamship traffic across the ocean was still in the early stages.

Rasmus Sørensen was replaced as an idealistic emigration agent by a person with even more pungent and implacable opinions, Mogens Abraham Sommer, spokesman of the extreme political and religious radicalism of the nineteenth century in Denmark. Sommer was born in Haderslev in a Jewish family, originally called Schomer, i.e., watchman. He received sufficient education to start a career at the local cathedral school in 1853. But during the following years, his religious and political fanaticism was aroused, and from 1856 on he lived as a ceaselessly wandering preacher and speaker. He traveled on foot from one end of the country to the other, arranging meetings everywhere. He was frequently accused of slander and sentenced to prison on several occasions; these humiliations furthered his fanaticism and his feelings of being a martyr. The interesting thing here is his activity as an emigration intermediary, beginning in the first half of the 1860s, just about the time when Rasmus Sørensen's work stopped. In 1861 Sommer sold all his belongings and went to the United States, where he spent 12 weeks handing out Christian tracts to soldiers serving in the Civil War. Then he undertook the 4-week crossing back to Denmark. It was characteristic of this restless man that he was unable to remain for any length of time in the same place, and during the following years he traveled constantly between Denmark and the midwestern states of America. When he died, a poor and forgotten man, in Ålborg in 1901, he had crossed the Atlantic more than 20 times.

In the spring of 1864, Sommer added emigration to his activities as a lay preacher, book canvasser, homeopathic doctor, and photographer. In addition to his indisputable eloquence, he possessed an equally indisputable business talent; and he obviously realized that the disheartened atmosphere in Denmark after the fatal Schleswig war against the German powers offered a possibility of recruiting large numbers of returning soldiers and other dissatisfied persons for his emigration plan. With the purpose of forwarding this program, he began to publish a periodical, *Emigranten* (The Emigrant), which was issued regularly until February, 1872, except for the periods when Sommer was accompanying groups of emigrants to the United States. In 1864, Sommer established an emigration agency in Copenhagen. He found his customers by arranging hundreds of meetings in Copenhagen and in Jutland, during which he served God, his political career, his book canvassing, and his emigration agency all at the same time. Between January and April in 1865 alone, he held 134 meetings, and he sold, according to his own account, 60,000 copies of his many publications. These publications, *Emigranten, Den lille Amerikaner, Vejledning for Udvandere* (Instructions for Emigrants), and several edifying publications that were rather less edifying to the middle classes than to the poor, because of their very outspoken and frequently vulgar defamation of the king, the government, and particularly the members of the clergy.

But Sommer was not simply a blind fanatic; he was an intelligent man with penetrating understanding of the serious social problems of the day, as study of *Emigranten* shows. Apart from the taunts about the clergy, his religious ideas were not expressed here; *Emigranten* was mostly a political periodical aimed at arousing the poverty-stricken rural and urban workers to consciousness of their miserable conditions, and thus at promoting emigration. In his article, "What is the reason for the steadily increasing emigration?," Sommer touched on something vital in the problem:

While people are living in the darkness of complete ignorance, they never think about the pressures and wrongs which they suffer from the powerful. But with freedom comes enlightenment, and if that freedom is limited or only a formality, then dissatisfaction will increase constantly with the growing realization of the existence of suppression.

He mentions some activities that may be described as suppression: the revision of the Constitution in 1866, compulsory military service, the direct tax (a war tax levied from 1864–1872), and the tyranny exercised by the vicars over their parishioners—all things which would necessarily make a considerable impression on poor people, particularly in Jutland. His watchword, "Do not become slaves of men," borrowed from the Bible, probably aroused many people to social consciousness, and did, as he claimed himself, spread America fever. In many ways, Sommer's political agitation resembled that conducted by Lars Bjørnbak in Århus Amtstidende (a newspaper) at about the same time. Like Bjørnbak, Sommer was an anti-militarist.

On several occasions Sommer traveled to America with groups of hundreds of Danish emigrants, but unfortunately it is not possible to give exact figures for the number of emigrants for which he was responsible. However, there is no doubt that his work as a lay preacher was of considerable importance in starting a movement that formed a background to mass emigration. Thus it was no exaggeration for the obituary writer to comment, on his death in 1901, "The number of Danes which he, directly or indirectly, has helped to convey across the sea must be reckoned in the tens of thousands."

In 1871, Louis Pio began the organization of the Danish social movement. The Paris Commune and the ideas of the French socialists were probably an impetus at the very beginning, but another incentive was the social distress existing in the Danish towns, which caused unrest among the workers. Low wages and unemployment, particularly in the provincial towns, added fuel to the flames. A first high point for the movement occurred in the spring of 1872 with widespread strikes and unrest. Interference from the authorities together with increasing differences of opinion among the socialists themselves caused the party to begin to disintegrate during the next few years. The lost "battle" and the economic crisis after 1873 resulted in a feeling both within the party organization and among its voters that political means were insufficient and that other methods would have to be tried. Emigration to America was then one way out of the misery, an idea which, as we shall see later, was adopted by the socialist leaders in 1876 when conditions inside the party were at their worst. The question is how this idea came to the leading socialists.

A study of the party's paper, *Socialisten,* does not offer an answer. In 1871–1876, the paper regarded emigration with passive benevolence. But on March 19, 1876, there appeared a conspicuous article about plans for an organized socialist emigration. The writer begins by referring to Malthus's theories on overpopulation and maintains that while emigration used to be a token of extreme distress, the means of transportation were now at a level where large emigrations could take place before the final crisis occurred and perhaps could even prevent it. The article referred to the system employed by the English trade unions: The Moulders' Union, for instance, had in the year 1867 spent 23,000 crowns on arranging emigration for distressed members, and the Machine Workers' Union decided that if the percentage of unemployed members exceeded 7.5, organized emigration should be arranged. Pio, probably the author of the article, then suggested a plan to the effect that one part of the United States should be chosen, large enough to take hundreds of thousands of fellow party members, who would then establish "a large active socialist society." After the publication of this article, the central committee of the party put forward a suggestion that they organize emigration from Scandinavia "in a manner which would be beneficial to the spreading of our teachings."

On January 14, 1877, the great colonization project was launched as the most prominent concern of the party. In the meantime, Geleff, one of the party leaders, had been to the United States (his voyage paid for by the party), and he suggested Kansas as the place. During the following months, the front page of *Socialisten* constantly called for emigrants. For men over the age of 18 (but under 50), the cost of participation was 400 crowns, for women, 230 crowns, and for children under 12 years, 50 crowns. These prices were to cover tickets to Kansas and to purchase land, tools, cattle, and food for the first months. The conditions were, apart from having no criminal record and, for women, not being pregnant beyond the third month, an acknowledgment of:

> our fundamental principles such as the colony being responsible for the rearing of children whose parents were unwilling to undertake it; easier divorce possibilities, cooperative cultivation of the land, distribution of necessary work by a commission, and equal rights for women in society.

In 1876–1877, the situation was critical for the Social Democratic party, and the idea of emigration was therefore not wholly unrealistic. But still the thought of transplanting a complete political movement to foreign parts was so fantastic that somebody must have inspired Pio with the plan. It seems possible that the person behind the socialist colonization project was also Mogens Abraham Sommer. Sommer was engrossed by the cause of socialism. He regarded it as the way to abolish social inequality. Sommer was in contact with Louis Pio during the summer of 1871, and after that Sommer placed all his energy and violent manner into propaganda for the International.

The reason why Kansas was chosen as the place for the socialist colony, despite the fact that very cheap land was still available in agricultural states such as Minnesota, Iowa, Nebraska, or the Dakotas, seems to have been a visit paid to Copenhagen in 1875 by a special representative of the Kansas immigration authorities. Very likely Pio met this agent.

The emigration project was run at the highest level of the party. The central committee of the party set itself up as the "emigration committee," and in addition to numerous meetings in Jutland about the project, one large meeting was held in Copenhagen. Here it was decided that a demand should be made to the Rigsdag for a public grant of 200,000 crowns for the purpose of easing the prevailing serious economic difficulties by financing the emigration of unemployed workers. In this period *Socialisten* ran large front-page invitations to join in the emigration scheme. On February 16, the deadline for enrollment was deferred to March 14, as "several participants have found it impossible to sell their belongings and houses so soon." Requests were issued to fellow partisans in Norway, Sweden, and Schleswig, too. But on March 23, 1877, an event occurred which left all of Denmark gaping and which, for a long time, left the Danish Social Democratic party on the verge of disintegration. On that day both the top leaders of the party emigrated. Pio and his colleague sneaked quietly aboard a ship, accompanied by two policemen who were to ensure that the two socialists kept their secret agreement with Police Inspector Hertz. As a reward for absenting themselves to the United States and staying out of Denmark, Pio was to receive 10,000 crowns and Geleff a little less.

Pio seems to have tried to make his departure part of the project, but as time passed the police became increasingly nervous about the situation, and somehow they succeeded in forcing him to depart on March 23. A flight of this kind, both from the party and from all moral and economic responsibilities, was an obvious advantage to the police. The scandal might enhance the chances of total disaster for the socialist party, and at any rate the authorities could avoid socialist demonstrations in connection with the passage of the controversial provisional Finance Act on April 12th.

As a matter of fact, a small group of about 18 courageous socialists did set out on April 16 with the aim of establishing the colony. They began to break land near Hays City in Ellis County, Kansas, and Pio

joined them there. The fate of this colony was described by a Danish–
American historian in the following words:

> There were 18 colonists, some married, some unmarried. They at
> once set to work to build a log cabin with separate apartments
> for the married and the unmarried. Tools and stocks were pur-
> chased. The men worked "like Hell." The women quarreled. And
> the naked prairie—save for an abundance of buffalo bones, rattle-
> snakes, prairie dogs, owls and an occasional soldier—seemed so
> unresponsive to the demands for a better social order that the
> colonists could stand it no longer than six weeks. The property
> was then sold and the proceeds divided among the colonists, net-
> ting each some thirty dollars.

The recruiting of emigrants was claimed as the monopoly of profes-
sional emigration agents. An almost comical expression of this is found
in a letter from one agent on behalf of all the Copenhagen agents, addressed to Crone, the commissioner of the Copenhagen police. It is a
complaint about Pio's emigration propaganda and a demand that he be
punished for having trespassed on their preserves: "Otherwise I do not
see how my colleagues and I shall be able to pay taxes, keep up offices
and deposit the guarantee, when any socialist gambler can with impunity
work as our competitor."

Crone, who was very well informed in the matter, wrote in his shaky
handwriting the words, "nothing further to be done." He had already taken
steps to bring Pio's emigration agency to an end.

Although the political situation in Denmark was unusually unsettled in
the years after 1870, this seems to have been of little importance as a
motive for emigration. We have seen that the socialist experiment with
organized emigration failed; not one instance of public resentment against
the extremely conservative rulers among the adherents of the Liberal party
(who constituted a majority of the Danish population) has been uncovered
in all the source materials treated in this study that could be interpreted
as emigration resulting from political protest. Something of this nature
would not have been unexpected around 1885, when political tensions
reached a peak, but surprisingly, the emigration curve shows a striking
drop in that year in the number of emigrants. This feature is found in
practically all European countries.

It is curious and of some significance that while the ordinary emigration
from Denmark was smaller than that of most other European countries,
and particularly that of Norway and Sweden, emigration determined by

religious conviction was of quite a different extent, far above that in our two neighboring Nordic countries. Seen in relation to the population of the country, it was probably the largest in Europe. This raises the question of whether the Danes were more susceptible to religious revivals than were other nationalities. From about 1820, revivals of many different kinds mushroomed in Denmark and were probably connected with the social and economic tensions characteristic of the rural districts—the same kind of tensions that later gave rise to large-scale emigration.

Generally the revivals fall into two groups, according to place of origin: One group consisted of the "homemade" ones—the Strong Jutlanders, the Funen Layman's movement centered around Peder Larsen Skræppenborg —and the other group comprised the "imported" ones, among which two were particularly important—the Baptists and the Mormons. The purely Danish revivals were, as far as we can see, connected with organized emigration only to a very limited extent. One exception should be mentioned, and that was Sommer's peculiar movement which included, moreover, a strong current of politics and business.

But with the two foreign sects, the Baptists and especially the Mormons, we find organized emigration, and in the case of the Mormons even direct urging. The difference exists probably because these two sects had their origins in England and the United States. The earliest Baptist congregation in Denmark was established in October, 1839, probably as a result of missionary work from Hamburg, where the first congregation was created in April, 1834, by American missionaries. The Danish church authorities were extremely intolerant toward the Baptists; their congregations were prohibited and several of the leaders of the sect were sent to prison for long periods. Furthermore, an equally disturbing sabotage was practiced by the local population. According to American sources, organized emigration of Baptists from Denmark began in 1854 and was still going on in 1870, as indicated by remarks in a report from Captain Wilhelm Sommer to the Minister of Justice:

> I particularly want to mention the Baptist leader, Lars Henriksen, a farmer, of Skee Tostrup near Ringsted, who has for a long time been arranging the emigration of co-religionists (to America) through the Baptist preacher and hostler Braunn (Bramm?) of Hamburg.

It seems clear that the Baptists had their own channels for emigration, obviously independent of the official ones. They did not contract with Danish emigration agents. That the Baptist emigration from Denmark seems to have remained at a relatively low level must be due to two facts:

(1) that the number of proselytes was limited, and (2) that the spokesmen of the sect never painted emigration to America as a travel to the Holy Land, but solely as a way out of persecutions in Denmark.

The Morman preachers, on the other hand, tried directly to summon emigrants. They preached about the Salt Lake Valley in Utah as "Zion" on earth, roused people to go there and join the Latter-Day Saints. Mormonism (a name, by the way, which is not used by its adherents), is perhaps the most peculiar and most complex of all the more recent revivals, a mixture of Christianity and exuberantly imaginative ingredients fitted into a set of extremely rigid rules, all strictly governed by a system of officials. The carefully planned organization is one of the more important reasons why this sect enjoyed widespread acceptance.

The pronounced religious zeal characteristic of the first pioneers in Utah and the unusually effective organization and government of the Church made it possible for the Mormons to establish a mission across the Atlantic shortly after their arrival at Salt Lake. The only place where this had been tried previously was England. Here Brigham Young himself had started a mission in 1840–1841: The first cargo of new converts set out across the sea as early as June, 1840, and then across the prairie to "Zion."

This is not the place to give a detailed description of the inception and quick spread of Mormonism in Denmark after the first missionaries arrived in Copenhagen in May and June, 1850. However, it may be useful to point out certain circumstances of fundamental importance in the earliest phase of the Mormon mission in Denmark. This way we may find part of the answer to the question we asked earlier, whether Danes were more susceptible to the Mormon message than were other nationalities. What we find indicates that there were, here as well as abroad, purely practical circumstances that contributed to the Mormon success in Denmark.

The starting point of the mission was a decision made by the leaders in Salt Lake City in October, 1849, to the effect that one man was to be sent to Germany to cover the whole of the German area including Austria, one man to Italy and France, but three to Scandinavia—two to Denmark and one to Sweden. This very marked stress on the mission in Scandinavia was probably due to the fact that among the persons in the inner circle were two Danish brothers, Hans Christian and Peter O. Hansen, who had some weight with the Mormon leaders. At the request of Brigham Young, one of the brothers had translated the Book of Mormon into Danish even before the Mormons had reached Utah. This was the first translation of the book which formed the foundation of Mormonism.

No special success in spreading the sect throughout Denmark came about because the Danish translation was the very first of all, nor because two missionaries were sent to Denmark while France and Italy shared one. But the reception which the missionaries received varied greatly from one country to another. The two persons who came to Denmark, according to the decision made in Utah in October, 1849, were Erastus Snow, one of the 12 apostles of the Church, and Peter O. Hansen. They were joined by a third, George P. Dykes, a pioneer whom Snow had met in England and persuaded to go with them across the North Sea. Next they were very soon joined by a fourth missionary, John Erik Forsgren, who had been sent to Sweden but expelled from there after a few days' work. Consequently, from the very beginning, the so-called Scandinavian campaign became a purely Danish affair.

Although the Mormons had already won many adherents among Norwegian settlers in the northern part of Illinois during the Nauvoo period, no missions in Norway itself seem to have been established until about 1853. The Norwegian authorities looked upon revivals with relatively unfriendly eyes.

Denmark was the only country in which the authorities did not interfere with the Mormons. The first democratic constitution, which was passed the year before the arrival of the missionaries, granted the right to free worship provided it did not conflict with public decency. Admittedly there was the problem of polygamy, but despite several indignant pamphlets against the Mormons and reports to the bishops from the vicars about the same thing, the authorities seem at no time to have tried to hamper the activities of the missionaries. When the emigration legislation was passed in 1868, the police did begin to reflect on whether the Mormon missionaries' direct invitation to emigration in Utah was not in conflict with the law, but no trace can be found of intervention.

The one real difficulty for the missionaries was the public attacks on the Mormon meetings, fights, and street riots—all of them reactions which the missionaries knew well from the United States and which might harm their work, but also help by stimulating interest and activating sympathizers. The missionaries seem, furthermore, to have had benevolent support from the American envoy to Copenhagen, Walter Forward.

Among the advantages that might have given Mormonism a head start in Denmark was the fact that the four missionaries found a most favorable starting point for their activity in the numerous Danish Baptist communities, a fertile soil which they probably were familiar with from England. Among other things, the two sects held common views on the baptismal ritual. It is therefore immediately understandable that the missionaries began their work among the Baptist congregations in Copenhagen, who, in February 1850, numbered about 400 members. A few months later, an independent Mormon congregation of about 60 persons was established.

practically all of them former Baptists who had been re-baptized. From then on the path of the Mormon missionaries through Denmark was clear: They went from one Baptist congregation to the next. As early as 1850, George P. Dykes went to Aalborg, where the Baptists had gained more ground than anywhere else in the country, and in spite of furious indignation among the Baptist leaders there, a considerable number of its members were immediately converted to Mormonism. Similar things happened in Falster and Bornholm a short time later.

We may conclude from this description that Mormonism enjoyed extremely advantageous working conditions in Denmark compared with other countries. This was one important reason why Mormonism made such strong gains and brought such large numbers of converts to the holy land across the Rockies. The effectiveness of the drive undertaken by the four missionaries in 1850 is evident from the information that one out of every three or four religious tracts in Danish which they had printed by 1850, such as Snow's *En Sandheds Røst* (A Voice of Truth), was issued in no less than 20,000 copies. A new printing in 1882 numbered 140,000 copies. According to a calculation in *Morgenstjernen* in 1884 (a Danish periodical published in Salt Lake City), 750 Mormon pamphlets and other items had been printed in Denmark up to 1881. Thus the idea that Danes were particularly susceptible to the message of Mormonism should obviously be taken with some reservation. In missionary work as in other activities, there is a certain relationship between seed and harvest.

The missions of the Latter-Day Saints were organized with an effectiveness and method that was otherwise unknown at that time, when the well-tested advertising schemes of today had not yet been developed. While the management of the Baptist church was decentralized to such an extent that each congregation was an autonomous unit, the Mormon church was held together by a firm organization under a hierarchical leadership. Mormonism in Denmark was divided into so-called conferences and branches, and at the head of the total number of Mormon congregations was a president subject to the authority of the 12 apostles in Utah. From the beginning the purpose of the missions was that converts were to emigrate to Utah, and any obstacles to the accomplishment of this purpose were removed. All the anxiety common among other emigrants who were traveling alone to a foreign country that had an unfamiliar language were at least partly eliminated for the Danish Mormons by gathering them into large groups under the leadership of American missionaries. The Mormons chartered vessels of their own, and the long journey from New York to Utah was so well organized that the lambs had only to follow the shepherds.

From the very beginning, the Mormon church solved the economic problems with amazing effectiveness. All adherents both in the United States and in Europe tithed to the church. In order to anticipate objections from poor, recently converted persons who lacked the money to go to Zion although their hearts were longing to do so, a Perpetual Emigration Fund was established at Salt Lake City in 1850. This fund became the economic keystone of the missions and pumped the necessary credit into any areas where missions were sent. New converts did not pay anything to set out, and they could get their entire transportation on credit. Later, they paid back the expenses of the crossing (food along the way, railroad tickets, a place in an ox-cart or whatever) a year or two after their arrival in produce: wheat, hay, or vegetables. Consequently the fund never ran dry. It grew steadily as a result of constant payments being made into it from both sides of the Atlantic. In 1850 it was started with a basic capital of $5000, and by 1877 it had passed $1 million, a part of which, however, consisted of outstanding debts. In that same year 19,000 debtors were kindly requested to make their remaining payments!

The Mormon communities in Denmark were largely made up of extremely poor families who would gather around the missionary every year when it was announced how large an amount was available that year from the fund for emigration purposes. Moreover, considerable altruism was displayed by wealthier members, who contributed to make it possible for the poor to emigrate.

During the period before 1869, faith alone was not enough for an emigrant to Utah. Good health was needed, too, as the voyage would normally take some 4 or 5 months: up to $1\frac{1}{2}$ months to cross the Atlantic to New York and 2 or 3 weeks by river steamer and railroad to the banks of the Missouri, where the long trail across the prairie and mountains started (see Figure 12.1). When sails were supplanted by steam and a railroad was built across the Rocky Mountains, the trip was reduced to approximately 27 days.

The statement that Mormons did not suffer persecution from the Danish authorities must be taken with reservation, because police supervision of the missionaries was intensified in the late 1890s. This was probably caused partly by pressure from America. As early as 1879, the Danish foreign minister had received a long official note from the American chargé d'affaires, Cramer, in which it was recommended that Denmark put an end to the emigration of Mormons because they were, presumably, emigrating to Utah for the purpose of committing polygamy, a violation of the American legislation of 1862. In January, 1880, the minister replied that the authorities had no intention of stopping the emigration of Mor-

Figure 12.1 Ole Peersen tells a wondering neighbor about the horrible things he and his wife Dorthe experienced when they emigrated with the Mormons to Utah. (Broadsheet ballad of 1874 in the Royal Library, Copenhagen.)

mons, "however regrettable we find it that Danish subjects should be inveigled into joining the said community as a result of the activities of missionaries from the United States."

In Norway and Sweden, where similar notes were delivered, the governments reacted by publishing in the press a declaration stating that polygamy was prohibited in Utah just as in Europe. Cramer's successor in Copenhagen, Payson, tried in 1881 to make the Danish government take similar steps, but in vain.

A decade later the situation was more or less the opposite. Now the Danish government wanted to restrain the activities of the missionaries, while the American government tried to protect them. Early in 1897, the Danish minister of justice expelled two American (Danish born) missionaries for preaching Mormonism. They appealed to the ambassador in Copenhagen, who received instructions from Washington to render them assistance, provided they had not violated Danish laws. However, his endeavors were of no avail. In March, 1900, a similar incident occurred. Another two missionaries were expelled, and again the ambassador approached the Danish authorities in vain. The missionaries were given 2 months to leave. After that, the Danish authorities did not repeat this experiment.

The most reliable statistical material on the Mormon emigration is provided by Professor William Mulder in his Ph.D. thesis, written in 1954.[2] The thesis is based on a critical examination of the printed statistical data compared with unprinted basic material filed at Salt Lake City. Mulder has a table showing the number of baptized, apostates, and emigrants, covering a period from 1850 to 1904, when large-scale immigration to Utah was brought to a halt by the leaders of the sect. During that period, they succeeded in baptizing 46,500 persons in Scandinavia as a whole. One-half of them (i.e., 23,443) were Danes, a good third were Swedes (16,714), and only between a seventh and an eighth were Norwegians (6340). The Danish predominance is quite clear, particularly if the populations of the countries are taken into consideration. The greatest increase among Mormons came in the 1860s, when the annual number of baptisms in Denmark averaged more than 700. After this peak period, the number of conversions showed a constant decline. In Denmark, more than one-half the proselytes were won over before 1870.

An inquiry into the corresponding disaffection percentages over the decades shows that the highest one—38%—appears in the 1860s, and

---

[2] The thesis is unpublished. One copy is on deposit with the Utah Historical Society, Salt Lake City. I thank Prof. Mulder for permission to publish part of his material.

this was reduced to about 15% at the turn of the century. This might indicate that more or less anyone was accepted for baptism during the 1860s, while the converts in the following period were subjected to some kind of test of religious constancy before the actual baptism took place. Furthermore, it seems very likely that a certain number of poor people chose the spiritual raiment of Mormonism in the hope of being able to get a new start in the United States.

When we see the very large percentages of the congregations that emigrated to Utah, we must understand that in the Mormonism of that time conversion and emigration were almost inseparable elements. Mulder's table shows that a total of 22,650 Mormons over the age of 8 (the age of baptism) emigrated from Scandinavia, which means that approximately one-half of all the converts emigrated. And in this calculation, the disaffected have not been left out, as might have been expected. If they are deducted, we reach a figure of no less than 70% of all persons of firm conviction who went as pilgrims to their Holy Land.

From Mulder's survey, we can see that the percentage of emigrating converts from Denmark was larger than from Sweden and Norway. Out of all Danish converts, 54% emigrated during the period before 1904, while the corresponding figures for Sweden and Norway were 44% and 40%, respectively. An explanation of this difference must be found among other factors in the different periods during which Mormonism caught on in each of these countries. In the 1880s, when conversions were really numerous (and there were more conversions in Sweden than in Denmark), the missionaries had become more cautious about whom they sent to Utah.

The character of the Mormon emigration was in many respects unlike that of ordinary emigration. Especially striking is the way in which the structure with regard to men, women, and children was fundamentally different. There was an amazing preponderance of women, and the number of children brought along was correspondingly large. Out of 8344 Mormons from the period 1872–1894, almost 2700 were adult women, 2425 were adult men, and 3225 were children under 14 years of age. The difference between the Mormon emigration and other emigrations is clearly illustrated in Table 12.2.

TABLE 12.2

Mormon Emigration Compared with Other Emigration (in percentages)

	Men	Women	Children	Total
Mormon emigration	29.3	32.2	38.5	100
Other emigration	52.0	30.0	18.0	100

The preponderance of women and children among Mormon emigrants is surprising. Many people now (as others did at the time), tend to connect this with the Mormon acceptance of polygamy, the idea being that all these excess women would end up as the third or fourth wives of believers in their Zion. It is perfectly possible that some did in fact end up like that, but as to the distribution of men and women, the Mormons did not differ from the other Danish sects and revival groups of the time. It was a general trend that the majority of persons who joined all these movements—Irvingians, Baptists, or Adventists—were women, and the Mormons were not exceptional here. The reason that Joseph Smith and his successors encouraged polygamy may be found in the example of the Old Testament, but an additional, rather more practical justification may have been the social problems resulting from the large number of excess women arriving in the Mormon state. A change in family structure helped to solve these problems. As far as Danish Mormons go, however, it is worth noting that while there was a preponderance of women in the rural districts and in the provincial towns, the opposite was the case in Copenhagen. Among emigrants from the capital, the relation was 126 men per 100 women, while, for instance, Ålborg County had 77 men per 100 women. No reasonable explanation can be found for this.

While the majority of the emigrants were individual persons about whose motives statistics can only indirectly yield information, the emigration movements among Socialists, Baptists, and Mormons led to organized popular movements. But it should not be forgotten that a political or religious motive was unlikely to be the sole reason why the adherents of these groups set out for America. Besides their idealistic reasons, they were probably prompted by the same set of social and economic motives as other emigrants.

13

DANISH EMIGRANTS
IN THE NEW WORLD

The settlement of the huge American continent, the enormous empty region from the Alleghany Mountains to California, is one of the most fascinating chapters of modern history. Although they were inconspicuous in the large panorama, thousands of Danish emigrants were part of the building of this new world. In the course of approximately 75 years, this enormous area was brought under the plough and made the massive core of an empire inhabited by people who had shed everything they had been bound to beyond the sea in order to sweat and toil in a fight against the rebellious countryside. Settlement occurred by stages, increasing in speed after the 1840s. The vanguard toward the West was made up of trappers armed with axes, rifles, knives, and a frying pan to face life in the wilderness. Such frontiersmen may have cleared small pieces of land to cultivate a few vegetables, but their principal food was the game they shot with a rifle. For these early white men, the Indian's war cry and tomahawks were not romantic spicing, but harsh reality. Where the Indians were aggressive, several trappers would join forces and build a fort—the germ of a town. But many of them, probably the majority, preferred to live in solitude, and when they heard several rifle shots in their vicinity, they gathered their sparse equipment and set out further toward the West—not necessarily to avoid the company of others, but because the hunting would not support so many.

The next group of arrivals in the process of settlement was the early farmers—the pioneers. Theirs was the heavy job of breaking the land, cutting trees, and ploughing the centuries old prairie turf. Horses as draft animals were a luxury, whereas oxen were obtainable but slow when measured by the pioneers' necessity to get the harvest in before winter came. Unlike the frontiersmen, the pioneer farmers were socially inclined. They settled in colonies, especially in the early decades, and often created settlements where emigrants of the same origin, German, English, or Scandinavian, maybe even from the same village, gathered together. Farmers saw to it that sons and sons-in-law got neighboring land, and they formed a small state within a state. From about 1860, the federal government began taking an interest in emigration to the West. New states were incorporated in the federation, and the same rational administrative plan for land division as in the eastern states was established earlier. The country was ruled in square counties and square townships, each consisting of 36 sections of land, 1 mile on each side. In each township (an area of 6 miles x 6 miles) special sections were reserved for schools and churches. Admittedly this was a dull, geometric grid placed on a vast, varied land, but it was uniquely rational and practical from an administrative point of view. Every newcomer was able to find his future home by counting his way through the numbers of townships and sections.

The famous Homestead Act of 1862 gave any person over 21 years of age (and all breadwinners) the right to take 160 acres of land, i.e., one-quarter of a section. Anyone who obtained a homestead had to guarantee that he would not use the land for speculation and swear that he did not hold land anywhere else. After 5 years of habitation, the holding would be the property of the holder, free of debt. It is hardly an exaggeration to call the Homestead Act an event of worldwide importance. It started the avalanche of emigrating European masses, for a most effective propaganda machine saw to it that the provisions of the Homestead Act did not remain unknown across the Atlantic. The idea of being able to obtain free, fertile land became an unparalleled magnet to the European masses, and even the indirect effects of the legislation were immense. The large number of immigrants who obtained free land brought it under cultivation. In the course of a few years, the United States had a large production of wheat and corn, part of which was exported to Europe on board the empty returning emigrant ships. The consequence of this enormous export is well known. The falling grain prices in Europe after 1865–1870 caused a serious shock to the European agricultural system, especially to Danish farming, which was forced to readjust to new production within a few years. There is a curious historical quality of going around in circles about this mutual connection between the European mass emigration and the agricultural crisis that caused renewed emigration to the United States. Thus these first Danish emigrants may have contributed to the readjustment of Danish farming and to the cooperative movement in Denmark.

To a young peasant in Denmark or any other European country, the idea of obtaining 160 acres free of charge was fascinating, considering the size of the average holding in Europe and the difficulty of acquiring any land of one's own at all. But the queer thing is that when the size of the homesteads was decided by Congress, it was clearly done with the aim of making the United States a country of small-holders. With the type of farming that was commonly practiced (the soil was exploited heavily, and manure and fallow were practically unknown), 160 acres was just enough to offer a family a reasonably good living. It would correspond to a Danish farm of approximately 90 acres. But as early as the first years of the twentieth century, there were complaints that the homesteads were too small, and a long, protracted process of amalgamation began and is still going on.

Soon after the first pioneers were breaking the soil here and there, the railroads arrived, a system of veins into the endless wilderness that created a never-ending circulation: people going West and money and goods going East. The large capital concentrations centered around the building of railroads were an important basis for the westward expansion; they were investments that produced unfathomable yields. Curiously enough, around 1880–1890, when the first stage of the settlement was past, the same capital organizations that had been a sine qua non of building the country now became the principal object of conflict in American politics.

Danish participation in the development described earlier began relatively late. A sparse flow of Danish immigrants can be traced quite early in the nineteenth century, but the stream did not gain importance until the time when the railroad construction reached its height, i.e., the late 1860s. Admittedly there were Danish emigrants who did not go to the United States, but those who did formed a majority so large that a description of the principal phases of their assimilation can serve as an introduction to the treatment of the emigrants' geographical destinations in the following section.

To tell the fates of the various Danish emigrants after they had left their home country could easily take years and fill volume after volume. Such an endeavor is clearly outside the scope of this work. The source materials concerning the development of the numerous Danish minorities that grew up gradually in the United States, Canada, Australia, and South America are far too extensive and widely spread. Furthermore, the subject has been treated by other historians. Few if any problems have enjoyed more thorough research than the subject of Danish overseas emigration before World War I. The demand for descriptions of the popular Danish movements in the United States developed in communities with Danish schools and congregations, especially in the Danish churches in Blair, Nebraska, and Grand View College of Des Moines, Iowa. The great period of Danish–American historiography was between the turn of the century and World War I, but even between the wars many valuable books and articles were published on the subject. The two major works, both with considerable breadth of outlook, are the Reverend P. S. Vig's book in two volumes, *Danske i Amerika* (1908), and Arne Hall-Jensen's *Den Dansk-americanske Historie* (1937). However, like the great majority of minor articles, both these books concentrate on biographies and on the histories of institutions. The aim of the authors was to portray the important personalities among the emigrants, which was perfectly understandable in their situation. Also, they believed that descriptions of the Danish–American high schools and churches would render an indirect description of the Danish minority. To a certain extent this is true, but still one feels the lack of an exhaustive sociohistorical description of Danish assimilation into American society. A study of this nature would be difficult to make now, so long after the era of mass emigration, but it is undoubtedly still possible to collect this valuable source material.

In Sweden various parties have recently undertaken the collection and processing of source material concerning assimilation. Even philologists may profitably take up the study of Danish–Americans. In some cases, the mother tongue of the emigrant has remained uninfluenced by the developments that changed the language in his home country since his departure. Very often the native dialect will be traceable through the American surface, even after the emigrant has been away for several decades. The process of assimilation is clearly distinguishable in the emigrant's letters to his native country. A cursory study of this material indicates that it was frequently a very short time before an emigrant was so affected by the new language as to let foreign words and phrases sneak into his Danish. In some cases this corruption of the native language would begin as early as a few months after the arrival of the immigrants.

The emigration registers that formed the basis of the present study give information on the destinations of the emigrants, and to a certain extent such data have also been computer processed. The statements in the registers are very exact, giving for the United States not only the state to which the emigrant planned to travel, but even the name of the minutest settlement on the prairie. Often there was not even a railroad station: The agent arranged transportation by ox-cart or with horses from the nearest station in the wilderness, and all was paid for in Copenhagen. In many ways it would have been valuable to include all these destinations in data in the computer files. We would have obtained a picture of the way in which a Danish settlement began, grew, or stagnated. But on the other hand, it would have incurred considerable difficulties and costs. For one thing, the number of localities is very large. During the year 1884, the emigration from the town of Odense alone contains statements of destination which include approximately 100 names of tiny settlements in the United States —not even including the larger, more well-known towns. The number would swell to something enormous if we were to collect the registrations from every county during the entire 32-year period.

Consequently, for this study detailed registering of American destination was abandoned. Only the state of destination is included, and within

Figure 13.1 The skyline of Manhattan in the background indicates that the emigrants are quite near their goal—the New World. The passage from Denmark to New York took 10–14 days in the 1880s, but only 1 week after about 1900. (This photo dates from the turn of the century and is part of the collection of the Genealogic Society, Salt Lake City, Utah.)

the state only one or two towns or settlements have been treated separately. A particularly strong argument against a detailed registration was that in many cases the stated destination may well not have been identical with the place where the emigrants finally settled. Mobility was much greater in the United States than in Denmark, and newly arrived immigrants tended to move far before choosing their new homes. If the destination chosen before departure from Denmark was a tiny group of farms on the plains the emigrant had heard about through correspondence, he may have intended to get a homestead or buy land there. But before he had reached that goal, the immigrant usually moved around to get work at other farms, or frequently became a railroad worker in order to earn the money to set up in farming.

In the course of 45 years, almost 285,000 Danes spread over most of the globe. But considering the number of new overseas countries that were competing for European immigrants, it would certainly not be true to say that these emigrants spead out at all evenly. As can be seen from Table 13.1, almost nine-tenths of them went to the United States. America was the big magnet at that time; and there was no exaggeration in the contemporary practice of speaking about the phenomenon as "America fever." If we include Canada in the United States emigration, we see that as few as 6 out of every 100 emigrants went to any other part of the world, a very small number indeed when we think of the natural resources and riches offered by all the other parts of the world, countries favored by far better climates and without the enormous competition from the other 94 immigrants to the United States. It is understandable that the America fever belonged primarily to the period before World War I. If we look at the emigration figures from the 1920s, we find that at that time the United States no

TABLE 13.1

Distribution of Danish Emigrants by Destination, 1869–1914

Country	Number	Percentage
United States	254,693	89.1
Canada	11,618	4.7
South America	9,315	3.3
Australia and New Zealand	6,973	2.3
South Africa	1,411	0.4
Asia	745	0.2
Other localities	12	0.0
Total	284,767	100.0

longer had the same importance it did previously. During the period 1921–1931, when there was still considerable overseas emigration, the total number of emigrants was almost 63,000 persons, and out of them only 34,200 (approximately 54%) chose the United States as their destination. The Canadian share of the total, on the other hand, rose to about 30%, so that these two destinations between them absorbed about 10% fewer than before the war. This reduction cannot be explained solely by the quota legislation introduced in 1921 and 1924 in the United States to limit immigration. The share of the Danish emigration going to America shows a constantly decreasing tendency as we get closer to the present. Table 13.2 shows that a somewhat altered distribution is reflected by the 36,800 emigrants of the period 1956–1960.

After 1945, the rigid American immigration restrictions made themselves felt. During the period before World War I, the Danish emigration appeared small compared to the great exodus from Norway and Sweden. Now the relation is the opposite: Danish overseas emigration during the same 5-year period, 1956–1960, is approximately double that of the other Scandinavian countries. The figures for Danish, Swedish, and Norwegian emigration in 1956–1960 follow:

Denmark	36,798
Norway	11,363
Sweden	18,280

Compared with earlier periods, Scandinavian countries have changed from being countries of emigration to actually having an immigration. Thus during the period mentioned, about 54,000 more persons immigrated to Sweden than departed. The flood of workers from southern European countries to Switzerland, West Germany, and Scandinavia has become the headache of northern Europe since World War II. This modern phenom-

TABLE 13.2

*Danish Emigration 1956–1960 and 1868–1924, Showing the Percentage
Going to Each Destination*

	1956–1960	1868–1924
United States	28.2	89.2
Canada	40.8	4.6
South America	6.1	3.3
Australia and New Zealand	11.6	2.3
Africa	6.4	0.4
Asia	6.9	0.2
Total	100.0	100.0

enon confirms the general impression that there is a close connection between migration and differences in the tempo of industrial expansion.

But during the time before 1914, America was a power that attracted millions. Within Scandinavia, the share of the emigration that went to the States varied considerably (see Table 13.3).

Although Danish emigrants obviously preferred the United States, a comparison with Norway and Sweden shows equally clearly that the Danes also had a certain tendency to try other destinations. Or it might be more exact to say that emigration from the other two Scandinavian countries showed an absolutely incredible one-sidedness. If we look at a sea-faring nation like Norway, whose merchant marine sailed all over the world, it is surprising to find that this cosmopolitanism resulted in 99.4% of its emigrants going to North America, while only a mere 0.6% investigated the rest of the world. Sweden was a little better on this point: The non-American world appealed to rather more than 1 out of every 100 Swedes. Obviously, special factors must have played a role as far as Denmark was concerned. If we look at the situation south of the Danish border, at the distribution of the German emigration, we find that the figure is just a little lower than the Danish one in roughly the same period: In 1871–1926, 84.6% of the German emigrants went to America. The difference is especially pronounced in the later years, 1918–1926. If these years are left out, the German level is approximately 89%.

It is difficult to offer an exact explanation for the difference between emigration from Denmark and that from Norway and Sweden. A hint may be found, however, in the observation that emigration to continents other

TABLE 13.3

Danish, Swedish, and Norwegian Emigration, 1871–1925, Showing the Percentage Going to Each Destination [a]

	Denmark	Sweden	Norway
United States	87.9	97.6	95.6
Canada	5.4	1.2	3.8
Central and South America	3.8	0.6	0.0
Australia and New Zealand	2.3	0.0	0.4
Africa	0.4	0.6	0.2
Asia	0.2	0.0	0.0
Total	100.0	100.0	100.0

[a] From Walter Wilcox, ed. *International Migration*, Vol. 18. New York: National Bureau of Economic Research, 1931, p. 299.

than North America is strongly concentrated around the urban areas, particularly Copenhagen. This may lead to the conclusion that the volume of emigrants to Australia, South America, etc., must be connected with the concentration of towns in the countries of emigration. We have already seen that towns played a more important part in Denmark (and likewise in Germany) than in Sweden and Norway. The emigration to Australia and South America especially was closely connected with propaganda campaigns arranged by the two receiving continents through immigration agents who usually settled in the capitals. Agents could establish contact with the urban population much more easily through the press than with the inhabitants of rural areas.

At any rate, it seems certain that the phenomenon does not have an explanation in a chronological development, i.e., that Denmark began just like Sweden and Norway, and then gradually invented destinations other than the United States. It is striking that once emigration has been directed almost solely toward one country, it will tend to continue in the same direction. Norwegian emigration provides a clear example of this: In 1914, 99.4% of the Norwegian emigrants went to the United States; and as late as 1956–1960, 96% of Norwegian emigrants still had the same destination, even though the volume was reduced.

The data shown in Table 13.4 depict the decennial American censuses on the number of Danish-born inhabitants in the United States. These figures give an impression of how Danish immigrants gradually came to form a not inconsiderable minority.

At the beginning, the increase approximates the emigration figures known from Denmark. Gradually the growth drops off: For 1900–1910, the increase is only 27,000, though we know that approximately 65,000 Danes came to the United States during the same 10 years. One reason

TABLE 13.4

Number of Danish-Born Persons in the United States and Decennial Increase, 1850–1910[a]

	Number	Increase
1850	1,838	
1860	9,950	8,112
1870	30,098	20,138
1880	64,196	34,098
1890	132,543	68,347
1900	154,616	22,043
1910	181,649	27,033

[a] Data from the 13th Census of the United States, 1910, Vol. 1. p. 784.

for this disparity is that death took its toll abroad as well as at home. Many of the early pioneers of Danish immigration died around the turn of the century, and during the years just before World War I, Danish immigrants consisted almost solely of a new generation. The old tanned emigrants of the sailing-ship era had become rare.

Measured against the Danish population, 250,000 persons is a huge number. But when a quarter of a million people mingle with the entire population of the United States, it does not appear to be much more than a few, especially if spread thinly across the whole country. In 1850, the Danish-born Americans amounted to only 0.1% of the population. By 1880 they formed 1%, and in 1900 as much as 1.5%. That was the peak, and since then the proportion of Danish as well as other western European immigrants has been on the wane, partly as a result of the new flood of immigration from Russia, the Balkans, and Italy. But the fact that the number of Danish emigrants increased constantly up until 1900 shows that emigration from Denmark, irrespective of its volume, was accelerating more quickly than emigration from other countries in western Europe during that period.

Aside from the reduction of the minorities caused by death and return emigration, the number of "Danish" Americans was increased by births. Thus it was found that in 1900, the Danish minority, apart from the 132,000 who were actually born in Denmark, consisted of another group of 151,415 persons born in the United States but whose parents were both born in Denmark. Is it really possible to call them second-generation Danes in the true sense of the word? Danes I have met in the United States have frequently stressed that this second generation showed a pronounced tendency to react against the national affiliation of their parents. They were working determinedly to become assimilated. But among the following generation—the third—one could find an increasing interest in national origins. The problems concerning assimilation among national minorities, a subject intensely cultivated in international sociological literature, is outside the scope of this book. The Danish minority in America, however, does seem to have special features compared with other nationalities, and it is tempting to touch on a few of these. But this attempt should only be taken as a sketch of possible future studies into the problem.

The density with which the immigrants from one country huddle together in the new country can be taken as a yardstick of the speed at which assimilation takes place. If they tend to build up independent societies in which the "natives" or immigrants of other nationalities form a minority, assimilation advances slowly. And conversely, where a national migration spreads thinly over a large area and the immigrants settle among

Americans and other immigrants, adaptation to the milieu of the new country and particularly its language will happen more quickly.

If we apply this criterion to immigration from various European countries to the United States, we find that the Danish group seems to be exceptional in that it spread out over many more states than did other European nationalities. Table 13.5 illustrates this situation. Several European countries are listed, with the three American states in which the largest number of emigrants from each country settled. The figures are from 1910, a time when the era of mass emigration was coming to an end.

Italy, with its more than 2 million emigrants, is a unique example of concentration. But even Denmark's near neighbor, Norway, had its emigrants grouped within a relatively narrow area, three northern states that border on Canada and the Great Lakes. A total of well over a quarter million persons (57.3% of all Norwegian immigrants) settled in Minnesota, North Dakota, and Wisconsin. For Denmark, however, the distribution is far more even. No single state received more than 11% of the Danish immigrants, the lowest figure that can be found for any of the 18 European countries analyzed in the census. Switzerland comes closest, with a percentage just above 11. When we note that emigration from that country was even smaller than that from Denmark, we might be inclined to conclude that the smaller the volume of emigration from a country, the less the emigrants will tend to group in colonies overseas.

Danish and Norwegian emigrations spread very differently, but the difference between Danish and Swedish emigrations is much less. Admit-

TABLE 13.5

Concentrations of National Minorities in American States, 1910 (expressed as percentages of all emigrants) [a]

Denmark		Sweden		Norway	
Iowa	10.4	Minnesota	19.6	Minnesota	28.6
Wisconsin	9.6	Illinois	16.9	Wisconsin	16.1
Minnesota	9.4	New York	6.9	North Dakota	12.6
Germany		*England*		*Ireland*	
New York	14.9	New York	14.7	New York	24.2
Illinois	12.2	Pennsylvania	12.5	Massachusets	14.1
Wisconsin	9.6	Massachusets	7.9	Pennsylvania	12.7
		Italy			
		New York	35.2		
		Pennsylvania	14.2		
		New Jersey	9.1		

[a] Data from the 13th Census of the United States, 1910, Vol. 1, pp. 898–899.

tedly the Swedes concentrated in Minnesota, where some 270,000 out of a total 1.3 million immigrants settled. But apart from this, the Swedish immigrants showed a considerable tendency to scatter. The so-called north central division had been the destination of 84% of the Norwegians in 1900, while only 64% of Swedes and Danes went to this part of the United States. The Swedes tended to stay in the towns, while the Norwegians and Danes generally became farmers.

In 1896, the Danish–American author John H. Bille published an account of Danish civilization in America, a polemic article with harsh attacks on the Grundvigian wing of the Danish church in the United States, but all the same containing a considerable amount of convincing statistical material concerning the problem of the exceptional tendency among the Danes to disperse widely in America. Bille tries to explain the reluctance of the Danes to gather in large groups, and he gives anything but a kind picture of his compatriots:

> His [the Dane's] love of personal advantage is liable to be greater than his love of country, home, and friends, for he is willing to part with them in order to better his fortune.

From the very detailed tables of the American censuses as to the "native" and "foreign-born" inhabitants of the country, one can read much about the assimilation of the Scandinavian minorities. One table, for instance, gives the parental situation of children of immigrants. It shows that out of the total number of children of Swedish immigrants, 72% had both parents of Swedish origin, while the other 28% had one parent of some other nationality. Out of 255,000 Danish emigrant children, only 57% had parents who were both Danish. Another 28% had one parent of American origin, while the last 15% had a parent from some other national minority. The figures may mean that the Danes mingled more with the local population, but another interpretation is possible, too: These figures may merely confirm the earlier mentioned disparity between the numbers of male and female Danish emigrants compared to the almost even balance found among the Swedish emigrants. Many Danish men were forced to look for a wife among the other nationalities. Out of second-generation Danish–Americans in 1910, 37,700 had a Danish-born father while the mother belonged to some other national minority. The census even tells which of these minorities Danish men preferred.

We learn that approximately one-third chose German-born immigrants, and that the other Nordic countries came behind Germany, although the prevailing Danish nationalist point of view at the time might suggest that Scandinavian girls would be preferable. Admittedly, the German element of the American population was so numerous that the distribution is indeed reasonable. But if we draw in the corresponding figures for Norway, we find that the 33,800 Norwegian men of "mixed" marriages had a dominating preference for other Scandinavians as wives: Sixty-seven percent had a Danish or Swedish wife. The situation is exactly the same where the wife is Danish or Norwegian and the husband is the "foreign" element.

One more piece of evidence of the Danish disinclination to stick together with other Danes, compared to the attitude of the Swedes and the Norwegians, should be mentioned. The yardstick used here is the support of the Danish church in America by the immigrants, seen in relation to the total Danish minority and compared with the corresponding situation in the Swedish and Norwegian minorities. The data come from a statistical survey published in 1906 by the Reverend A. M. Andersen of Blair, Nebraska, and according to Andersen the data are based on public statistics. The following of the churches is measured by the number of communicants, i.e., those taking part in the services of the churches. In 1902, the Danish churches in America were divided into two synods: the United Danish Lutheran Church and the Danish Lutheran Church, the distinction between them being that the former was "united" and the latter was not. Together they mustered a total of a little more than 41,000 churchgoers. The number of Danish-born immigrants, according to the 1900 census, was about 154,000, so that just over 25% supported the church. Almost 259,000 Norwegian immigrants out of a total of 338,000, or more than 75%, supported the four existing Norwegian church organizations in America in 1900. As for the Swedes, one common church group, the Augustana Synod, had been established, and approximately 40% of the Swedish immigrants were associated with the group. Even if these "numbers of communicants" are undoubtedly defective in some ways, the tendency is so clear that we can maintain that the Danes took less part in nationalistic activities in America, and that therefore they assimilated with the local population more quickly than did the other Scandinavians.

The question as to whether Danish–Americans should strive to keep their native language alive and force the next generation to learn it, or whether it was more important to assimilate as quickly as possible among the Americans, was one that divided the different Danish church organizations. Enok Mortensen has given a picture of their perpetual warfare, which covered many other problems besides language. The Grundtvig wing, led by Frederik Lange Grundtvig, son of the famous Danish prophet, maintained the first view: that representatives of Danish civilization should stick together and keep their patriotic feelings alive by being brought up with the Danish language, school, and church. For this purpose, the Grundtvig wing established five folk high schools between the years 1878 and 1888: Elk Horn in Iowa, Ashland in Michigan, Polk in Wisconsin, Nysted in Nebraska, and Tyler in Minnesota. They even tried their hand at bigger projects, according to which the scattered Danes were to gather in large colonies like the Norwegians and Swedes and form purely Danish settlements. In 1883, the Grundtvig church organization entered into business relations with a "land company" and obtained an option on 35,000 acres of land in Lincoln County, Minnesota, which were sold to Danish settlers. The project became a success. Within 1 year, 100 Danish families had bought land there and formed a colony around the town of Tyler with their own school, church, and folk high school. Another attempt at the same thing in 1888 in western Kansas proved a failure, however.

The followers of the Inner Mission (the other faction of the Danish church) in the United States were fiercely opposed to these efforts at keeping up Danish culture. The leader of this movement, the Reverend P. S. Vig of Blair, Nebraska, wrote an article in 1888 which became a kind of manifesto. He believed that:

> We should indeed serve ourselves and our children poorly by
> doing all in our power to prevent them from becoming American-
> ized. . . . Even if the Danish language is lost to our posterity, they
> might retain all that is good and true in the Danish character.

Disagreement on this vital point contributed to the vehement fighting and distintegration within the Danish Lutheran Church, which reached a state of crisis after 1894. There was a constant unrest in these organizations, which may have been the reason why so many Danish–Americans avoided them.

The explanation for the Danish tendency to keep little contact with fellow countrymen in the new country was hardly the one given by John A. Bille, that their desire for personal wealth was stronger than their love for their country. The whole problem is more complex than that. One reason seems particularly to stand out, namely, that the Danish emigration began so much later than that from Norway and Sweden. During the earliest phase of emigration, in the time of the sailing ships before 1860, emigration was to a very large extent confined to large groups that set out for America under the leadership of an experienced person and intended to settle at a definite location.

The Swedish and Norwegian emigration of the 1840s and the 1850s may have established a tradition that survived even after the shipowners and agents began to organize most of the emigration after 1866. The larger the settlements that had been formed before the Civil War, the greater their attraction to new emigrants who flocked across the Atlantic on their own. The number of Scandinavians in the United States by 1860 seems consequently to indicate the extent to which the members of the individual nationalities would settle close together in the following years:

Norwegians	44,000
Swedes	18,625
Danes	9,900

Since 80% of the Norwegians in 1890 were living in almost purely Norwegian settlements, this may indicate that these settlements or areas were already thriving, and therefore attractive, by 1860. And conversely, in 1860, there were only a few small Danish settlements, and they offered little attraction when mass emigration began around 1880.

The choice of destination is one of the major problems in connection with mass emigration overseas. When a young farmer's son from some Danish island contacted a Copenhagen emigration agent in April, 1884, with the intention of going to the United States, how would he know that he wanted to go to Monoa, a tiny settlement in the western part of Iowa? Nevertheless that was what happened every day of the year. By far the majority of the Danish emigrants before 1914 asked for a ticket to a very specific spot on the American continent. Only a few traveled in the way we normally expect emigrants to travel: a ticket to New York and the rest left to fate. Out of the total Danish emigration during the years 1868-1900, only one-third (35%) or 54,792 persons set out with tickets to New York and no further. From there they spread over the rest of the country, except for some 5600 Danes who got "caught" in the metropolis. Chicago was another junction where hundreds of thousands of immigrants stayed for shorter or longer periods before fanning out to the small towns and rural areas of the prairies. The total Danish emigration to Chicago amounted to about 15,000, or 10% of the entire Danish emigration.

The rest of the Danes emigrating to America before 1900, over 88,800 persons, knew before they set out precisely to which state, county, and settlement they were going, possibly to spend the rest of their lives. How did they know?

The two figures tempt us to see the problem in a larger context. Could the explanation be that the 88,800 emigrants with a definite destination represent the number of persons who were pulled across the Atlantic by encouraging letters, prepaid tickets, and sums of money sent home? Is that the true reason why they knew all about their destinations? Are they, in other words, the objects of the genuine pull factor in emigration? Such a large number — 88,800 persons, or 56% of all the emigrants — can hardly have had such definite destinations without something quite concrete to pull them to that place, either a job or a certain person. Conversely, the other 69,000 who went to New York or Chicago represent those who traveled without an "invitation," seeking happiness at random wherever it might be. That does not mean that we can call these 69,000 persons representatives of a push movement. Their way of migrating merely means that generally it was not a concrete offer that enticed them to leave home. Admittedly we are out on thin ice here, because the entire material comprises a number of individual fates, each with its own history. But the figures presented later concerning the number of prepaid tickets and money transferred to the relations and friends of Danish emigrants illustrates that the figures cannot be completely wrong: Approximately 55% of the emigrants were pulled across the Atlantic by personal contacts. If anything, the figure is probably too low.

One of the combinations in the data processing which might help to shed light on emigration is a juxtaposition of the destination abroad and latest residence in Denmark. This might give us an idea whether certain parts of Denmark had favorite destinations abroad—whether people from Funen or Zealand tended to settle in specific areas in the United States.

It is practical to start by examining the origin of those who merely went to New York and spread out from there later, i.e., the group of 54,000 persons mentioned earlier. There is a clear tendency for urban emigrants to dominate among emigrants in this category. An especially large part of the Copenhagen emigration followed this pattern. Out of 31,800 emigrants from Copenhagen, more than 13,800 had tickets to New York in their pockets. It seems possible that a very large number of these emigrants had the intention of settling in some American city, wherever they might find work. Many of them may have been craftsmen planning to go on the tramp from New York in hopes of making a living from their craft as they traveled. It seems safe to assume that if an emigrant intended to get a homestead, he would not go to New York alone, but would take a ticket directly to the farming regions or possibly to Chicago.

A particularly pronounced example of urban emigrants preferring tickets only as far as New York is found in emigration from Bornholm, which was of a dominantly urban character. Out of 3300 emigrants from the seven picturesque towns on Bornholm, more than 45% went to New York. Generally, people from Bornholm went to different places in the United States from their fellow countrymen. Thus a large part of them went to the old New England states and Pennsylvania, which may be the reason that so many preferred tickets to New York only. Out of the rural emigration from Bornholm, not less than 10% went to Pennsylvania alone, a very high percentage when we remember that only 1.8% of the total

Danish emigration settled there. So a considerable fraction of the 2500 Danish-born Pennsylvanians in 1900 must have spoken the melodic Bornholm language, perhaps with an American accent.

If we look more closely at the Danish-born settlers in the big farming states west of Chicago and map out the approximately 50,000 persons according to their origin in Denmark, we find, predictably, that they came mostly from rural Denmark. That was where a large part of the landless Danish rural population would settle if they did not want to make a complete change and become factory workers.

But it is a surprise, however, to see how differently the Danes in the individual American states dispersed in relation to their origin in the various parts of Denmark. We see it from Table 13.6, which gives the origins of the Danes living in the four farming states—the region where we most often find them: Wisconsin, Minnesota, Iowa, and Nebraska. The first three states mentioned received about 11,000 Danes each, and Nebraska only about 8000. For the sake of clarity, Denmark is divided into very few regions.

Copenhagen and to some extent the provincial towns are clearly underrepresented. This is particularly the case in Iowa, where the largest number of Danes settled. About 75% of the more than 11,800 Danes who traveled directly to Iowa came from Danish rural areas, and only 25% from the capital and other towns. In the other states in Table 13.6, the rural percentage of the emigrants is not quite as high as that, generally in the neighborhood of 70%.

TABLE 13.6

Danish-Born Immigrants to Four American States, Grouped According to Last Residence in Denmark, 1868–1900 (in percentages)

Region in Denmark	Total emigration	Wisconsin	Minnesota	Iowa	Nebraska
Copenhagen	18.5	7.5	9.3	5.6	7.8
Urban areas:					
in east Denmark	11.6	13.5	9.9	7.5	7.9
in Jutland	15.3	8.5	9.1	8.8	11.2
Rural areas:					
in east Denmark	26.7	47.6	41.3	36.0	31.9
in Jutland	24.0	21.9	28.6	37.3	39.0
Schleswig and unknown	3.9	1.0	1.8	4.8	2.2
Total	100.0	100.0	100.0	100.0	100.0

A particularly interesting aspect clearly illustrated in this table is that eastern Denmark and Jutland contributed so differently to the populations of the four states. If we look at the two states mentioned first, Wisconsin and Minnesota, we find that the rural areas of eastern Denmark are represented by approximately double the number from rural Jutland. This is particularly so in Wisconsin: Here the dominance of eastern Denmark is even clearer in the figures for provincial towns. We can establish that more than 60% of the Danish population of Wisconsin was from eastern Denmark minus Copenhagen. But it can be defined even more precisely, namely, that the emigration to Wisconsin was distinctly concentrated in two Danish counties, southern Zealand and Lolland-Falster, which between them contributed more than one-half of the 60% (31.6%).

Michigan has not been included in Table 13.6, as the Danish immigration to that area was only half that to the other states. Out of 6000 Danish immigrants to Michigan, 4160 came from eastern Denmark minus Copenhagen, i.e., about 70%, and among them again more than one-half from southern Zealand and Lolland-Falster.

An examination of the Danish population of Minnesota shows a more even distribution by origin in Denmark, but still with a clear domination of rural people from the islands but without marked predominance of specific localities.

The last two states in Table 13.6, Iowa and especially Nebraska, were dominated not by emigrants from eastern Denmark but from Jutland. Out of 100 Danish-born immigrants, 40 came from eastern Denmark (outside Copenhagen) and almost 50 from Jutland, although at that time the Jutland emigration represented roughly 41% of the registered emigration. In Iowa the region of Jutland north of the Limfjord dominated. In Nebraska the distribution is more even; the northern part of Jutland is of relatively less importance, and the Århus region alone provided one-fourth of the emigrants.

In the Dakotas, the Danish contribution to the population was small, only about 2500 persons. Consequently the majority of the approximately 7000 Danish-born persons who lived in those two states in 1900 must have been arrivals from other states. Among those who came without detours to the Dakotas, the region of Thy was particularly heavily represented, i.e., by one-third of the total. In Zealand, there was a special interest in the Dakota prairie in Sorø county, which provided more immigrants to the Dakotas than did the whole of Copenhagen.

We see then that these four Midwestern states have varying mixtures of people from Jutland and eastern Denmark. In Wisconsin and Minnesota (as in Michigan), most emigrants came from the eastern area of Denmark, whereas in Iowa and Nebraska, Jutland dominated. This can hardly be pure coincidence, and a highly probable explanation is found in the time factor, which has so far not been taken into consideration. Until about 1875, Wisconsin, Michigan, and Minnesota were among the open states which carried on propaganda campaigns to attract immigrants. Partly as a result of the huge wave of Swedish and Norwegian emigrants in the late 1860s, these two states were soon peopled and all homesteads were brought under cultivation. Iowa and Nebraska, on the contrary, were still "open space" as late as 1880, where untilled and consequently cheap homesteads were obtainable for new arrivals. In 1885, emigration from Denmark was still absolutely dominated by the eastern regions. Jutland did not really come into the picture until after 1885, but then it dominated until the turn of the century.

The aim of this chapter has been to give some indications of problems and perspectives in connection with distribution and assimilation, revealed by a cursory study of the basic statistical material. It is a subject that ought to be studied as an independent work based mainly on American materials.

14

RETURN EMIGRATION

Homesickness became an important factor in the emotional life of the emigrants. To some it was an unbearable pain which could not be relieved until they were aboard the steamer that was to carry them past the Statue of Liberty back to Europe. To others it was just a sentiment that was satisfied through intense correspondence with relatives in Europe. In any case, the European large-scale migration caused emotional conflicts of untold numbers among the 50 million people involved. Practically everyone in modern times knows examples of the emigrant's psychological dilemma, the feeling of rootlessness after years spent abroad. In numerous cases where homesickness was a constant evil to the emigrants, they returned to their starting point, in this case, Denmark. But often they found it difficult to fit in again. The home country was not what it had been when they left it. Its idyllic cast was gone; the people were not the same ones; and the longing reverted toward the overseas country they had left with the milieu, friends, and possibly children who stayed abroad. The result was sometimes complicated cases of restlessness, psychological difficulties, perhaps especially among those who became wealthy abroad, for whom a move was of minor economic consequence.

But among the emigrants, there must have been many who, on the day of departure, had no feeling of being about to take leave of their home country forever. Many, perhaps even a majority, found comfort in the thought that after a few years in America they would return. After having "struck gold" in the states, they would go home and enjoy their wealth, some in open-handed lavishness, others in some specific investment such as a small shop or farm. (See Figure 14.1.)

This expectation of a happy return tempered the bitterness of the leave-taking, relieved the minds of those left behind, but was often eclipsed after arrival by the new exciting surroundings overseas, and by the fact that the gold was not quite so near at hand as the emigrants had been led to believe. The idea of returning to the Old Country with hardly more riches than one had taken along seemed less attractive, even if the longing was great.

This confused mixture of human emotions forms an important element in the system of causes and effects in migrations. The emotional factor influenced all aspects of the statistics of emigrations: the annual emigration, the statistical relationship between men and women, and the age structure of the national minorities that gradually developed in the countries of immigration. But in no other connection was the emotional element of such importance as with return emigration, a movement of sizable dimensions.

Unfortunately the true size of the return migration of several countries is a statistically obscure subject. This is particularly the case in Denmark. As early as the late 1890s, the arrival of the annual "Christmas ships" from the United States was a well-known and much discussed event. Danish–Americans crowded down the gangways eager to see the Old Country again. But how many in these crowds were just visiting, and how many came to stay for the rest of their lives? The Danish statistics are of no help in this problem. That a person had spent half his life in the United States was not entered anywhere. What figures we do have indicate that a return emigration of any importance did not begin until after 1890, and this fact was the result of several natural causes. One of them is that the Danish minority did not reach any considerable number until then; another that the means of transportation were so primitive prior to that point that only a few of those who had tried a crossing once would have the courage to repeat the experience. Also one must remember that after 1890 it became very difficult to find free homesteads. After the 1893 crisis in America very few farms were established, and it seems that these were the very years in which return emigration grew to a considerable level.

Figure 14.1 The returning emigrant with his elegant dress, his Yankee manners, and his many dollars was much admired in provincial Denmark—but sometimes the public also made some fun of him as in this ballad from 1904 about the piano worker who had lived in good circumstances in America, loved many girls, but in spite of all preferred his Danish girlfriend.

But even in the early period of mass emigration there were quite a few who ventured to return to Denmark for shorter visits. From the police archives, the number of persons departing to the United States with Danish names who had stated America as their last place of residence can be ascertained. Although the figures belong to the years 1875–1878, i.e., a period of depression in America as well as in Denmark, they are not negligible: In these 4 years there were 233, 218, 258, and 260 persons respectively. Another group of returned Danish–Americans had come to stay in Denmark, and by 1876 they were apparently numerous enough to establish a club. In the newspapers of March 12, 1876, the following advertisement appeared:

> *United States Club.* In accordance with the mandate given at the meeting at No. 3, Jernbanegade, all Danes returned from the United States are hereby called upon to attend a first general meeting at 8 o'clock on March 18th at No. 7, Kronprinsessegade, the old Free Masons' building.

The effect of economic trends upon the figures for return emigration is clearly visible from Swedish statistics, which give the annual return emigration from 1875 without interruption. There is even evidence that some returning persons had not given up the United States, but were merely returning home to wait for more favorable times before emigrating once more. In 1884 a Danish newspaper wrote:

> Because of the present extremely low wages in the U.S.A., some of the Scandinavian emigrants there have found it profitable, in spite of considerable traveling expenses incurred, to spend the winter in their native countries. *Skånska Aftonbladet* reports that on November 22, 600 Danish, Swedish, and Norwegian workers returned to their home countries, and that on December 6, another 400 arrived from New York. When spring arrives with increasing wages, the majority of them will very likely return to the U.S.A.

Seasonal migrations of this kind must obviously impair the importance of returned emigration statistics.

How many of the 285,000 Danish emigrants did in fact return to Denmark? Probably more than we might expect. An estimate based on the total European immigration to North and South America during the period 1821–1924 showed that no less than 30% must have migrated back to their home countries. For Argentina, the figure is as high as 47%.

Some facts seem to indicate that the corresponding figures for the Scandinavian countries cannot have a similar magnitude. The Swedish figures for the period 1871–1908 are about 109,000 persons out of a total emigration of about 900,000, or about 12 returns per 100 emigrants.

From 1908, the United States recorded return emigration by use of the registration of the number of "citizens" who left America with the intention of abandoning their citizenship to settle in some other country. For Denmark, the return emigration figures from the United States to Denmark for the subsequent years (1908–1914) were as follows:

1908	689	1912	665
1909	460	1913	608
1910	433	1914	629
1911	468		

On an average, these figures give a return emigration of 8.6%, which is less than the corresponding figure for Sweden. The American records should clearly be viewed with some skepticism. Ingrid Semmingsen has demonstrated that they are too low for Norwegians by comparing them to Norwegian statistics on returned Americans, which showed a total of 58,000 persons who had resettled in Norway in 1920.

The Norwegian study of returned Americans, included in the ordinary census in 1920, is of considerable interest to other countries as well. Among other things, an investigation was made as to the length of time the returned persons had spent in the United States before leaving. The results are given in Table 14.1.

Three-quarters of all return emigrants had been away for 9 years or less. Old people from the pioneer period returned as pensioners only to a very limited extent; the majority were still able-bodied. Women especially showed a tendency to return relatively soon.

TABLE 14.1

Length of Stay in America for Norwegian Return Emigrants (in percentages) [a]

	Men	Women
2–4 years	33.5	37.3
5–9 years	38.4	39.6
10–19 years	21.3	16.8
20 years and more	6.0	4.6
Not stated	0.8	1.7
Total	100.0	100.0

[a] Data from Ingrid Semmingsen, *Veien mot Vest*, Vol. 2, 1950, p. 570.

Another interesting feature is the occupational flexibility seen among the Norwegian returned emigrants. While in the United States most of them had been employed in mining and industry, only one-tenth of them had been farmers. But home in Norway the picture was different: Now some 40% of them took up farming, while only 10% found work in industry. They all returned to their childhood milieu, the place where they were born and still hoped to find romance. Of all the returned male Americans, 82% settled in the rural parishes where they were born. For women, the percentage was lower, as a wife tended to accompany her husband to his home place.

15

PERSONAL CONTACT
ACROSS THE ATLANTIC

When an emigrant vessel was about to sail from Copenhagen and hundreds of emigrants were taking a tear-stained leave of an even larger number of friends and relations, a comforting word was needed to make the farewell less painful. This might be either "I'll be back soon," or, more likely, solemn promises to write many letters to those at home. The majority of the emigrants were not practiced letter writers. Proficiency of expression was limited among the masses in Denmark, but separation from family as well as exciting new experiences forced many an emigrant to take up his pen. However brief and clumsy such letters were, they were read and even studied intensely, read aloud to many people, passed from one house to the next, and even occasionally printed in a newspaper. Here is an example of a letter from a paper in Jutland, given in part:

Omaha, 5th October, 1862

My dear father, dear friends, sisters, brothers and friends,

It is with pleasure I take my pen into my hand to tell you of our present home, Omaha, where we are very satisfied. We have one big black cow and one heifer. I have built a cowshed and have got 6 cartloads of hay. I immediately found work with a carriage factory where I am making 60 rigsdaler of Danish money per month, on which I can easily support myself as food is much cheaper here than in Denmark. A worker earns one dollar or about 2 Danish rigsdaler per day. One sack of good wheat flour, 100 pounds, costs 2 dollars, meat 8 skilling Danish money per pound, butter 20 skilling; everything is so cheap that poverty is unknown.

It is only after this minor treatise on national economics that our emigrant arrives at the sad news that four of his children died during the recent voyage. The order of the various news items was not due merely to lack of writing skill, but also the vivid impression American plenty made on a poverty-stricken Dane who had lived his entire life close to starvation. The realization that one could obtain food and clothing without continual struggle was the unique piece of news that had to be told to those still at home.

As a whole these letters conveyed a relatively attractive impression of conditions in America, Canada, or Australia. Emigrants who did not succeed in the New World (and they were a not inconsiderable number) would probably be less inclined to grasp the pen to describe their misery, except in cases where the description ended in an appeal for a return ticket. Others might chose to hide the rags of their existence under an enthusiastic picture of America. But the large majority, those who landed in the northwestern states or on the Canadian prairie, gave a relatively accurate view of what the individual person saw of the details of this macrocosm, a picture that may easily have tempted the readers. The letters from across the ocean became one of the most important incentives in mass emigration, an unparalleled pull factor.

The influence of the letters on the volume of emigration is generally accepted, but, nevertheless, emigration literature seems to show no endeavor to give a concrete impression of personal communication between emigrants and their home country. From Danish source material it is possible to make a quantitative calculation of the personal communication across the Atlantic and present a comparison with the fluctuations of the emigration. There were three ways emigrants could give personal stimulus to further emigration. One was by means of the already mentioned letters; another (and more direct way) was by remitting money to relatives at home; and a third way was the very direct one of sending prepaid tickets for the trip.

Let us first treat letter communication between North America and

Denmark. Two years before the establishment of the International Postal Union, the Danish Post Office began making statistics on the number of arriving and departing letters between Denmark and foreign countries. These tables were published in the annual reports of the Danish Post Office from 1872–1873. Figure 15.1 illustrates the number of letters passing between America and Denmark during the period 1872–1914.

Until 1886, the figures cover the entire American continent including South America and Central America, after that time only the United States and Canada. If we assume, as seems very likely, that the majority of these letters were sent by immigrants and their relations, the general impression one gets from the graph is that more letters were sent from immigrants to their families at home than vice versa. Particularly noticeable in the graph is that the exchange of letters had fluctuations just like the flow of emigrants. In the case of letters from the United States to Denmark, the first major increase begins about 1880, concurrent with the increase in emigra-

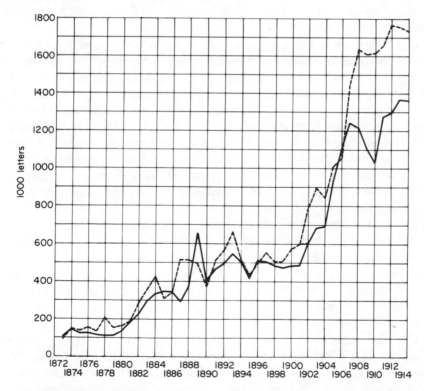

Figure 15.1 Number of letters between the United States and Denmark, 1872–1914. Those from Denmark to the United States are represented by a solid line; those from the United States to Denmark are represented by a dashed line.

tion. The flow of letters from America culminates in 1883–1884, when 423,500 letters were sent across the Atlantic to Denmark, whereas the peak in the emigration was the previous year, 1882. The fact that the flow of letters continued to increase after this peak year is presumably the consequence of the large number of new immigrants who wrote home very frequently, especially during the first period after arrival. However, from the summer of 1884, the effects of the severe economic crisis in America that culminated in 1885 began to make themselves felt. The flow of letters from the United States suddenly fell by more than 25%. Smarting from the recession, Danish emigrants wrote 110,000 letters less than in the year before. They were ducking under during the crisis, and, be it cause or effect, the immigration of 1885 was 32% lower than that of the previous year. After the crisis, the number of letters reached new heights. During the following years, emigration ran more or less parallel to the stream of letters from the United States. Both have peaks in 1887 and 1893. The big collapse in the first months of 1893, "the panic of '93," was followed by a depression, and a pronounced drop in the volume of both letters and emigrants.

After 1900 there was a considerable increase in the number of letters between the United States and Denmark, and surprisingly, the volume of Europe-bound mail was much larger than the westbound mail after the year 1905. It seems likely that part of the explanation lies in commercial correspondence from the United States, as the same period saw a tenfold increase in imports from America to Denmark. Between 1895 and 1906, the value of imports rose from 10 million to 129 million crowns per year. In 1910, however, it fell to 52 million. It ought to be mentioned here that after the 1880s these imports comprised, aside from cotton and tobacco, fresh pork and beef that were directly re-exported from pork-producing Denmark to Germany.

The increase in the number of letters to Denmark after 1900 must be viewed as a result of the steadily increasing number of Danish-born immigrants in the United States, a development that was in line with the general increase in emigration from Denmark. But a calculation of the average annual number of letters home per immigrant from Denmark suggests that part of the increase after 1900 must be commercial correspondence, as Table 15.1 shows.

The rise after 1905 is so large and sudden (the number of letters doubled), that it would be unreasonable to explain it as an increased inclination toward letter writing, even if improvements in education made letter writing less of a burden. Between three and four letters per year must be regarded as the average. But even just one letter might cause emigration

TABLE 15.1

Average Annual Number of Letters from Denmark to the United States

Period	Danish-born in the U.S.A.	Average number of letters	Letters per year per Danish immigrant
1875–1885	64,200	238,200	3.6
1885–1895	132,500	493,600	3.7
1895–1905	154,600	586,500	3.8
1905–1914	181,600	1,283,000	7.1

to spread throughout a region, like circles from a stone dropped in water, if it arrived at the right time and in the right place.

From the beginning of large-scale emigration, the "rich uncle in America" became a legendary person to the population of Europe. To many immigrants, even if they were fighting a harsh struggle for existence against severe economic difficulties, it was a matter of pride to be able to send money to the family in Europe. To some national groups, particularly Italian and Spanish rural laborers, who had left behind a numerous family of several generations, the postal order to the Old Country became an obligation of immense dimensions.

An investigation in the United States showed that in 1907 alone, immigrants sent home a total of $275 million to Europe. A distribution among the different nationalities gives the interesting picture seen in Table 15.2. The national dissimilarities in this table are obvious. Immigrants from the Mediterranean countries sent home every dollar they could save, while German and English immigrants tended to send an occasional trifle to their families. The phenomenon is particularly clear in the case of the

TABLE 15.2

Capital Sent Home by Immigrants in the United States in 1907, Grouped by Nationality

Country	Total dollars in millions	Dollars per immigrant
Italy	70	30.0
Austria–Hungary	65	28.1
England	25	7.1
Scandinavia	25	15.0
Russia	25	14.5
Germany	15	4.1
Greece	5	50.0

relatively small number of Greeks in the United States, who sent home by far the largest amounts per person. An inquiry in the 1920s made by Fairchild showed how the transmitted capital was the direct cause of a serious financial crisis in Greece. The rate of exchange of the current standard, the gold franc, fell from 160 to 108 and caused a pronounced rise in the Greek cost of living. The problem was that the capital sent home was not invested: Families who received money from America frequently stopped working or spent the money on a new tower for the village church! But by and large, such transferred capital was a considerable advantage for the receiving countries, which thus gained a chance to invest capital and import goods. The fact that the value of Danish imports from the United States for the period 1905–1910 was greater than that of English imports may be connected with the considerable dollar resources created by transferred capital.

In the case of Denmark, we are able to study the amounts of money sent home by Danish emigrants to the United States as far back as 1879, this being the year when the Danish Post Office started publishing details as to postal order remittances between Denmark and the United States. The only problem is whether the figures are a true expression of the volume of money remitted by immigrants. The postal order was the most frequently used means of money transfer for private persons, while banks and stockbrokers were mostly used by businessmen. The maximum limit of $50 per postal order made them virtually useless for import or export business.

But then it is also probable that money was, particularly during the earlier periods, sent across the Atlantic through other channels besides the mail service. European emigration agents made extensive use of money orders, a money transfer dependent on agency connections in the United States.

From Table 15.2 we see that in 1907 Scandinavians sent home an average of $15, or, in Danish money at an estimated rate of exchange of 3.60, 54 crowns. In 1907–1908, the amount conveyed by postal order from the United States to Denmark totaled 2,338,994 crowns, or about 13 crowns per Danish-born American at that time. This indicates that only part of the amounts sent home from the United States went by mail.

Figure 15.2, which shows the money transfers from the United States to Denmark, is very similar to that showing the volume of letters. The most striking detail is the increase after the turn of the century. This graph shows the fall after 1893, an unmistakable reaction to the panic in January, 1893. The income of the immigrants suffered and there was less to spare for those in the Old Country. Both graphs also show a temporary improvement in 1896, which again was superseded by a new decline lasting

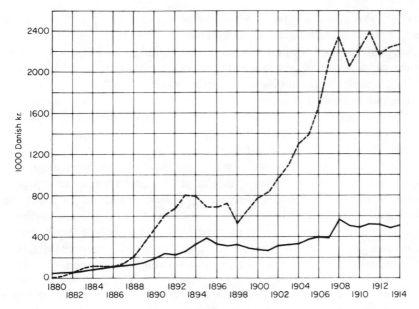

Figure 15.2 Money transfers between the United States and Denmark by postal order, 1879–1914. Money sent from the United States to Denmark is represented by a dashed line; money sent from Denmark to the United States is represented by a solid line.

until the great rise after 1898. The solid line of the graph describes money transfers from Denmark to the United States, and shows among other things a small rise in 1894, the worst year of the depression. This would seem to indicate a certain amount of help sent from Denmark to immigrants suffering from unemployment in America. The 1908 crisis shows a similar drop in money sent home, but here it is significant that the corresponding increase in money sent from Denmark occurred 1 year earlier.

A large part of the amounts from the United States was presumably sent home to families whose breadwinners had emigrated first, and were supporting them from abroad until they could afford to send money for their tickets to America. It is a surprising fact, however, that a calculation of the average amount per postal order within the individual years showed relatively small figures, and remained, contrary to expectation, remarkably unchanged during the entire period. For orders sent from the United States to Denmark, the average started at about 80 crowns, but by 1886 it was down to about 62 crowns per order. Until 1914, it remained on the whole at roughly 60 crowns. This suggests that some of the payments may have been of a particularly obligatory nature: contributions toward the maintenance of illegitimate children were approximately 50 crowns a year in 1886. This was the kind of obligation that could not be left behind, at least morally, even by emigration.

Another kind of regular payment from immigrants might be money for the support of their parents in Denmark. At that time social legislation was still undeveloped, and old-age support was to a large extent dependent on the old system of the previous owner of a farm receiving a pension from his successor, and similar arrangements. When the younger generation emigrated, they would obviously retain their obligations to their parents. It will hardly suffice to interpret all the large amounts of money sent to Europe from the United States as generous donations from rich uncles, but they did exist to an extent large enough to tempt many a poor Danish worker. The hope of obtaining riches enough to distribute to others was indeed attractive. In many cases the money was accompanied by a letter saying that it was to be used for a ticket to New York, but in such cases there was another, more direct, method, the prepaid ticket. This solution was, as we shall see in the following, widely used.

Letters with picturesque descriptions of conditions in overseas countries might make a poor European restless and be an incentive to emigration. Money sent from America might convert a dream into reality, but the most direct way of pulling thousands of new emigrants across the Atlantic to the new countries was to send prepaid tickets for the entire voyage from Denmark to the sender. Letters and money sent home might leave the receiver in some doubt as to whether emigration was the right thing to do; but once the prepaid ticket arrived the decision was made. It would be difficult to refuse, and the risk could not be so great after all when the transportation in one direction was already paid.

The prepayment system was naturally used often by the heads of families who had left their wives and children behind until they found work and homes in America. Many men emigrated with the intention of obtaining a homestead, working for 1 year for the railroad to save money for equipment, a house, and tickets for the rest of the family. The same system must in many cases have served to bring less remote relations from Europe to America.

From 1877, we have lists compiled every 3 months showing all transactions executed by some Danish emigration agents stating the amount of cash paid and the number of prepaid tickets. At the beginning, the compilation work was done by a policeman as an extra job and covered only a certain number of the agents. Until the mid-1880s, only one group of departing emigrants was registered this way, i.e., those who set out via Liverpool. But even so, the figures can probably be taken as representative of the entire emigration, as it was possible to buy and send home tickets for the German lines and the Danish Thingvalla Line. Table 15.3 shows an annual survey of the percentage of the total emigrants of these lines who held prepaid tickets.

Between one-fourth and one-third of the emigrants during the 1880s were pulled across the Atlantic to the New World in this way. We can almost say that for this large group of emigrants, the decision to emigrate was made in America.

Irrespective of whether these prepaid tickets were sent by fathers to their families or by other immigrants, the percentages given in this table are virtually an expression of the pull exerted on the countries of emigration from the overseas countries. In itself, the realization that about one-fourth of the Danish emigration wave of the 1880s was prepaid from the United States may seem impressive, and may indeed open up new perspectives for understanding the dynamics of mass emigration. But a comparison with the very few clues that exist in the Norwegian and Swedish sources shows that the share of prepaid tickets in Danish emigration is particularly small. In the case of Norway we know that out of 18,372 emigrants departing from Christiania between 1872 and 1875, 7247, or almost 40%, held prepaid tickets. From the Danish source material, in-

TABLE 15.3

Prepaid Tickets in Relation to the Annual Total Emigration, 1877–1895

Year	Emigration	Prepaids	Percentage of prepaids in total
1877	1,932	283	14.6
1878	3,151	449	14.2
1879	3,848	495	12.9
1880		figures missing	
1881	6,984	1,063	15.2
1882	6,486	1,188	18.3
1883	8,980	2,379	26.5
1884	5,570	1,535	27.6
1885	5,770	1,865	32.3
1886	8,022	2,017	25.1
1887	15,345	3,382	22.0
1888	12,302	2,751	22.4
1889	10,440	2,630	25.2
1890	11,634	3,108	26.4
1891	12,396	3,286	26.5
1892	12,479	3,332	26.7
1893	11,383	2,936	25.8
1894	5,874	1,191	20.3
1895	6,478	1,851	28.6

conclusive though it is, it is clear that the Danish share of prepaid tickets did not exceed 20%.

Even more surprising are the figures we get from the as yet unprocessed archives of the emigration agents, Larsson Brothers, which are deposited in the district archive of Gothenburg. Quarterly lists of the emigration transactions by the English lines were compiled in Sweden, too, similar to the Danish ones which provided the material for Table 15.3. In the Larsson archive, there are such lists for Gothenburg (in which the heading "Return of Emigration" was used) covering the period 1883–1886. The figures comprise the 10 largest emigration shipping lines, which probably handled about 80% of the total emigration from Sweden.

In the case of Sweden, 50% of the emigrants were "imported" to America by means of prepaid tickets, an absolutely astonishing demonstration of the power of the pull effect. The difference among the effects of the pull factor in the different Scandinavian countries leads directly to the thought that the effect of the pull in the country of emigration must be directly proportional to the volume of the emigrated population already abroad. Norwegian and Swedish emigration was already considerable in the 1840s. By 1880, there were 182,000 immigrants born in Norway and 194,000 born in Sweden who were living in the United States, whereas the number of Danes was only 64,000. These figures indicate the potential purchasers of prepaid tickets, and consequently the power of the pull effect on the individual countries—a power that at least theoretically would tend to increase concurrently with the increase of the immigrant population. In actual fact it did not work that way. As far as Denmark is concerned, the share of prepaid tickets remained at a level which was a little above the average for the 1880s, approximately 28%. In Sweden, the share for 1923 was as small as 20%.

However, a calculation of the number of nonprepaid emigrants from the Scandinavian countries, i.e., all the persons who made the decision themselves and paid for their own crossings, gives the result that the difference in intensity between Denmark and the other two Scandinavian countries was more or less eliminated. With all possible reservations, this suggests that the push effect in all three countries tended to be the same, whereas the pull effect varied.

Naturally the number of transferred emigrants' tickets varied over the years, just like any other aspect of emigration. But the percentages given in Table 15.4 show that the yearly variations in the volume of prepaid emigration do not fluctuate parallel with the rest of the emigration. The prepaid share culminates at 32% in 1885, a pronounced crisis year as far as emigration was concerned. After that comes first a drop and then a rise that continued for the rest of the period, except for a sudden fall

TABLE 15.4

Prepaid Tickets among Swedish Emigrants to the United States and Canada, 1883–1886

	Total number of emigrants	Emigrants traveling on prepaid tickets	Prepaids in percentage of total
1883	21,195	10,634	50.2
1884	14,473	7,243	50.0
1885	13,114	7,135	53.2
1886	20,950	7,195	34.3

in 1894. It is tempting to connect these variations with differences in the economic cycles of Europe and the United States by interpreting a large share of prepaids as an expression of boom conditions in the United States and depression in Europe. But the figures probably provide an insufficient basis for a conclusion of that type. The fluctuations seem to reflect another and much more obvious circumstance. A comparison between these figures and the variations in the total emigration shows that the volume of prepaids increased after the great emigration years. A peak of the curve will be followed by an aftermath during the following years, presumably because the men who had emigrated during the peak years would be established securely enough a few years later to be able to send for others —their family or friends. The decrease in the proportion of prepaid travelers during 1877–1879 is not solely explained by the depression that occurred during those years, but also by the fact that the large number of emigrants who came to America during the peak period, 1871–1873, had already sent for their families and friends. The fall in emigration in 1884–1885 affected the prepaid volume during the following years; but when emigration reached a high level again after 1887, prepaid emigrants increased proportionally. The great economic reversal occurred in 1892–1893, and by 1894 the economic conditions of the United States were so difficult that only very few were able to send prepaid tickets home.

One more factor seems to indicate that the system of prepaid tickets was to a certain extent used by immigrants who had arrived fairly recently. If we inquire into the relative distribution between paying and prepaid emigrants within the four quarters of the individual years, we find that the percentage of prepaids was largest practically every year in the last months of the year. The reason for this is probably that emigrants who set out early in the year became sufficiently settled in the course of the summer to send for their families before the approaching winter. At any rate, this time lag for prepaid emigrants within the individual years and over longer periods is a phenomenon of considerable interest, as it would of necessity influence the curve of immigration. The lag is less liable to obey the trends of the economic cycles than the rest of emigration, and therefore when nearly one-fourth of total emigration was prepaid, the result would be a flattening out of the emigration curve. There is, however, one small matter to be treated later which indicates the necessity for discretion when conclusions are drawn as to the influence of the economic cycles on the yearly fluctuations of the emigration curve. Personal contact between immigrants in countries overseas and their home country was, as we see, intense. Letters, money, and prepaid tickets came in a constant stream, the volume of which would quite likely surprise most people, since the emigrants were generally believed to have formed the poorest part of the population and to have been characterized by intellectual narrowness and insufficient education. Improved economic conditions in the United States combined with the emotional longings inherent in emigration furthered both letter writing and sending tickets home. These personal contacts with the Old Country may well be sufficient explanation of why mass emigration accelerated whenever economic conditions permitted.

16

GENERAL PERSPECTIVES

Hans Christian Clausen, a learned clergyman from Brande in Jutland, wrote a treatise in the 1780s that places the large-scale emigration overseas in a broad perspective. The treatise, a prize paper for the Academy of Lyons, was called *An Inquiry into the Problem of Whether the Discovery of America Has Been More Harmful Than Useful to Humanity*.

Seen through the eyes of modern man, the title is almost ludicrous. To us America is an important part of the political, economic, and cultural map of the world, so that the idea of inquiring into whether Columbus would have done better not to make his discovery seems grotesque. But if we place the vicar's treatise in its proper temporal context, we understand Clausen's perspective of 1785. He wrote:

> This large continent, known as America, has come to our knowledge during the time of our ancestors. Our fathers saw it in infancy, we see its childhood, our children its youth, their descendants its manhood, and the last generation will be in a position to judge its old age.

The vicar of Brande witnessed American society in its childhood stage, and he felt no doubt that the arrival of this continent on the scene had caused more harm than good. But the development of the United States since 1785 served to change this view. The fates of Europe and North America were welded together as millions of European emigrants contributed to the economic expansion of the United States that characterized the "manhood" of the continent.

We are left with the question of why the 50 million emigrants left Europe. A satisfactory explanation will only be obtained through a long series of detailed studies similar to this one, which has made special use of the Danish source materials. The method, at least, should aim at discovering whether there are features common to the great masses of emigrants that distinguish them materially from the rest of the population from which they were drawn. Observation of such characteristics has led scholars to speculate on whether it is a matter of chance who emigrates and who remains behind within a particular population section, or whether it is possible from empirical evidence to predict which subgroups are likely to emigrate.

Numerous examples have been given earlier from which a model of "migratory selection" might be constructed: distinct patterns with respect to the emigrants' age, sex, latest residence, and occupations. It should be possible to say, with reasonable certainty, that in Denmark in the 1880s a young man aged 18–20 years, employed as a farm hand on Langeland, would be likely to emigrate. A certain pattern of emigration has been established that indicates which tensions in the socioeconomic conditions of Denmark induced particular sections of the population to leave home. So it seems that, while the pull factor was a rather uniform attraction from the overseas countries, the push factor was the force that set population groups moving out of Europe, and was identical with the migration selection process. It is that latter force that determined that just those people, rather than others, emigrated. However, the general question of push versus pull effects has not been taken up for detailed examination in this book. I feel that overseas emigration should be viewed in a larger context —as just one aspect of the great migrations that characterized population conditions in the period before 1900.

The 285,000 Danes who emigrated in the years 1868–1914 made up only a very small fraction of all those who made a decisive change of residence during this period. The difference between the two kinds of migration is a matter of the distance involved. But almost all the other factors that may be listed as causes of migration are common to both: economic, social, geographical, and even emotional. For there are push and pull aspects in internal as well as in external migrations. The push is common to the entire phenomenon of mobility, while the pull theoretically differed between the two kinds of migration, since different objectives were involved. In reality, however, the pattern of motivation behind internal migration most often has been much clearer in the minds of the migrants, and more realistic, than that associated with overseas emigration. To most emigrants, America was a very vague concept.

One of the main purposes of the previous analysis has consequently been to demonstrate similarities and differences between internal and external migrations. The crucial point is that after the middle of the nineteenth century a movement of population set in, stimulated partly by cheaper and easier transportation and partly by new social aspirations in certain sections of the population. These groups were confronted with a choice between the shorter, internal migration and the far-reaching emigration overseas. The question now is whether the characteristic features of the migration trend that have been found here are an isolated Danish phenomenon, or whether similar features can be found in other European countries.

A comparison with the efforts of demographic theorists to establish general laws of mobility shows that most of the major results fit into the theoretical framework. As early as 1885, the English scholar Ravenstein advanced a set of "Laws of Migration," and in spite of extensive work on this subject since then, his theories have remained more or less unchallenged. The Ravenstein model was based on studies of mobility in 20 different countries. For instance, he examined stage migrations from the countryside to a nearby town to the big city, and found a tendency for women to predominate in short-distance migration and men in long-distance migration. The seven Ravenstein "laws" on the whole confirm the observations made in Denmark, but some of them seem to leave overseas emigration out of consideration. Such is the case with his theory that "migrants proceeding long distances generally go by preference to one of the great centers of commerce and industry." On this point Ravenstein has recently been corrected by Everett Lee who, like myself, underlines the error involved in treating internal and external migration as two separate phenomena.

The seventh and last "law" of the Ravenstein series establishes, as should also appear clearly from the previous chapters of this book, that economic motives are of absolutely supreme importance in migration, whether the distance is long or short. A striking confirmation can be found in a Norwegian questionnaire that was presented to all departing emigrants during the period 1905–1916. They were to state one out of five main reasons for their emigration. The reason given by 85% of the 13,000 men who left in 1905 and 64% of the 18,000 women was "a lack of opportunity for well-paid work."

But the concept of "economic motive" is in many ways obscure. It includes many diverse elements that come to light when one observes, from the data available, the structure of emigration over a period of many years, and finds that the character of emigration from a country changes as the current accelerates, culminates, and then subsides. It passes through different social stages: The customers of the emigration agents after 1900 were different from the customers of the 1870s. While emigration in the earliest stages seems typically to have been a desperate measure taken by the most poverty-stricken members of the population, it seems later on to have become more a movement of adventurous young people. In all of the European countries, emigration passed through these stages of the "economic motive."

The frequent references to Swedish and Norwegian material in this past section reflect an effort to answer the question that haunts every student of Danish emigration: Why was Danish emigration so relatively insignificant compared with the emigration from Sweden and Norway? The explanations which have been pointed to here, especially on the basis of comparisons between Danish and Swedish emigration, can be briefly summed up in two points: (1) the differences in processes of urbanization—the Danish towns were less scattered and their ability to absorb rural migrants was greater. The point is illustrated, among other things, by the considerably larger share of women in Swedish emigration than in Danish. (2) A difference in the structure of agriculture—the intensive process of subdivision of farms in Sweden in the early nineteenth century, the "hemmansklyvningen," had resulted in holdings of a size too small to be economically viable, particularly when the slump in grain prices set in. What happened was that, in contrast to Denmark, a large number of Swedish landowners were forced out of farming. Subdivision of land holdings (together with reclamation of moorland) was sufficient to retain part of the Danish rural proletariat.

Apart from these two points a third, less certain factor should be mentioned: The volume of emigration may have depended to some extent on how early in the period emigration reached a high level. The fact that the Swedish and, particularly, the Norwegian settlements in the United States reached impressive sizes in the 1850s must mean that these "colonies" acted as intensifying stimuli once the era of large-scale emigration began about 1865.

When we study the international population movements collectively from the 1860s to the present, we find much that resembles such physical phenomena as electric currents, water moving in a certain rhythm or direction, or ripples that grow into waves in minor migrations that unite into mass movements. It is the scholar's aim to find a pattern in these waves of people, outline the regularity of the movements of the masses, and find an answer to the question of what made these millions depart from Europe, which until about 1800 possessed a relatively static population structure. What was the impetus that caused more than 50 million Europeans to cross the oceans in less than a century?

Many prominent scholars have contributed answers to these questions through detailed inquiries into immense amounts of source material. During the last decades such studies have tended to concentrate on the relationship between the economic cycles of countries on either side of the Atlantic and the yearly fluctuations of the stream of emigrants. The study of economic cycles has particularly contributed to our insight into the causality of the problem. This work has attempted to go beyond the narrowly defined economic, and rather theoretical, examination of fluctuations, and to study emigration and its motivation from a more general historical point of view.

The certainty that mass emigration was nothing like an even stream, but subject to fluctuations, is not nearly so significant as the fact that the 52 million did actually set out within such a relatively short period of years. Thanks to the work of Jerome and Dorothy S. Thomas, the concepts of push and pull in emigration were defined in detail and now provide a profitable basis for a study of this subject. On the other hand, it should not be forgotten that push and pull effects remain unsatisfactory explanations for the causes and effects of emigration.

Both emigration figures and statistics on economic cycles cause the critical historian several problems when he ventures into detailed evaluation of the causal relationships in the fluctuations of the stream of emigrants. Furthermore, other circumstances besides the plain pull and push effects may have helped to shape the curve of emigration fluctuations, such as the stage emigration of families. If, say, in one year, 500 married men set out alone, the curve of the following year would show a rise indicating the departure of some 1000 or 1500 persons (the families of these men). This peak in the curve could not be interpreted as to whether a push or a pull was dominating that of the previous year. To some extent, circumstances of this nature hide some aspects of fluctuations that depend on economic cycles. The same can be said about the entire prepaid system, described previously.

What especially serves to reduce the validity of the "classical" conception of push–pull is the realization that the push effect cannot be regarded as an isolated emigration phenomenon, but must be seen as the common denominator of the "migration fever," characteristic of Europe after 1800, which caused internal migrations that far exceeded emigration. The next question is whether emigration should be seen as a counterpart to internal migrations or as an alternative. Brinley Thomas maintains that the two alternated; this opinion is based on an apparent counterrhythm in the two currents that he fits into a larger economic cycle. There are, however, considerable weaknesses in the material on which Brinley Thomas developed this theory concerning countereffects of internal and external migrations, a problem that must still be described as unsolved.

According to the opinions of other scholars, it was not a case of actual interplay, but of internal mobility, which was a rather stable factor compared to emigration but was liable to react to economic fluctuations. The final solution will have to wait until more reliable statistical material is available and the unreliable figures of net migration can be disregarded.

The pronounced population increase contributed to the rise in mobility. People at that time were of the opinion that Denmark was overpopulated, and that this found expression in emigration. Thus in 1873 the Danish economist Falbe-Hansen regarded emigration solely as a result of the "too pronounced reproduction of the working classes." Subsequent generations would hardly accept the dictum that Denmark was overpopulated in the Malthusian sense of the word. In a relative sense, however, the expression is perhaps permissible. The awakening of economic and political self-realization, which occurred in Europe after the French Revolution, gave rise to a "social buoyancy," a pressure from below toward a better social status. The movement went from the plough to the factory, from the machine to an office desk. The actual manifestation of this buoyancy was the migration from country to town, and the basis of the urbanization process was industrialization. The problem was that industrialization, and with it the demand for labor in the towns, seems to have lagged compared to the influx of people, thus creating the impression of overpopulation. This additional population could not be absorbed by the towns. We see the consequences in the marked rise in urban emigration from Denmark in 1872–1873. To a certain degree, the large emigration during the 1880s was due to a similar situation, whereas in 1895–1900, the extremely low emigration in spite of favorable economic conditions was a consequence of the growth in Danish industry and an accompanyingly greater demand for labor.

In the light of this it seems generally possible to divide Danish emigrants into two large groups. One, numerically the smaller but, in relation to the population distribution, the larger, was the urban emigration of people who were caught in the delay in industrialization, and who therefore moved on to overseas countries. The other group was the part of the rural population possessing the same buoyancy as those who migrated to the towns, but who preferred to stay in an agrarian milieu. They ended up as farmers on the American prairie. For them, attaining independence was the main goal. Though there was a Danish rural proletariat, this does not imply that migration away from the countryside was caused by unemployment. The departure of the rural population did not abate even when the demand for rural labor became very large indeed. A typical example in this respect is the situation on Lolland-Falster, where the number of people who left the region was larger than anywhere else, and yet at the same time a large-scale importation of labor to this region occurred from Sweden and Poland.

The structure of Danish emigration changed in several respects during the period in question. During the 1870s, it had a high degree of family emigration and was characterized by a fairly high age level; but from 1885–1890 it became more of a young people's movement: lower age levels, fewer families, and more single women. The decisive factor in this development was probably the conjunction of two economic conditions: the slow but constant increase in both rural and urban real wages, and a steady decline in prices for transportation across the Atlantic. This meant an enormous increase in the potential number of emigrants after 1885. Even the very young could afford a ticket to America. Transportation facilities also improved constantly; the between-deck accommodations might still be cramped, but the crossing was now so quick and the vessels so large that there was little cause for hesitation.

Unsatisfied ambitions and wrecked hopes frequently led to departure from home, but in most cases only for the neighboring town or for the capital, unless the migrant had previously heard of the outside world. The pull factor of emigration took effect through the spread of information, and without this constant stimulant no mass emigration would have taken place. Part of the spread of news came automatically: Emigrants' letters home had a considerable pull effect. The figures offered by the Danish material as to the number of letters and fund transfers from America are surprisingly large, a telling testimony of the self-generating element in overseas migrations. When we remember that on top of this up to one-third of all Danish emigrants traveled on prepaid tickets, and in certain periods as many as one-half of all Swedish emigrants did, it is obvious that an important part of the governing mechanism of mass emigration must be sought in personal contacts across the Atlantic.

SELECTED REFERENCES

Andersen, A. M. *Hvor danskerne i Amerika findes. Statistik oversigt.* Blair, Nebraska, 1906.

Barkley, G. W. *Techniques of Population Analyses.* New York: Wiley, 1958.

Beijbom, U. *Swedes in Chicago. A Demographic and Social Study of the 1846–1880 Immigration.* Chicago, Illinois. Chicago Historical Society, 1972.

Bille, J. H. *A History of the Danes in America.* Wisconsin Academy of Science, **XI**, 1896.

Brattne, B. *Bröderna Larssen. En studie i svensk emigrant-agentverksamhet under 1880-talet.* Uppsala, 1973. English summary also in *Review: American Studies in Scandinavia,* no. 9, winter 1972.

Cairncross, A. K. *Internal Migration in Victorian England.* The Manchester School, 1949, pp. 67–83.

Carlsson, S. *Den sociala omgrupperingen i Sverige efter 1866.* Samhälle och Riksdag I, 1966.

Carlsson, S. *Från familjutvandring till ensamutvandring. Emigrationer.* Festskrift till Vilhelm Moberg, Stockholm, 1968, pp. 101–122.

Christensen, T. P. *Dansk amerikansk historie.* Cedar Falls, Iowa, 1927.

Christensen, T. P. *The Danish Settlements in Kansas.* Kansas Historical Collections 1926–1928, **17**, pp. 300–305.

Claussen, H. C. *Undersøgelse om Amerikas Opdagelse har mere skadet end gavnet det menneskelige kjøn?* København, 1785.

Danmarks Jordbrug 1850-1907. Statistiske Meddelelser, series IV, vol. 24, 1907.

Dansk Folketidende, 1873.

Degler, C. N. *Out of Our Past: The Forces that Shaped Modern America.* New York: Harper & Row, 1959.

Dillard, D. *Economic Development of the North Atlantic Community.* Englewood Cliffs, New Jersey: Prentice-Hall, 1967.

Encyclopedia on Social Science, vols. I–XVII.

Falbe-Hansen, V., *Udvandringen i vor tid.* Nationaløkonomisk Tidsskrift, 1873, pp. 273–295.

Grove-Rasmussen, A. C. L. *En rejse i Amerika.* Nordisk Månedskrift, **II**, 1873, pp. 241–293.

Hall-Jensen, A. *Den dansk-amerikanske historie.* København, 1937.

Hansen, M. L. Official encouragement of immigration to Iowa. *Iowa Journal of History and Politics,* **XIX**, 1921, pp. 175 ff.

Hansen, M. L. *The History of American Immigration as a Field of Research.* Cambridge, Massachusetts: Harvard Univ. Press, 1927.

Hansen, M. L. *The Immigrant in American History.* New York: Harper & Row, 1940.

Hvidt, K. *Flugten til Amerika,* Aarhus, 1972.

Hvidt, K. Danish emigration prior to 1914. Trends and problems. *Scandinavian Economic History Review* **XIV**, 1966.

Isaac, J. *Economics of Migration.* London, 1947.

Jacobsen, A. *Hvad har bevirket de nuværende høje priser på jordejendomme?* Copenhagen, 1866.

Jensen, A. *Udvandring.* Nationaløkonomisk Tidsskrift, 1904, pp. 65–90.

Jensen, A. *Udvandring i vor Tid.* Socialt Tidsskrift, 1972, pp. 225–243.

Jensen, A. *Befolkningsspørgsmålet i Danmark.* Studentersamfundets oplysningsforenings serie nr. 55, 1937.

Jensen, A. og H. Koefoed, *Befolkningsforholdene i det 19.århundrede.* Det nittende århundrede, **VIII**, 1919.

Jerome, H. *Migration and Business Cycles.* Publication issued by the National Bureau of Economic Research, 1926.

Jones, M. *American Immigration,* 4th ed. Chicago, Illinois: Univ. of Chicago Press, 1965.

Larsen, E. *Urovækkeren Abraham Sommer.* Kirkehistoriske studier, 2.række nr.17. 1963.

Lee, E. S. Empirical generalizations concerning migration. Demography, 3, no. 1, 1966, pp. 47–57. Reprinted in *Readings on Population* (David M. Heer, ed.). Englewood Cliffs, New Jersey: Prentice-Hall, 1968.

Malthus, T. R. *An Essay on the Principles of Population.* London, 1798.

Moberg, V. *Utvandrarne.* Stockholm, 1949.

Mortensen, E. *The Danish Lutheran Church in America. The History and Heritage of the American Evangelic Lutheran Church.* Philadelphia, Pennsylvania, 1967.

Mulder, W. *Mormon Conversion, Disaffection and Emigration in Scandinavia 1850–1904.* Dissertation unprinted. Copies in Harvard University Library and Utah State Historical Society, 1954.

Mulder, W. *Mormons from Scandinavia 1850–1900. A Shepherded Migration.* Pacific Historical Review **23**, 1954, pp. 228 ff.

Mulder, W. Image of Zion. Mormonism as an influence in Scandinavia. *Mississippi Valley Historical Review*, **43**, 1956.

Mulder, W. *Homeward to Zion. The Mormon Migration from Scandinavia.* Minneapolis, Minnesota: Univ. of Minnesota Press, 1957.

Nilsson, F. *Emigrationen från Stockholm till Nordamerika 1880–93.* Monografier utg. av Stockholm Kommunalförvaltning, no. 31. Stockholm, 1970.

Nyholm, P. *The Americanization of the Danish Lutheran Church in America.* Minneapolis, Minnesota, 1953.

Olsen, E. *Danmarks økonomiske historie siden 1750.* Copenhagen, Akademisk forlag, 1962.

Oversigt over det danske postvæsens statistik, 1872–1914.

Ravenstein, E. G. The laws of migration. *Journal of the Royal Statistical Society*, **48**, 1885, pp. 167–227.

Semmingsen, I. *Vejen mot Vest*, vols. I and II. 1942 and 1950.

Smith, Adam. *Wealth of Nations*, vols. 1 and II. 1776.

Snow, Erastus. *En sandheds røst.* Tract. 1850.

Sommer, Wilhelm, *Til belysning af udvandringssagen.* 1867.

Sonne, C. *Langbrugets forsyning med arbejdskraft.* Dansk forening for Socialpolitik. 1.hefte, 1915.

Sundbärg, Gustav, *Emigrationsutredningen*, Stockhen, 1909-1913. With Appendix Vol. I–XX.

Thistlethwaite, F. *Migration from Europe in the 19th and 20th Century.* XI Congrés International des Sciences Historiques, Stockholm. Rapport V, pp. 32–58, 1960.

Thomas, B. *Migration and the Rhythm of Economic Growth, 1850–1913.* Manchester School of Economics and Social Studies, vol. 19. 1951.

Thomas, B. *Migration and Economic Growth. A study in Great Britain and the Atlantic Economy.* The National Institute of Economic and Social Research. Economic and Social Studies, Series no. XII. Cambridge: Cambridge Univ. Press, 1954.

Thomas, B. *Seen from the Other Side.* Annals of the American Academy, 1966, pp. 63–72.

Thomas, D. S. *Social and Economic Aspects of Swedish Population Movements 1750–1933.* New York: Macmillan, 1941.

Vig, P. S. *Danske i Amerika.* Blair, Nebraska, 1908.

Warming, J. Danmarks Statistik. Copenhagen, 1913.

Wilcox, W. (Ed.) *International Migration.* I. Statistics, 1929. II. Interpretations, 1931. National Bureau of Economic Research, vols. 14 and 18.

INDEX

A

Age
  declining, 76
  distribution among emigrants, 73–74, 84, 85–86, 114
  economic conditions and, 77
  falsification of, 72–73
  inability to enter agriculture and, 76–77
  at marriage, 95–96
  tendency to migrate and, 71
  urban versus rural emigration and, 74–75
Agricultural crisis
  American exports and, 158–159
  Swedish, 121
Agriculture, *see also* Farmers
  age of emigrants and, 76–77
  common-field, 7
  influence on urban emigration, 56
  in Malthusian theory, 18
  in North Schleswig, 139
  reforms in, 123–124
  structure of, 38, 127, *see also* Land division
Alborg, emigration intensity in, 50
Assimilation, 159–160, 166–171
  Dillingham Committee's report on, 12–13
Atlantic economy, 34, 66
Austria–Hungary,
  government-subsidized emigration from, 20
  volume of emigration from, 11

B

Bakers, marital status of, 114
Balkans, volume of emigration from, 11
Baptists, 147–148, 150
  Mormon missions among, 149–150

207